LUNCH WITH A **BIGOT**

LUNCH WITH A **BIGOT**

The Writer in the World · AMITAVA KUMAR

For Patrick and the lovely Andy,

Thank you for your hospitality.

Amitava K

DUKE UNIVERSITY PRESS · DURHAM AND LONDON · 2015

Printed in the United States of America on acid-free paper ∞
Designed by Heather Hensley
Typeset in Chaparral Pro by Westchester Publishing Services

Library of Congress Cataloging-in-Publication Data
Kumar, Amitava, 1963–
Lunch with a bigot : the writer in the world / Amitava Kumar.
pages cm
Includes bibliographical references and index.
ISBN 978-0-8223-5911-1 (hardcover : alk. paper)
ISBN 978-0-8223-5930-2 (pbk. : alk. paper)
ISBN 978-0-8223-7539-5 (e-book)
1. Kumar, Amitava, 1963– 2. Kumar, Amitava, 1963-—Criticism
and interpretation. I. Title.
PR9499.4.K8618Z46 2015
824'.92—dc23   2014040367

Cover art: Subodh Gupta, *Full Moon*, 2011. Oil on canvas,
228 × 168 cm (89 ¾ × 66 ⅛ in.). Courtesy the artist and Hauser &
Wirth. Photo by Thomas Müller.

In memory of my mother,
Lakshmi Nidhi Singh (1937–2014)

After forty years,
what I came
to care about most
was not style,
but the breath of life.

. . .

WILLIAM MAXWELL

· CONTENTS ·

· AUTHOR'S NOTE ·

I must have been nineteen or twenty at that time. I was enrolled as a student in political science at Delhi's Hindu College, but in a vague and desultory way I thought of myself as a writer. On thin sheets of typing paper, I wrote bad poems. Once there was a poetry competition at Lady Shri Ram College. I went. It is possible that I won a prize, but what made the occasion difficult to forget was that one of the judges said to the poets who had presented their work, "If you have nothing to say, don't write. Please."

The man who had offered this suggestion taught Hindi at my own college. He was a short, chubby fellow. Balding at the top, he kept his hair long and carefully combed. Like a former middle-order batsman of my acquaintance, a Ranji player who in the decades that followed retained some of his earlier flamboyance amid general seediness, the Hindi lecturer was a bit of a dandy. He was always to be seen in the company of young female students. I disliked him without having any particular reason to do so, and his statement at the event made me hate him more. But he was right, of course, and I must have known this even then. Like everyone else, I had failed in love and had written about it—except that I didn't know then that it wasn't even love that I had failed at. If I were to now hear a teacher tell young writers what the professor said after that poetry competition, I would at least be curious. I'd want to know how he dealt with that ascetic logic in his own writing life, and what had been the process through which he had arrived at it. What were the impulses in his own heart—or art—that he encouraged without being dogged by doubt? Most important, what had he written himself? What did he have to say in his own work?

Three decades have passed since that afternoon. During this time, I've written several books, but I'm taken back now to the events that took place during those years when I was studying in Hindu College: the poisonous leak in the Union Carbide factory in Bhopal; the street performances of Safdar Hashmi, the activist who was murdered two years after I left India; the innocent Sikhs who were killed in Delhi and elsewhere after the assassination of Indira Gandhi. Why did I not write about those events as they were happening? In my own role now as a teacher, I encourage my students to become journalists. It is not only that I want them to escape the prison of their petty love stories; I want them to go out into the world. The world is an extraordinarily rich place, full of stories, and it is marvelous to see how stories feed the curiosity of the young. I also offer specific technical advice. For instance, I repeat to them an anecdote I read in a journalism textbook about Gene Roberts, a former editor of the *New York Times*, whose first job was writing farm columns for a small newspaper in North Carolina: "Roberts' editor was Henry Belk, who was blind. Roberts recalls that when he showed up for work in the morning, Belk would call him over and inform the young reporter that his writing was insufficiently descriptive. 'Make me see,' he would order."[1] *Make me see, make me see!*

Writers are observers. Recently, I read an essay in which the author had quoted her mentor in college, the writer Annie Dillard. Dillard had told her class, somewhat provocatively, that rather than travel to a far-flung place they would be better off if they read a book about it. She had just returned from Alaska and informed her class that the only thing she hadn't already known about Alaska from her reading were the sunflowers: "Apparently, in midsummer, as they work to follow the sun circling tightly overhead, their stalks twist until their bright, oversize heads break right off their slender necks."[2] If a book had contained that tidbit, Dillard said, it would be worth reading. When I read that anecdote I immediately saw in it a lesson not about choosing books over travel, but about developing an eye for a story or at least for unusual details.

The writer who for me has been a master of narrative, expert at seeing and also at seeing through, is V. S. Naipaul. Here is Tim Adams describing what Naipaul told him during an interview in the *Guardian*: "My wish is to fix a scene with a very bright picture and to move along like that. . . . People can never remember long descriptions. Just one or two images. But you have to choose them very carefully. That has always come naturally to me, of course."[3] One of the recurrent themes of Naipaul's writing is seeing—or showing—how writing is learned. In his epic novel *A House for Mr. Biswas*, a newspaper editor named Mr. Burnett, a London man, gives Mr. Biswas the sense that the city was populated with stories waiting to be told. He encourages Mr. Biswas to write stories with a jaunty edge. Mr. Burnett also offers his younger protégé elementary lessons in precision and clarity (" 'Several' has seven letters. 'Many' has only four and oddly enough has exactly the same meaning.").[4] Mr. Burnett's instructions to Mr. Biswas were notable, but what pierced me was Naipaul's account that the single line that came to Mr. Biswas every time he wished to test a new ribbon in the typewriter was the following one: "At the age of thirty-three, when he was already the father of four children . . . ."[5] The half-finished sentence momentarily lights up a whole dark universe of desire and futility. The despair got to me, and I was unable to finish reading the book while still a student at Hindu College. When I began reading the book again, I had come to America. This time I read it to the end; I had already published my first book, and the threat of extinction was not so immediate anymore. During this reading, I noticed the comedy in the novel. Life had become bearable. I was no longer reading *Mr. Biswas* as a self-help book.

The windows of the A. H. Wheeler Booksellers kiosk at the railway station in my hometown, Patna, are full of self-help books. Books that teach you how to become successful; the art of writing letters; how to be healthy; how to think and grow rich; and twenty ways to remove worries. There is a specificity to the eclecticism that I recognize: thrillers by James Hadley Chase and Jeffrey Archer, astrology books in Hindi, a book on numerology, and autobiographies of Swami Vivekananda and Adolf Hitler. The self that is assumed in *self-help* is a submissive and yielding one, unusually open to any and all comers; it takes any struggle, even that of a mass murderer, as a lesson in self-improvement. Personal transformation, understood as advancement in social status, is the goal. That is the moral of the visit to the Patna station book kiosk: the train always stops for success.

In May 2014, India elected a new government by a landslide. The vote was widely seen as a mandate for Narendra Modi, the chief minister of Gujarat State and leader of the right-wing Bharatiya Janata Party. Modi's platform had stressed development in an economy that had been in decline for decades; this stress on economic revival was in sharp contrast to Modi's previous avatar as a nationalist with sectarian prejudices. He is accused by many of abetting the deaths of more than a thousand Muslims in the riots in Gujarat back in 2002. Modi's new focus, on the perils of a stagnant economy instead of on his party's earlier support of Hindu assertion against claims made by minorities, was accepted by his voters as a lesson in self-transformation. One might even go so far as to call it self-improvement. And as with other stories of such transformation, there was a great deal of simplification. There was also a great deal of forgetting. The belief in development is impossible without a degree of unquestioning optimism and amnesia. For the moment, there are many people in India who are eager to forget the murders of Muslims and instead put their faith in the promise of economic self-help. The essays in this volume are memorial acts. Like a photograph that shows abandoned shoes, stones, and dried blood on an empty street after a riot, this collection insists on what is absent. Who once stood at this place? What happened here? What is the story?

Thirty years after my encounter with the Hindi lecturer in Delhi, I present here a record of what I have to say and the ways in which I have learned to say it. There is self-help in these pages (How to be a writer?), but the writer here is interested in examining the borders of the self (What divides the writer from the rioter?). Written or published over nearly a decade and a half, the pieces are assembled here in four sections: reading, writing, places, and people. Those four themes are my north, my south, my east and west. I want to thank the editors of various publications or anthologies who commissioned these writings and helped put them in print; my immense debt to Shruti Debi at Aitken Alexander Literary Agency, who read the manuscript and guided it toward publication; and the team at Duke University Press, particularly Elizabeth Ault, Laura Sell, Michael McCullough, Willa Armstrong, Danielle Szulczewski, and, last but first, Ken Wissoker, who has been a true collaborator in my writing over the past several years.

NOTES

1. Melvin Mencher, *Melvin Mencher's News Reporting and Writing* (New York: McGraw Hill, 2011), 249.
2. Virginia Pye, "China of My Mind," *New York Times*, December 29, 2013. Accessed July 31, 2014. http://opinionator.blogs.nytimes.com/2013/12/29 /china-of-my-mind/.
3. Tim Adams, "A Home for Mr Naipaul," *Observer*, September 11, 2004. Accessed July 31, 2014. http://www.theguardian.com/books/2004/sep/12 /fiction.vsnaipaul.
4. V. S. Naipaul, *A House for Mr. Biswas* (New York: Alfred A. Knopf, 1995), 311.
5. Naipaul, *A House for Mr. Biswas*, 330.

I
READING

· **1** ·

Paper

In my childhood home, paper, of any kind, was to be touched only by hand. If you stepped on a book by accident, you were to pick it up and raise it respectfully to your forehead. I am not from a culture, although that seems the wrong word here for any number of reasons, where you rubbed paper on your arse.

I did not know what to write on the notebooks I first bought as a child when I visited my birthplace, Ara. The nibs we were given were of wood. We dipped them in ink. My cousins and I sat in a row near our elderly aunt who had become crippled with grief after her husband died young. His blood had turned black before his death; when he died, my aunt didn't move for months. Her legs swelled up and she could no longer walk. That is what at least I had heard my mother and others say. When she lay on her back in bed, my aunt couldn't sit up or raise herself without help. Through most of the day, she would sit with her legs immobile, on the side of the bed that faced the door. Her son was studying to be a doctor. We were told that he wanted to be a doctor because his father had died of an incurable disease, *kalaazar*. And his mother was waiting to be able to walk again. There was reverence and also a faintly morbid, perhaps dread, expectation in that house. My aunt told me not to buy notebooks that had the pictures of Bombay film stars on them, and to always remember to touch the notebook with my forehead if I stepped on it. Her crippled hand gave to the alphabets she wrote out for me a larger, rounder form. I remember her as being neat and very strict, this aunt who wore a widow's white sari. Her room smelled of Dettol. In her presence, I wrote my first letters on the plain sheets of my notebook, always afraid that I would make mistakes. I always made mistakes and as soon as I had made one, I didn't want to use that notebook anymore.

It was in that same house in Ara, where my aunt lived, in which Naniji, my grandmother on my mother's side, died a few days short of my seventh birthday. When Naniji died, her sons' wives tore out the blank pages from our notebooks. The women rubbed clarified butter—"pure ghee"—on my grandmother's feet and then placed the sheets of paper against her soles. In the months that followed, these oily prints were filled with heavy embroidery and hung on the walls of the houses of all the relatives on my mother's side, including my old aunt. This is what remains of my earliest lessons in writing: the red footprints of my dead grandmother pointing toward eternity. On those sheets of the notebooks that I used to so quickly tire of when I made mistakes, the creases on Naniji's soles were stitched stiff with green silk.

Paper was to be worshipped, like money or the *Gita*. This freed you from the burden of doing any reading. My maternal uncles worked in the prison bureaucracy. I looked up to cousins who, on the flimsy wooden doors of the rooms that they shared, wrote down in chalk their names with fancy titles. There were notebooks around, and some textbooks with their covers wrapped in pages taken from newspapers or magazines, but I do not remember any other books. There was certainly no library. The comfortable ritual that I enter into now—a part of the privilege of living in a place like the United States—of choosing and reading books from the shelves that line my study, could not have been imagined at that time. The rituals in my grandmother's house, in that small town in India's most backward province, had more to do with cleaning your teeth with tooth powders that had tobacco in them or concentrating on a cure for constipation.

. . .

There is a short story I like in which a young man comes to the United States from India and becomes obsessed with the desire to know everything about the Indian tradition. The story was written in Kannada by A. K. Ramanujan, who taught for many years at the University of Chicago. In the story, the young man named Annayya is amazed at how, unlike him, the American anthropologists knew so much about Indian culture. Annayya begins to read books on India: "On the second floor of the Chicago library were stacks and stacks of those books which had to be reached by climbing the ladders and holding on to the wooden railings. Library call number PK 321. The East had at last found a niche in the West."[1]

The number PK 321 is tied, in my mind, with another code or number, a cryptic marker of mid-twentieth-century globalization. It is PL 480, short for Public Law 480, 83rd Congress. Beginning in 1951, the United States provided wheat to India and other newly independent nations and accepted payment for the grain in local currency. The money that was "interest payable by the Government of India on the Wheat Loan of 1951" was used to fund "cultural exchange."[2] In other words, monies to buy Indian books for American libraries in return for the regulated disposal of wheat from the American Midwest. The PL 480 library program for India and Pakistan began in January 1962. The library at the University of Chicago was selected by the Library of Congress as one of the top beneficiaries of the program. The books about ancient Hindu traditions that Ramanujan's Annayya was reading concealed a more contemporary exchange involving, among other things, the regulation on the open market of the price of thousands of tons of wheat from places like Kansas.

It was after coming to America as a foreign student that I read "Annayya's Anthropology" for the first time. For me, there was even a glimmer of self-recognition in Ramanujan's description of Annayya in

America: "He read the *Gita*. In Mysore, he had made his father angry by refusing to read it. Here he drank beer and whisky, ate beef, used toilet paper instead of washing himself with water, lapped up the *Playboy* magazines with their pictures of naked breasts, thighs, and some navels as big as rupee coins."[3] But what caught my attention during a subsequent reading was a detail in Ramanujan's story: the American anthropologist whose book Annayya was reading in the Chicago library stacks was a Ford Foundation fellow in India. In this fact hides the repetition of the link with PL 480.

Under the National Defense Education Act of 1958, a South Asia Language and Area Center was started at Chicago; as a result, the university received substantial Ford Foundation long-term grants. The same Ford Foundation was, of course, also interested in grains. India, with help from the Americans, was trying to succeed at launching the Green Revolution, which was to later make grain transfer to India unnecessary. But that was not the only aim of the Green Revolution. The environmental scientist Vandana Shiva has written that under the Ford Foundation program in India, "agriculture was transformed from one that is based on internal inputs that are easily available at no costs, to one that is dependent on external inputs for which credits become necessary."[4] The creditor was going to be America. We begin to see the further irony hidden in Ramanujan's remark that the East had found a niche in the West under the call number PK 321: the ghost that lurks beside that call number is the PL 480 program and the story of American grains and even gain. As Shiva points out, "the social and political planning that went into the Green Revolution aimed at engineering not just seeds but social relations as well."[5]

In Ramanujan's story, however, it is in a different way that Annayya brushes against the grain of history. The book that he is reading in the library stacks contains photographs that reveal to Annayya scenes that appear familiar. When looking at the photograph showing a Hindu cremation, Annayya recognizes his cousin Sundararaya, who owned a photography studio in their hometown. Annayya reads the foreword and finds a mention of his cousin's name. He returns to the photograph of the funeral. He realizes that the picture was taken in his own home. He looks at the corpse. Now the truth dawns on him: this is a photograph of his father's funeral. His father is dead.

I had only recently left my home in India when I read this story and was drawn by the drama of Annayya's loss. There was a lesson there, too, about books and libraries. I saw that the book is not removed from the world, from the realities of trade and profits and power. There was certainly a lesson there also about travel and what it grants in terms of awareness that results from displacement. The act of opening a book or entering a library also produces results akin to travel. All of this was present in Annayya's experience. And also in mine, when I read Ramanujan's story.

This lesson about the worldliness of books and libraries, and the reality or even illusion of travel, pervades those pages of Raj Kamal Jha's novel *The Blue Bedspread* where he describes a visit to the American Center Library in Calcutta. The chapter is titled "American Dream." People step in carefully in ones or twos, shuffling past the metal detectors and the uniformed guards, and enter another world. The visitors leave sweat marks on the glass-topped counters. These visitors, Jha writes, wipe away carefully, surreptitiously, those marks with their shirt sleeves. And then the visitors sit down. "The sweat begins to evaporate; outside, the wind continues to blow across the desert, the waves continue to churn in the ocean, through the Venetian blinds in the window, they can see the air shimmer as if in a mirage."[6]

This memory shimmers for me through the mirage of time. It returns me to my youth, when I would go to the American Center Library near Connaught Place in Delhi. It was one of those libraries that granted students like me entry whereas Indian libraries, controlled by the regulations of the bureaucracy and the elite intelligentsia, barred their doors to us. We would need letters of attestation from two "gazetted officers" to get admission to the Indian government libraries. The U.S. library or the British library, even if they made you feel more alien in your own land, allowed easier entrance. Apart from the freedom of entry, there were also other distinct, sensual pleasures that appeared wholly luxurious. I recognize Jha's description of the civic comforts offered by the library: in the bathroom, "the cold faucet is blue, the warm is red, they wash their faces, pour out the liquid soap that floats, like cool green jelly, in their palms. They tear out the tissue paper for the first time in their lives, watch it stain dark in patches as it soaks in the water from their washed hands." In Jha's narrative, the visitors pick up last week's *New York Times Sunday Magazine* and look at the haute couture ads. They peel off the perfume strips and rub the smell on their wrists. Such smells are a prelude to a reverie. They flip back to the ads for expensive houses near Central Park West that are available for sale. They even manage to fall asleep, for half an hour.

That detail stops me. The half-hour nap. It is statement about limits. It reminds one of the duration of a fantasy and, therefore, of the material conditions of the real world. Perhaps what stirs in me is the memory of a desire to fall asleep in the American Center Library, the cool metal of the chair on which I was sitting in touch with my skin. The desire, at that point of my life, might have had a name: America. But as with Annayya, to come to America means to discover anew what had till now been home. The scrutiny takes banal forms. Why doesn't liquid soap float, "like cool green jelly," in the bathrooms in the town in which I was born? I return to a childhood memory of the home in Ara where I was learning to write alphabets during my visits to the town with my mother. In the corner of the house was the toilet: it had a hole in the floor and underneath it a bucket that was removed by an "untouchable" each morning. The bucket, foul and always tilting, was visible from the narrow back street that ran past the house. A bucket stood under each house on the street. When you were inside in the toilet, you could watch through the hole under you the *mohallah*'s pigs that had wandered in from the street. You would see them grunting over the bucket, fighting among themselves to eat your waste.

The sight fascinated me as a boy. I return to that memory now when I read in a book by an Indian novelist a description of a bathroom in a library run by the U.S. government in India. The contrasting images that arise in my mind make me reflect on the strange process through which books—and libraries—help you mark and discover the stations of your displacement. Books narrate history, and not simply by what they tell you between their pages. It is the same with libraries, as the narrator of Jha's novel finds during his visit to the bathroom of the American Center Library. In this process of discovery of the divided world, and the motion within it, lies nothing as narrow as a static lesson about inequality, undeniable as it may be. Rather, I ask myself whether there isn't an invitation to come close to the insight shared in that wonderful memoir *Beyond a Boundary*, by C. L. R. James: "Time would pass, old empires would fall and new ones take their place. The relations of classes had to change before I discovered that it's not the quality of goods and utility that matter, but movement, not where you are or what you have, but where you come from, where you are going and the rate at which you are getting there."[7]

. . .

The movement I am most conscious of now is the movement of memory, shuttling between places. One place is home, the other the world. In one place, paper is worshipped; in the other, there is reading. But this is a false distinction. The two divided zones enter each other. There was such worldliness in the use of paper at home. I am suddenly reminded of Hindi newspapers being read in the trains that ran between Ara and Patna. For twenty paise, someone sitting around me would buy a newspaper like the *Indian Nation* or *Aryavarta*. A man on the adjoining berth, a complete stranger, would ask for a page from the paper. The newspaper would circulate among readers in the compartment, its individual pages sometimes torn and separated for easy reading by all. The news would incite conversation and debate. The one who had originally bought the newspaper could very well choose to be less generous and, spreading out the newspaper on the upper berth like a bedsheet, promptly go to sleep under the ineffectual railway fan screwed to the compartment's ceiling. When peanuts and puffed rice would be eaten, the pages from the newspaper would serve as makeshift plates. Outside, rain would begin to fall and people would roll up their newspapers to be unfurled later and used to cover their heads as they rushed to their homes or offices. The newspaper could also serve other ends. Sometimes, the toilets in the train would have no water. On those occasions, the newspaper would be put to more uncustomary use.

When I think of Annayya in the library at the University of Chicago, I also think that what he was beginning to learn, in some complex sense, was that you do not know love or death's loss except through language. And that language is changing. It dies. This sense of weighted mortality was perhaps not Annayya's, but it certainly is mine when I think about language. Unlike Annayya, who had learned about the death of his father, I have experienced in slow and small ways the death, in at least my own private universe, of my mother tongue. For the past fifteen years, I wrote in Hindi only when I bought the pale blue aerograms to post letters to my old grandmother living in a village in Bihar. My grandmother died two years ago. I seldom use Hindi anymore in my writing. All the news I get from India, either on the web or in print, is in English. The loss that Annayya was feeling is experienced by me as the loss also of the language in which that loss would first be felt and communicated. I discover myself as stranded at a distance. I am united with the people I am no longer among only by the dispossession of a common tongue.

There is a moment in a short story by a contemporary Hindi writer, Uday Prakash, where in the loss of a language what is also seen is the arrival of the triumphalist West. The protagonist of Prakash's tale is a Hindi poet, Paul Gomra. His real name is Ram Gopal Saksena, but upon witnessing the popularity of foreign brands in the market, "names like Maruti, Cielo, Zen, Sierra, Sumo, Honda, Kawasaki, Suzuki and whatnot," Ram Gopal reverses his name and comes up with Paul Gomra. Standing at the turbulent borders of a changing age, the Hindi poet feels bewildered. Gomra has seen nations like Yugoslavia and East Germany and superpowers like the Soviet Union vanish from the political map of the world. With the demise of socialism in Europe, people have been waiting with great anticipation for its disappearance from Asia and the Third World. Prakash writes: "If matters had stopped there, Paul Gomra would not have been too much worried. But he could see that with the same speed with which socialism had been wiped out of Eastern Europe, now all the Hindi magazines and newspapers were being wiped out in Delhi."[8] When I think about the transformation that Uday Prakash is describing, I am struck by another fact. It is only in books and in language that the disappearance of books and languages is to be mourned. And also fought.

In my hometown, Patna, there is a general consensus that culture, like the surrounding economy, lies in ruins. And yet a visit to the Khuda Bakhsh Library reveals another world, distant from the cramped, dusty streets outside filled with rickshaws and cars with loud, blasting horns. A librarian, his right hand shaky, pulls out a book on medicine that was written two thousand years ago. The book is titled *Kitab-ul-Hashaish*. The edition the librarian holds in his hands is from the thirteenth century A.D. The book was translated from Greek to Arabic by the order of

Haroun-ul-Rashid; it carries beautiful illustrations painted with herbal and mineral colors that still appear clean and bright. The librarian is old; his spectacles sit crookedly over his bulging eyes. He wants to show you ancient paintings of war scenes where, he says, "no two faces are alike." He keeps using the phrase "hidden treasures." There are twenty-two thousand handwritten books in this library; about five thousand to seven thousand of them are rare manuscripts.

A well-known historian, Surendra Gopal, accompanies me on my visit to this library. Gopal tells me that the library was gifted to the government in 1891 and is today "the richest manuscript library on Islam in the world." When I hear this, I am only conscious of the wretchedness on the streets outside. A stone's throw away is the Patna Medical College and Hospital, where I had been treated and operated upon when I was a boy. My mother, too, was a patient there. Later, my sister worked in its wards as a doctor. Medical procedures in the hospital were sometimes performed in the light of lanterns and torches: when it was raining, flying ants would crowd in and settle down on the open wounds during operations. Even during the day, stray dogs pulled away at bandages on patients. Patna is a place where rats carried away my mother's dentures.

The librarian at the Khuda Bakhsh has taken out from his safe another book. He tells me that it is a priceless book of poems by the Persian poet Hafiz. The book was presented to the Mughal ruler Humanyun by the emperor of Iran. The Mughal rulers used the book to read omens, or *shakun*: they would turn to a page and try to foretell the future from the words on the page that was open before them. Akbar was emperor when his son Jahangir, banished to Allahabad for his philandering, sought the help of the book to divine his future. The lines that the young prince came across were *"Gham-e-garibi wa mehnat chun barnamitabun / bashar-e khud rawam washaher yaar khud bashan"* (If it is intolerable for you to live in the foreign land, then you should return home. You will be emperor). In the margins of the book, Jahangir had written that he was in Allahabad and had been perplexed; he returned home to Fatehpur-Sikri on reading the augury and a few days later, following Akbar's death, was crowned emperor.

The librarian's dark finger hovers over the lines that the emperor had inscribed. The page is filigreed in gold, the bare portions stained with age. I want to touch the page myself. I ask the librarian's permission, and when he says yes, I gently place my index finger where the emperor has signed his name.

The librarian and the historian talk for a long time. I do not want to leave the library. It is hot outside. The temperature has exceeded 110 degrees Fahrenheit. The librarian, who knows Urdu, Arabic, and Persian, is reciting poetry. The words were written by the last Mughal governor of Bihar. The historian, Gopal, mentions his name. I ask the librarian to repeat the lines. The poet was addressing the deer in the forest, saying to them what they know, that Majnun, the lover, has died. But what the poet wants to know from the deer is what has passed over the wilderness, how the forest has suffered. The librarian is a man of courtesy, what is called *tahzeeb* in Urdu. When I am leaving his office, he gestures toward Gopal and says, "He is a museum of knowledge. There are very few people left like this in Patna." Patna is the wilderness; people like the librarian recall Majnun, who has departed.

Gopal has been affected by the conversation about Patna and the loss of cultural institutions. He says that there is a complete absence now of those kinds of conversations that he felt were essential to civilized life. He is nostalgic about his youth in a young India. We pass Patna's Gandhi Maidan, only a mile or so from the Khuda Bakhsh Library; this is the place where the most important political gatherings have taken place in Patna's history. Gopal repeats the two lines of poetry that he had heard the poet Sahir Ludhianvi recite at a socialist meeting there in the 1950s: "*Har cheez yahan bikti hai, har cheez ko bikte dekha hai*" (Everything here is for sale, I have seen everything being sold here). The historian is burdened by his memories. He talks about the lack of funds, the theft of public money, the closing of colleges and libraries.

I think of the librarian with his unsteady hand, lovingly laying out the volume that was brought to India by Humayun *badshah*.[9] The acquisition of those books was also a part of a process of trade and conquest. It was tied to commerce and, indeed, to the sale of both precious and ordinary goods. But this was not all. There are other truths too, like the words written by a reader in the margins of the text, about hopes, and fears, and the unknown. There are auguries of the future and a melancholia about the past. Libraries are haunted by the marketplace—but, it can be hoped, the opposite is true as well. At the same time, there is the enormous tussle of memory and desire that cannot all be neatly or fully regulated by the market or, for that matter, the rulers of nations and corporations. Writers bear witness to this uneven battle too: it is part of the reality of the writer's work, of struggling every day with the worldliness of the word. Writers are caught in the contradictory tasks of building imaginary worlds that are removed from everyday life and, at the same time, establishing how the imagination is not detached from the quotidian world and very much a vital part of it. To realize the truth of this condition is to know that books not only offer refuge from the world, they also return you to it. When I had understood this truth, I had stopped worshipping paper and become a reader.

NOTES

From Amitava Kumar, *Bombay-London-New York* (New York: Routledge, 2002), 1–15. Reprinted with permission of the publisher.

1. A. K. Ramanujan, "Annayya's Anthropology," trans. Narayan Hegde, in *From Cauvery to Godavari: Modern Kannada Short Stories*, ed. Ramachandra Sharma (New Delhi: Penguin, 1991), 47.
2. Maureen L. P. Patterson, ed., *South Asian Library Resources in North America: A Survey Prepared for the Boston Conference, 1974* (London: Inter Documentation, 1975), 11–12.
3. Ramanujan, "Annayya's Anthropology," 35–36.
4. Vandana Shiva, *The Violence of the Green Revolution: Third World Agriculture, Ecology and Politics* (New York: Zed Books, 1991), 35–36.
5. Shiva, *The Violence of the Green Revolution*, 16.
6. Raj Kamal Jha, *The Blue Bedspread* (New Delhi: Picador India, 1999), 179.
7. C. L. R. James, *Beyond a Boundary* (Durham, NC: Duke University Press, 1993), 113.
8. See Uday Prakash, *Paul Gomra Ka Scooter* (New Delhi: Radhakrishan Prakashan, 1997), 38–39. The translation is mine.
9. Or Emperor Humanyun.

2

My Hanif Kureishi Life

In the folder of papers that I collected during my first year as a new immigrant in the West, I have a newspaper clipping from the Indian newspaper the *Statesman*. The report is about the visit to Delhi of a literary critic who had emigrated from India in the early 1960s. The critic told the reporter that she liked to eavesdrop on conversations in Delhi's buses. She had noticed how people would switch to English whenever they wanted to express "a noble thought or a higher emotion." The literary critic went on: "It would be interesting to study how many people, who otherwise conducted their courtship in one Indian language or the other, have said that vital sentence 'I love you' in English."[1] While sitting in the basement of a library that offered the privilege of reading two Indian newspapers about a fortnight late, I read the report about the critic's visit, and that line about the use of the English language arrested me. The phenomenon that she had described was for her proof that we Indians had imbibed the colonizer's language, and, equally important, that there was no way of wishing away this fact. To deny the place that English had in our lives, she said, would be to deny our past. All this seemed quite indubitable to me. But the critic's remarks were actually of interest to me for an entirely different reason.

I had left India behind. In my new life, I wanted romance. It was not only my untried sexuality that bothered me; rather, the feeling of sexual inexperience seemed to gather into itself the more visible sense of social and financial insecurity in a new, foreign society. Love and sex, I had told myself, would make me an insider. However, there were obstacles in my path. I was worried that I would not know what to say when I was going to ask someone for a kiss. Or how exactly I would tell a woman I had fallen in love with, which I did with alarming frequency, that I wanted to be in love with her forever. As a result, I was extremely attentive to any insight into the language of love. The news item in the *Statesman* had posed a problem for me. In a place where everyone spoke English, how would I switch languages? This question didn't emerge in a vacuum. Although I wanted to fall in love with white women, women with golden hair and glittering smiles that I had seen in magazine ads, I was nostalgic for home. I would have given much to be able to say to someone in Hindi that I loved them very much.

During that first year I was away from India, *Masterpiece Theater* was screening the adaptation of Paul Scott's *The Jewel in the Crown* on television. Salman Rushdie had pilloried this film as a part of the Orientalizing "Raj revival."[2] He was right. But for me, the weekly screenings were a way to reenter a space of romance and Indianness. Within the frame of the film, I could still speak English and be at home. Perhaps it even gave me pleasure that the people around me were watching a television show that portrayed India, and therefore Indians, as erotic and dangerous. I wanted to look in the mirror and see Art Malik, the actor who played Hari Kumar. I longed for a tie, a jacket, and a British accent. In the weeks that followed, I acquired two of the three.

In those days, while I awaited the weekly screenings of *The Jewel in the Crown*, I also read other Raj fiction. I came across E. M. Forster's "Kanaya," a brief memoir of the writer's days as the secretary to a minor maharaja in Dewas, in central India, in the early 1920s.[3] I had not known that Forster was gay. As I learned later, the writer was putting some distance between himself and the England of the Oscar Wilde trial and the sodomy laws; his love affair with Mohommed el Edl in Egypt, and his later furtive relationships in India, were attempts to find a flawed fulfillment in the colonies. In Dewas, Forster was having trouble finding a suitable person to have sex with. The Englishman received advice from his Hindu employer—"you must not masturbate, that's awful"[4]—and also assurances that he could procure someone from among the hereditary servants. Kanaya was the name of the barber boy that His Highness thought Forster would like.

Kanaya was pretty, wrote Forster, "with a clear complexion, thick black eyebrows that met, and a thin black moustache." He was "somewhat overdressed, in too yellow a coat and too blue a turban," and, to Forster, "he rather suggested the part." But the barber-boy was amiable as he shaved Forster, and the writer was pleasant in return. At his next meeting, Forster "caressed the buttons of his coat." And when he drew the boy to him, Kanaya shook his head. Forster wrote: "To shake the head means 'yes' in that country." (Ah . . . the treacherous ambivalence of the sign in that alien country called sexuality. And also the ambivalence, of course, of colonial power, and the desire that meets domination.) "Are you willing?" Forster asked the boy.[5] But even as the question was posed, there was the sudden noise of water being splashed against the *tattie* that covered the door. A servant had returned. Kanaya went away.

At the third meeting, wrote Forster, "Kanaya was punctual and gratified my desires." But, the satisfaction, it seemed, didn't last. Forster had expected more by way of a friendship with Kanaya. But this seemed unlikely. Forster wrote, "I couldn't get from Kanaya the emotional response of an Egyptian, because he had the body and the soul of a slave, but he was always merry and he improved my health." There were other hindrances to the companionship that Forster seemed to be seeking. It was difficult for the two to meet, and then, after he had been away for ten days, Forster returned to Dewas to find that Kanaya had been talking to others. He had told someone that "Sahib's fond of boys." When the rumor spread, people responded with a change in their behavior; they acted with what Forster called "a good deal of impertinence and ill-breeding."[6]

The scandal spread. In another two months, Forster was to leave Dewas. And the tensions in the court persisted till he left. In Forster's account, there was little joy. The illusion of imperial romance, across races and classes, could not possibly have lasted, not in the form that Forster, a Cambridge intellectual, wanted it to take when he chose to have sex, almost exclusively, with illiterate, working-class men. This, too, is perhaps a part of the famous "not now, not yet" declaration in the novel that Forster was to write the following year, *A Passage to India*. The book ends with this lament about the impossibility of friendship between Aziz and Fielding, one man an Indian and the other British. Forster himself saw the division between the colonizer and the colonized clearly enough even when he was writing "Kanaya." But more clearly, he saw his own place in the state of things: "I see myself disintegrated and inert, like the dead cow among vultures at the edge of the road."[7] This was less about judging one of the two parties; Forster had decided that neither was any good. In a letter to his friend Syed Ross Masood, Forster confided why he had turned away from fashioning his novel as a bridge between the East and the West: "I think that most Indians, like most English people, are shits, and I am not interested whether they sympathize with one another or not."[8]

This unsentimental education was not proving a very great help to me in my search for romance. I had begun reading "Kanaya" with excitement because the writer's negotiation of the taboo against homosexuality could be instructive. It spoke to me about accepting desire and then speaking, or at least writing, about it. Forster's agonized presentation of his needs to His Highness, his sense of frustration, even the small, touching details about the Englishman fondling the buttons on Kanaya's coat, spoke to me of candor and even maturity. But my reading of "Kanaya" didn't lessen either my ignorance or my confusion, and there was a reason for it.

In India, when I was an adolescent, there was an incident in a nearby small town. I read about it in the papers. It was my first, shocking introduction to homosexuality. An upper-caste hoodlum had got into a quarrel with a teacher; he had picked up the teacher's son, taken him to a small house that served as the office of a political party, and sodomized the boy. Years later, in the mid-1990s, I was back in India, traveling with a group of Naxalites, the leftist activists organizing peasants in the Bihar countryside. A young man asked me I had come across any handbooks on guerrilla strategy, especially any that had come out of El Salvador or Nicaragua. I said I hadn't. He then asked me about the Persian Gulf War. He wanted to know whether I had made contacts with groups in the United States that had opposed the war. I said that I had. On the campus where I had been a student at that time, the leftist as well as the gay and lesbian organizations had been at the forefront of the protests against the war. I had many friends in those groups. After a pause, the young man asked me the meaning of the term "gays and lesbians." When I answered him, my interlocutor fell silent. Then he said, "In this region we are organizing a campaign against homosexuals." When I asked him why, he told me that the local landlords had taken to terrorizing the lower-caste landless peasants by raping their boys. The campaign was a part of the protest against this brutality.

I suddenly remembered that autumn some years ago when I had read Forster. I told the young man that, till I came to the United States, I was not aware of having met anyone who was gay. The signs of gayness, I could see with hindsight, were everywhere in India. I just did not read them as such. At the university that I joined in the United States, however, there was an active gay and lesbian organization. It had Indian members and, crucially, the members were progressive and active in a number of organizations. I considered myself a committed leftist when I left India, but the freedom of sexual choice had not before been articulated for me as an important right worth fighting for. I narrated all this to the young man in the village in Bihar and, later, our discussion that afternoon broadened, and the whole group discussed the difference between rape and homosexuality. I did not talk on that occasion about Forster, but he had been an important link in the story I was telling that day. Forster's brief piece had been an odd revelation to me: at one level, it offered me a new, empathic portrayal of gay sexuality, and even, more generally, of sexual desire; but at another level, it stirred in my mind, which might have been unguarded against prejudice, the memory of what I had read in the newspapers so long ago about the boy and the hoodlum in the town not far from my own.

When I look back at it now—my reading the news item in the library basement about English as the language of love in Delhi, or my search for writers who were broaching the subject of sex with Indians, or just the desire deep inside me of wanting to be in love—I am struck by a different thought. My desire to be welcomed into love by white women, the idealized sexuality of glossy magazines mixing somewhere with my tormented silence, did not exist alone. Its obverse was the limited—and limiting—view that Forster took of the Other. After Kanaya had come back to beg forgiveness for having said too much, Forster shunned him with the thought: "What relation beyond carnality could one establish with such people? He hadn't even the initiative to cut my throat."

. . .

Hanif Kureishi swam into my universe like a new planet. Here was an entirely other world, I thought. Kureishi was the right antidote to Forster. And to me. The first work of Kureishi's that I encountered was *My Beautiful Laundrette*. I watched the film in the university auditorium only months after I had begun dutifully sitting in front of the television whenever *The Jewel in the Crown* was being screened. The pathetic relics of the Raj, to which I had attached myself, were quickly washed away during the screening. There was India in Kureishi's film too, but this India was in the living rooms and laundrettes of England.

The people from the older generation were Indians I recognized: the hero's father was an over-the-hill socialist, alcoholic, and now dependent on the dole ("Oh dear," he says mournfully, mockingly, at one point in the film, "the working class are such a disappointment to me"). The youth in the film didn't say "sahib" every time they opened their mouths: they spoke in British accents and had skinheads for friends. Omar, the protagonist, was in love with a skinhead named Johnny. The gay theme was an important and very open part of the film. But it was also very much taken for granted; it wasn't a part of a big announcement or a program. And the film bound this story with other stories about large Indian and Pakistani families, and immigration, and the corroding power of Thatcherism. (When asked why he evicts people from his property, proving those people right who say that "Pakis just come here to hustle other people's lives and jobs and houses," Nasser, the entrepreneur, gives a response that would warm the cockles of a Thatcherite heart: "But we're professional businessmen. Not professional Pakistanis. There's no race question in the new enterprise culture.")

Some in the Indian and Pakistani community were shocked by the representation of gay sexuality and adultery in *Laundrette*. To them, the film was a betrayal by a renegade Muslim. In New York City, the film was picketed by the Pakistan Action Committee. The *New York Times*, reporting on a later visit by Kureishi to America, quoted the writer as saying: "People think you're supposed to show them [gays] exclusively as strong, truthful and beautiful. . . . It's just exactly what Philip Roth went through." Kureishi then added, "Looking back on it, I can see in it the seeds of the Rushdie situation."[9] The writer's own aunt, living in England, castigated him in a letter: "I tried to phone you, but I believe you were in the U.S.A. boring the pants off the Americans with your pornography. . . . We didn't know you were a 'poofter.' . . . Why oh why do you have to promote the widely held view of the British that all evil stems from Pakistani immigrants? Thank goodness for top quality films like *Gandhi*."[10] (The aunt was rewarded for her troubles when, in *Sammie and Rosie Get Laid*, Kureishi gave her name to the Asian lesbian.)

I came across more of Kureishi's writing in *Granta* magazine. After *Laundrette* came out, Kureishi published a novella in *Granta* with the not-so-easy-to-forget title *With Your Tongue Down My Throat*. Earlier, he had published in the same magazine travelogues like "Erotic Politicians and Mullahs" about a visit to Pakistan, and another one called "Bradford," about the discovery of the changes that have turned the city into what one later film was to call "Bradistan." I told myself that I was reading each word that Kureishi published—I later found out that this was not quite true—and talked to my friends about him. The first woman I kissed in America looked at Kureishi's photograph in a magazine and said, "What a face, what a face." I might be adding this to my memory of the moment, but I do seem to remember that I felt very close to my friend when she spoke those words.

When *Sammy and Rosie Get Laid* was released, it had the salient virtue of having as one of its stars a well-known actor from Bollywood films, Shashi Kapoor. He was playing the role of a Pakistani politician—he spoke all his lines in English—and reluctantly received lessons in London in deviant sexuality. I lapped it all up. The lesbian who had been named after Kureishi's aunt, and played by Meera Syal, dismisses heterosexual sex with the line: "You know, that stuff when the woman spends the whole time trying to come, but can't. And the man spends the whole time trying to stop himself from coming, but can't."

Rafi Rahman, Kapoor's character, has returned to a London where he had been a student. His youth lay in the memories of a city that had now changed beyond recognition. The city had changed, but so had its people. Now, for example, there were Bangladeshis in London who remembered what Rafi's army had done to their families. History came back to haunt Rafi. Kureishi had staged a dramatic confrontation in a restaurant between Rafi and his daughter-in-law, Rosie. Rosie asked Rafi, "What does it feel like to kill, to torture, to maim, and what did you do in the evenings?" In reply, Rafi rails at Rosie: "You are only concerned with homosexuals and women! A luxury that rich oppressors can afford! We were concerned with poverty, imperialism, feudalism! Real issues that burn people!" Rafi's paltry defense, a familiar left-nationalist argument, sounded so hollow. And yet, this is what, I thought, I too might have said earlier.

The most affecting exchange, however, took place between Rafi and Alice, the woman whom he had loved when he was a student in London. Rafi, it seemed, had found his white woman. She had loved him back. He had made promises to return, but never did. Alice, played with a kind of luminous fragility by Claire Bloom, takes Rafi to her cellar and shows the clothes she had packed, the books, the shoes, the bottles of perfume. She shows him the diaries from 1954, 1955, 1956, inscribed with letters to "My Darling Rafi." But Rafi has no response for Alice when she says to him bitterly, brilliantly uniting politics and passion: "I waited for you, for years! Every day I thought of you! Until I began to heal up. What I wanted was a true marriage. But you wanted power. Now you must be content with having introduced flogging for minor offenses, nuclear capability, and partridge shooting into your country."

In 1990, Kureishi published his debut novel, *The Buddha of Suburbia*. "My name is Karim Amir, and I am an Englishman born and bred, almost." That was the book's opening line; I loved the stumble at the end, which I read more as a feint, our own declaration of "not now, not yet."[11] The book presented an England strung out on what one character in *Buddha* called "race, class, fucking, and farce."[12] Kureishi was less Forster, and more Ackerley. J. R. Ackerley's *Hindoo Holiday*, which was a memoir written of his employment at an estate that his friend Forster had recommended to him, offered a hilarious portrait of colonial India. In Ackerley's writing, a kiss rarely carried the burden of gross cultural generalization. Once, Ackerley was kissed on the cheek by his young friend Narayan. Ackerley returned the kiss, but Narayan drew back immediately, saying: "Not the mouth! You eat meat! You eat meat!" Ackerley had written, "Yes, and I will eat you in a minute."[13] Then followed the writer's observation that this time when he kissed, Narayan did not draw away. There was kissing in Kureishi too, and it had a light, subversive quality to it. When Karim joins a theater group he meets another actor, Terry, an active Trotskyite, who asks him to join the Party. Karim narrates the exchange: "He said I should join to prove that my commitment to the ending of injustice wasn't all hot air. I said I would sign up with pleasure on one condition. He had to kiss me. This, I said, would prove his commitment to overcoming his inbred bourgeois morality. He said that maybe I wasn't ready to join the Party just yet."[14] Forster would not—could not—have accused Karim Amir of lacking the initiative to cut—or kiss—his throat.

When I read Kureishi, a whole generation of earlier writers who had written about race suddenly seemed dated—and old. In the presence of Kureishi's characters like Karim, the older writers could finally be seen for what they were in the England to which they had traveled from their old countries: aliens. In this new world, the white Englishmen who Karim met were, funnily enough, sometimes more Indian than he was. And those who weren't were right-wing reactionaries who wanted Karim to keep away from their daughters. One of them told Karim: "We're with Enoch. If you put one of your black'ands near my daughter I'll smash it with a'ammer! With a'ammer!"[15] (Then, he let loose his Great Dane on Karim. The dog, less racially prejudiced, put its paws on Karim's back and planted dog jissom on his jacket.)

Kureishi's candor appeared novel to me because it was both contemporary and sexual. I read later that while he was studying philosophy at the University of London, Kureishi had supported himself by writing pornography under the name Antonia French. That piece of information led me back to India and made me speculate on the place of the pornographic imagination in Indian fiction in English. Steamy, soft-porn writing has flourished in the books by very minor writers, Shobha De being one example, but no major writer, over a long span of time, had applied his or her talent to the elaboration of an erotic aesthetic. The only writer who comes close is Upamanyu Chatterjee, who had emerged as a voice in *desi* writing around the same time that Kureishi was gathering fans in the West. Chatterjee is a member of the Indian civil service, and, in my opinion, it is the juxtaposition of sex and bureaucracy in his writing (especially in his debut novel, *English, August,* and his latest, less impressive *The Mammaries of the Welfare State*) that gives his prose its particular touch of perversity.[16] In Chatterjee's writing, there is no trace of the reticence that many think is characteristic of Indian English writing about sex. It is not only that the dull acts of reading files and attending meetings are transformed by the fantasies of the eternally bored and stoned Agastya Sen, who serves in the above two novels as Chatterjee's doppelganger. Rather, Chatterjee's strength is that in his novels the more ordinary, everyday acts of Indians get imbued with sexuality. As a result, the whole world appears in a wonderfully sordid light.

Agastya Sen, and his colleagues with their families, go on a picnic to a forest area where there is a Shiv temple. The temple that the group is visiting had been built in the second half of the tenth century. The temple's walls are covered with intricate erotic sculptures. As can be expected, the sculptures invite bawdy jokes. But it is the more banal, perhaps repressed, practices of the people in front of Agastya, rather than those given form in the tenth century, that catch Chatterjee's eye, and as a consequence he produces writing that is more shocking and also revealing. Agastya is asked by someone, "Have you ever seen how women behave in front of a shivaling?" The narrative goes on: "There was a tube-light in the innermost sanctum directly above the black stone phallus of Shiv. There the wives came into their own. They took turns to gently smear the shivaling with sandalwood paste, sprinkle water and flowers over it, prostrate and pray before it, suffocate it with incense, kiss their fingers after touching it."[17]

There was a lesson here also about language. I had been carrying with me the knowledge imparted by the literary critic traveling in the Delhi bus, the knowledge that Indians switched to English whenever they wanted to express "a noble thought or a higher emotion." But in Chatterjee's writing, English was being made Indian precisely by expressing a less than noble thought and by giving voice to what would be called a lower emotion. An early chapter in *English, August* offered the lines: "District administration in India is largely a British creation, like the railways and the English language, another complex and unwieldy bequest of the Raj. But Indianization (of a method of administration, or of a language) is integral to the Indian story."[18]

An oft-quoted line from the novel, in fact from the opening page itself, is: "'Amazing mix, the English we speak. Hazaar fucked. Urdu and American,' Agastya laughed, 'a thousand fucked, really fucked. I'm sure nowhere else could languages be mixed *and* spoken with such ease.'"[19] But it isn't so much the mix of Urdu and American, I'd argue, that represents the abstract and somewhat elusive quality of Indianness. Instead, it is the quality of the burlesque: the staidness of colonial English tickled, harassed, abused, and caressed by proper as well as improper Indians. This is the world where memories, with a shift in the accent, get easily transmuted into mammaries. If anything separates me from that moment years ago in the library basement, where I sat contemplating a news item about the use of English in India, it is the realization that Indians, with all the ambiguity that accompanies the following term, get fucked in English.

．．．

"Your life is so pristine, mine's like the Hanif Kureishi scene," is a line from a song by the British Asian band Cornershop.

When I reminded Kureishi of this line in my interview with him, Kureishi laughed and said, "Yeah, I remember that. What were they talking about?" I said, "I think it has to do with sexuality, the idea that your life was rife with excitement." "It was!" Kureishi said. "At that time, it was. Until I had kids." He laughed again, and then looked at me. "You'll find that after you have kids, it just changes."[20]

I asked Kureishi how he might be different from a writer like Naipaul, and he began by talking of the similarities between his father and Naipaul's father. Both men had an interest in education and in writing. Kureishi said, "They were fastidious men who wanted to be journalists, but they were bitter men, failed men." Then he outlined the differences between himself and Naipaul. The two of us, he said, are "completely different." He didn't have Naipaul's interest in India, for example. Kureishi said of Naipaul, "He has a basically conservative sensibility, and I don't only mean politically. . . . Also, I like women. I like women and I've always been interested in sex and relationships between men and women." Naipaul's books fail, Kureishi said, because Naipaul "can't write about relationships between men and women, and he can't write about marriage, which seems to be the central institution of the West. Most of the great novels of the West are about sexual desire—*Anna Karenina*, *Madame Bovary*—they are all books about marriage and adultery."[21]

In 1998, Kureishi published *Intimacy*. It was a novella about a single night, when the protagonist, Jay, has decided to leave his unsuspecting wife and two kids for someone else. Kureishi's prose in the book was lucid and elegant. Jay was a mixture of doubt and desire. As a result, the clarity of the writing produced a strange effect, a tense sense of disquiet. In the novel, Jay is a screenwriter. And on that night, he wanted to record what he was feeling as he went through his separation, because he desired "an absolute honesty that doesn't merely involve saying how awful one is."[22] In other words, he wanted to achieve an intimacy with himself at the very moment he had become certain that he had lost every shred of it with his wife. Perhaps the tension that the reader experienced while reading the novella was that it mirrored the disturbing closeness that lies between the intimacy of the act of love and, on the other hand, the intimacy of the act of infidelity.

I asked Kureishi about *Intimacy*, and he described the book as an attempt to write a book "about how painful it is when a marriage falls apart. . . . I wrote a story about what happens on the night you leave. The violence of it. The viciousness, the hatred, the fury, the strength of feeling that you have when you fall out of love with somebody."[23] The book had very close autobiographical parallels to Kureishi's own life, and it was widely attacked for it. In the interview, Kureishi did not sound guilty, though one can imagine his critics wanted him to be precisely that, at least to start with.

Kureishi's own attitude has been to regard desire as liberation. When he was a kid, he read D. H. Lawrence, Henry Miller, Erica Jong, Philip Roth, the Beats, and others. Kureishi said to me, "You need other people to liberate you."[24] But liberation from what? What interests me, finally, about Kureishi's elaboration of the idea of sexuality and desire is that it comes into play in his work not as a nostalgic, return-to-the-1960s rebellion against bourgeois norms but as a way of coming to grips with the contemporary landscape that is mined with politics. In a 1988 article that I have saved from an era when I copied and kept everything about Kureishi, the writer told another interviewer: "I like to write about sex as a focus of social, psychological, emotional, political energy—it's so central to people's lives, who you fuck, how much you love them, the dance that goes around it, all the seduction, betrayal, loyalty, failure, loneliness."[25]

The following year, Khomeini's fatwa against Rushdie had a decisive impact on Kureishi. He was outraged by the threats to a writer's freedom. Many others were too, but, for Kureishi, sex now became a way of opposing fundamentalism. In *The Black Album*, and then in the short story "My Son the Fanatic," which was later made into a film, the absolutism of faith and its austerity is arrayed in battle against the human heart and its waywardness. Love, sex, alcohol, rock music, literature, fashion, and even food are defenses against the crushing certainties of strict religious doctrines. Not too long ago, I read a reviewer's comment on a film about Asians in England, *East Is East*, and I was struck by how much both the script and the review owed to Kureishi's pioneering work: "Sex in *East Is East* means a genital urge; but it also means the desire to eat pork sausage, or the aspiration to design hats, or the need to be admitted without hassle to the local disco, as if you were as good as white. For Dad, it's a drive toward rectitude, as much as power; for Mom, it's a longing for recognition and company, including that of her family."[26]

All this is a part of a liberal belief in openness and freedom. It is also a part of a strong belief in plurality. In many ways, the brilliance of the film *My Son the Fanatic* lies not simply in the moment in which the fundamentalist son, after being hit by the father, asks him, "You call me fanatic, dirty man, but who is the fanatic now?" Rather, beyond even this gesture of irony and reversal, is the father's desperate, loving statement to the son, as he watches the boy march away with his militant friends: "There are many ways of being a good man. . . ." This belief is combined in Kureishi with a commitment to the benefits of education. And the possibility that education offers an individual choices and the chance to grow. One can surmise that a faith in those liberal ideals, and in the promise of art to give shape to experience and lead to understanding, is the bedrock on which Kureishi bases his own practice as a writer.

Yet, as always, things are more complicated than that. Kureishi told me during our interview that the book burnings and the fatwa against Rushdie were only part of the reason why he wrote *The Black Album*. His own life, at that time, "was falling apart." Kureishi said that he was "very involved in drugs and all kinds of dissident sexuality" and scared that he would, if he continued in the same way, stop writing altogether. His father had died recently, and he was getting addicted to cocaine. He said: "And that's when I started getting interested in fundamentalist religion. I could see that a puritanical religion could be very helpful."[27] In other words, we begin to see that it is not liberalism pitched against fundamentalism, or even the other way around, but each of them acting as a check on the complete autonomy of the other. That essentially is the truth of the Hanif Kureishi scene, where life is not so much confusing as unstable and open-ended. It is also remarkable that in his fiction, Islam and the West have not clashed as opposing civilizations where one is modern and the other primitive, but, instead, they emerge as two contrary modernities. In the interview, Kureishi explained this point to me: "Islamic fundamentalism was a completely new phenomenon in the eighties. Of course, the fundamentalists would say, 'We're just following tradition,' but actually it was the invention of a brand new tradition. There hadn't been such a thing before."[28]

The talk of paradise and eternity is as much a part of the contemporary moment as fusion and Ecstasy. An aggressive, unequal form of globalization has produced as its equally dangerous underside a culture of fundamentalism. This is not a matter of the past and the future; instead, it has everything to do with our inseparable present. Kureishi's lucid lesson is that our desires, even when they are opposed to our more austere orders, are inextricably bound in conflict. The writer does not stand apart from this confusion. When we grasp this, we attain clarity.

In this way, we also learn that saying "I love you" is not so much a matter of choosing between English and Hindi, as I had believed when I first left India. Nor, for that matter, is it a case of choosing between promiscuity and commitment. Rather, we learn how our choices are threatened by, and even drawn toward, their opposites—and, forever famished, they crave language and, inevitably, also silence.

NOTES

From Amitava Kumar, *Bombay-London-New York* (New York: Routledge, 2002), 145–62. Reprinted with permission of the publisher.

1. Joydeep Gupta, "Cultural Politics Dissected," *Statesman*, February 13, 1987, 3.
2. Salman Rushdie, "Outside the Whale," *Granta* 11 (1983), 125.
3. E. M. Forster, "Kanaya," in E. M. Forster, *The Hill of Devi and Other Indian Writings* (London: Edward Arnold, 1983), 310–24.
4. Forester, "Kanaya," 315.
5. Forester, "Kanaya," 315.
6. Forester, "Kanaya," 319.
7. Forester, "Kanaya," 324.
8. Quoted in P. N. Furbank, *E. M. Forster: A Life* (Oxford: Oxford University Press, 1979), 106.
9. Quoted in Glenn Collins, "A Screenwriter Returns to the Themes of Race and Class in London," *New York Times*, May 24, 1990.
10. Hanif Kureishi, *Sammy and Rosie Get Laid: The Screenplay and the Screenwriter's Diary* (New York: Penguin, 1988), 64.
11. Hanif Kureishi, *The Buddha of Suburbia* (London: Faber and Faber, 1990), 3.
12. Kureishi, *The Buddha of Suburbia*, 189.
13. J. R. Ackerley, *Hindoo Holiday* (1932; New York: New York Review of Books, 2000), 240.
14. Kureishi, *The Buddha of Suburbia*, 149.
15. Kureishi, *The Buddha of Suburbia*, 40.
16. Upamanyu Chatterjee, *English, August* (London: Faber and Faber, 1988) and *The Mammaries of the Welfare State* (New Delhi: Viking, 2000).
17. Chatterjee, *English, August*, 127–28.
18. Chatterjee, *English, August*, 10.
19. Chatterjee, *English, August*, 1.
20. Amitava Kumar, "A Bang and a Whimper: A Conversation with Hanif Kureishi," *Transition* 10, no. 4 (2001), 124.
21. Kumar, "A Bang and a Whimper," 124.
22. Hanif Kureishi, *Intimacy* (London: Faber, 1998), 47.
23. Kumar, "A Bang and a Whimper," 131.
24. Kumar, "A Bang and a Whimper," 128.
25. Quoted in David Nicholson, "My Beautiful Britain," *Films and Filming*, January 1988, 10.
26. Stuart Klawans, "On Tyson vs. Downey," *Nation*, May 15, 2000, 36.
27. Kumar, "A Bang and a Whimper," 126.
28. Kumar, "A Bang and a Whimper," 127.

3

The Map of My Village

The house was in an alley, set away from the winding street, and in that house were three communists who, during my first visit, sold me a book and several magazines. This was in my hometown, Patna, in India. I had left Patna some years before; I was a graduate student in cultural studies in Minnesota; now, back home for a month, I was looking for a topic to research for a course in which I had taken an incomplete.

In one of the Hindi magazines I bought that afternoon, I read a long poem written by a poet I hadn't heard of before, but who, I found out from the biographical note, had been living in Patna for years. The poet's name was Alokdhanwa. He too had been a communist or a communist sympathizer, writing poetry about peasant struggles in the land. The poem I had come across was titled "Janata Ka Aadmi" (Man of the people). It was a long poem, and it started with a series of electrifying

declarations on behalf of poetry, a kind of bravely anti-aesthetic manifesto, and then it set its sights on what one might call media critique,
denouncing newspapers that carried everything but the news: "Woh log
peshewar khooni hain / jo nangi khabron ka gala ghoant dete hain /
Akhbaar ki sansanikhej surkhiyon ki aad mein / Weh baar-baar uss
ek chehre ke paaltu hain / Jiske peshaabghar ka naqsha mere gaon ke
naqshe she bada hai" (They are professional murderers / those who
strangle to death the naked news / in the shadow of sensational headlines / they show themselves again and again the serfs of that one face /
the map of whose urinal is bigger than the map of my village).[1]

That single line—"the map of whose urinal is bigger than the map of
my village"—enters my mind every time I step into a large, clean bathroom. This happens almost always only in the West, but it was for the
first time in India, in Delhi, when I was in my late teens, that the idea
of a spacious bathroom first filled my imagination. A friend of mine living in the same student hostel was a finalist for a Rhodes scholarship
to Oxford. He was interviewed at the home of a rich Parsi industrialist
who was an Oxford Blue in cricket. After his return from the interview,
my friend, whom I'll call S., reported that he had peed in a bathroom
where there hung paintings and whose walls were lined with shelves
containing countless rows of books. But wouldn't the water spill on the
bookshelves and the paintings? The idea of a shower curtain, and certainly a bathtub, was quite foreign to me; but more foreign still was the
idea of a large well-lit space whose purpose couldn't be reduced to a
filthy functionality. That unseen bathroom was my introduction to the
larger world that my friend was entering.

And later, returning from the West, during that long-ago afternoon
reading Alokdhanwa's line for the first time, what I was offered was a
map of my own private modernity: your class was revealed by what you
had—not in the bank, but in the bathroom.

I have been living for several years in upstate New York. While reading John Cheever's journals, I came across his critical note about Nabokov and his "sugared violets." Cheever had written: "The house I was
raised in had its charms, but my father hung his underwear from a nail
he had driven into the back of the bathroom door, and while I know
something about the Riviera I am not a Russian architect polished in

Paris. My prose style will always be to a degree matter-of-fact."[2] Ah, the bathroom door! That solitary nail! How it appealed to me.

Style reduced to class: at first it strikes me as true, and then, the next moment, not. There's so much elegance in Cheever's prose. Coming up with a phrase like "sugared violets" isn't a plumbing job, whatever that means. And that image of the nail driven into the bathroom door—there's a lot more than just the underwear hanging from it.

NOTES

From Amitava Kumar, "The Map of My Village," Maps special issue, PEN America no. 15 (2011), 12–13. Reprinted with permission of the publisher.

1. For the rest of my translation of Alokdhanwa's "Janata Ka Aadmi," see Amitava Kumar, "The Poet's Corpse in the Capitalist's Fish-Tank," *Critical Inquiry* 23 (Summer 1997): 894–909.
2. John Cheever, *The Journals of John Cheever* (New York: Vintage, 2008), 184.

· 4 ·

The Poetry of Gujarat Riots

If you type the words *Gujarat riots* into Google images, the photographs that pop up include the following: Narendra Modi; burned children; houses on fire; men armed with swords; and the face of a young woman I had met, during the months following the 2002 riots, in the Darya Khan Gumbat relief camp in Ahmedabad.

Her name was Noorjehan. When I saw her in the camp I recognized her from a photograph I had seen in the papers, the same photograph that was now appearing on my screen. When I asked what had happened to her, she said that her pets were killed on the first day of the riots. Then she began to speak about herself. She said that when the crowd came there were about seven or eight hundred of them, filling the streets. She had been watering the plants in her garden. Noorjehan used the English word *flowers*. She was watering her flowers when several men entered her house, hit her on the head with a sword, and then gang-raped her. Later, a young niece had to pull Noorjehan from the fire set by her assailants before they left her.

I came across Noorjehan's photograph again the other night because I had written a short piece for the *Indian Express*, about an Urdu poet in Gujarat, and I was looking for an image to accompany my article.[1] I had written about the Urdu poet, whose poems about the riots offered a testimony of survival. But the sight of Noorjehan's face made my stomach turn. I suddenly remembered what the little girls at the Shah-e-Alam camp had told the six female members of a fact-finding team when asked if they understood the meaning of the word *balatkaar* (rape). A nine-year-old gave this reply to the visiting women: "Mein bataoon Didi? Balatkar ka matlab jab aurat ko nanga karte hain aur phir use jala dete hain" (Shall I tell you, Didi? Rape is when a woman is stripped naked and then burned).[2]

And it was in this mood, then, that I settled back in my chair and looked at the picture of Narendra Modi on my monitor.

The Gujarat chief minister was on my mind because the piece I had written about the Urdu poet, Aqeel Shatir, was also very much a piece about Modi. A few days before Christmas, I had been sent a news story about Shatir, who had been asked to return the 10,000 rupees that he had been awarded by the Gujarat Urdu Sahitya Akademi.[3] The reason, according to the article, was that an anti–Narendra Modi remark had been found in a critical essay included in Shatir's book of poetry, *Abhi Zindaa Hoon Main* (I am still alive).

The offending lines were penned by Raunaq Afroz, in a commentary on Shatir's poems: "May good come the way of Narendra Modi who, as soon as he came to power, killed Urdu in Gujarat. Not only did Modi do that, but in 2002, under a well-thought-out plan for the whole of Gujarat, he played so nakedly with violence and barbaric riots that he shamed the whole of humanity. Everywhere, with loot and killings, murder and mayhem, rape, burning and genocide of the minority community, he created a climate of terror in the land."

When I called Shatir on the phone, he was sitting in the STD/PCO shop[4] that he owns in Ahmedabad. But as we talked, I realized he too had Modi on his mind. He told me that "Shatir" is his *takhallus*, or pen name; its literal meaning is "chess player," but it suggests a person who possesses cunning. And, he explained to me, true to his name, he wrote not about love or beauty but about the machinations of power.

To prove his point, he recited a few lines of his poetry:

Abhi zindaa hoon main, dekho meri pehchaan baaki hai
Badan zakhmi hai lekin abhi mujhmein jaan baaki hai
Tum apni hasraton ko zaalimon marne nahin dena
Shahadat ka mere dil mein abhi armaan baaki hai

(I am still alive, the person I was is left in me
This body is wounded but there is still life left in me
You, my killers, don't let your ambitions die
The desire for martyrdom is still left in me).

When he was reciting his lines on the phone, I tried to imagine Shatir reading them at a *mushaira*, or poetry reading, in Ahmedabad to an audience of riot victims. Think for a moment about the atmosphere at such a gathering in Gujarat where people, listening to a man reciting poems in Urdu, hear that despite the injury done to them they are still very much alive.

Earlier in our conversation, Shatir had told me that he wasn't too perturbed about the Akademi's actions. They were only making this demand, he said, because he had filed various official inquiries, under the Right to Information Act, asking about their use of public funds. But if things changed and the money needed to be returned, what would he do? Shatir was frank. He said, "It would be difficult. I am poor."

I then told him that in the week leading up to our conversation a small group of writers had come together to support him—financially, but also politically, to oppose censorship. This group had formed on Facebook and had borrowed its name from the opening phrase of the section that the Akademi had found offensive: "May Good Come to Narendra Modi." At last count, it had sixty-odd members, mostly writers who wrote in English but also a few others who used Hindi or Urdu. I didn't know many people in the group, even though I had met its founder, Peter Griffin, at the Jaipur Literature Festival. And I had read the work of some of the writers who had joined the list, like Indra Sinha, author of *Animal's People*, and others like Nilanjana Roy, Altaf Tyrewala, Annie Zaidi, and Vivek Narayanan.

In the last few days, with the reports in the news about Vibrant Gujarat, the international investors' summit, Narendra Modi has been again on my mind.[5] Over this two-day summit, which began on January 13, 2011, the state of Gujarat has purportedly attracted over $450 billion in promised investments. It would appear that a lot of good has already come to Narendra Modi.

On the phone, I had asked Shatir whether he thought Raunaq Afroz's words about Modi's role in the riots were incorrect. "No," Shatir replied, "Raunaq Afroz's views were no different from my own. And yet, if one were to remove that one page about the riots from the book of Modi's history, it could be said that Gujarat had never found a better chief minister." I then said to him that Modi had been chief minister when so many Muslims were killed, but was there any evidence that he had also killed Urdu? Again, Shatir was forthright. He said, "If the Muslim is killed, then his tongue, his *zubaan*, will die too."

My memory now takes me back to the camps in Ahmedabad. The last time I saw Noorjehan was when the weddings were being held in the school building where some of the riot victims had taken shelter. After the ceremony was over, the father of one of the brides told me that he was happy his daughter would now have a roof over her head. Parents were particularly fearful about their unmarried daughters. I wondered what would happen to Noorjehan.

I thought of her again when, before that year was over, elections were held in Gujarat. One week prior to the elections, in mid-December 2007, a report in *Time* magazine said that Modi asked his audience during an election rally, "Why are so many of you here?" In answer to his own question, referring to the train burning in Godhra, he shouted, "Because the fire that burns in my heart is the same as the fire in yours." The *Time* reporter wrote that, for anyone missing Modi's meaning, a young woman in the front had screamed out, "Kill the Muslim motherfuckers."[6] Modi won by a landslide.

During the Vibrant Gujarat summit, Modi has been hailed as a model leader. Big industrialists like Mukesh Ambani and Ratan Tata have cried themselves hoarse calling him a great visionary. Anil Ambani even likened him to Mahatma Gandhi. May I on this auspicious occasion once again reach for the words of Aqeel Shatir?

Aap teer-o-kamaan rakhte hain

Hum bhi seene mein jaan rakhte hain

Aur itna ooncha na boliye

Hum bhi moonh mein zubaan rakhte hain

(You have weapons in your arsenal

I too have this lust for life in my heart

And please don't shout so much

I too have a tongue in my mouth).[7]

NOTES

From Amitava Kumar, "A Testimony to Survival," *Caravan*, February 2011, 20–22. Reprinted with permission of the publisher.

1. Amitava Kumar, "I Am Still Alive," *Indian Express*, December 31, 2010.
2. Quoted in Amitava Kumar, "Weddings in a Camp," in *Husband of a Fanatic* (New York: New Press, 2005), 20.
3. Tanvir A. Siddiqui, "Poet Made to Pay for Anti-Modi Remark," *Indian Express*, December 20, 2010.
4. Essentially, a phone booth. STD stands for Standard Trunk Dialing and PCO for Public Call Office.
5. Shramana Ganguly Mehta and Himanshu Darji, "Vibrant Gujarat 2011: State May Get 1/3 of India's GDP in Two Days," *Economic Times*, January 12, 2011.
6. Kumar, "Weddings in a Camp," 47.
7. Shatir had recited this poem to me on the phone. The translation is mine.

Conversation with Arundhati Roy

We

Have to Be

Very

Careful

These Days

Because . . .

That is what I read on the little green, blue, and yellow stickers on the front door of Arundhati Roy's home in south Delhi. Earlier in the evening I had received a message from Roy asking me to text her before my arrival, so that she'd know that the person at her door wasn't from Times Now. Times Now is a TV channel in India that Roy memorably described, for non-Indian readers, as "Fox News on acid." The channel's right-wing anchor routinely calls Roy "provocative" and "antinational." Last year, when a mob vandalized the house in which Roy was then living, the media vans, including one from Times Now, were parked outside long before the attack began. No one had informed the police. To be fair, Times Now wasn't the only channel whose van was parked in front of Roy's house. But that too is a part of the larger point Roy has been making. Media outlets are not only complicit with the state, they are also indistinguishable from each other. The main anchor of a TV channel writes a column for a newspaper, the news editor has a talk show, etc. Roy told me that the monopoly of the media is like watching "an endless cocktail party where people are carrying their drinks from one room to the next."

In most other homes in rich localities of Delhi those stickers on the door could be taken as apology for the heavy locks. But in Roy's case the words assume another meaning. They mock the ways in which people rationalize their passivity and silence. You can shut your eyes, complacently turn your back on injustice, and acquiesce in a crime simply by saying, "We have to be very careful these days."

In November 2010, following a public speech she had made on the freedom struggle in Kashmir, a case of sedition was threatened against Roy. Several prominent members of the educated middle class in India spoke up on Roy's behalf, but a sizable section of this liberal set made it clear that their support of Roy was support for the right to free speech, not for her views. What is it about Roy that so irks the Indian middle class and elite? Is it the fact that she has no truck with the sober, scholarly, Brahmanical discourse of the respectable middle-of-the-road protectors of the status quo? Her critics, among whom are some of my friends, are also serious people. But their objections appear hollow to me because they have never courted unpopularity. They air their opinions in op-eds, dine at the corporate table, are fêted on national TV, and collect followers on Twitter. They don't have to face court orders. Naturally, I wanted to ask Roy whether she feels estranged from the people around her. She does, but also does not. Her point is, which people? A bit melodramatically, I asked, "Are you lonely?" Roy's wonderfully self-confident response was: "If I were lonely, I'd be doing something else. But I'm not. I deploy my writing from the heart of the crowd."

When I sat down for dinner with her, I noticed the pile of papers on the far end of the wooden table. These were legal charges filed against Roy because of her statements against Indian state atrocities. Roy said to me, "These are our paper napkins these days." What toll had these trials taken on her writing? Was her activism a source of a new political imagining, or was her political experience one of loneliness and exile in her own land? What would be the shape of any new fiction she would write? These and other questions were on my mind when I began an exchange with Roy by e-mail and then met with her twice at her home in Delhi in mid-January 2011.

· · ·

AMITAVA KUMAR: Before we begin, can you give me an example of a stupid question you are asked at interviews?

ARUNDHATI ROY: It is difficult to answer extremely stupid questions. Very, very difficult. Stupidity defeats you in some way. Especially when time is at a premium. And sometimes these questions are themselves mischievous.

AK: Give me an example.

AR: "The Maoists are blowing up schools and killing children. Do you approve? Is it right to kill children?" Where do you start?

AK: Yes.

AR: There was a *Hardtalk* once, I believe, between some BBC guy obviously, and a Palestinian activist. He was asking questions like this— "Do you believe in killing children?"—and any question he asked, the Palestinian just said, "Ariel Sharon is a war criminal." Once, I was on *The Charlie Rose Show*. Well, I was invited to be on *The Charlie Rose Show*. He said, "Tell me, Arundhati Roy, do you believe that India should have nuclear weapons?" So I said, "I don't think India should have nuclear weapons. I don't think Israel should have nuclear weapons. I don't think the United States should have nuclear weapons." "No, I asked you do you believe that India should have nuclear weapons." I answered exactly the same thing. About four times. . . . They never aired it!

AK: How old were you when you first became aware of the power of words?

AR: Pretty old, I think. Maybe two. I heard about it from my disappeared father whom I met for the first time when I was about twenty-four or twenty-five years old. He turned out to be an absolutely charming, unemployed, broke, irreverent alcoholic. (After being unnerved initially, I grew very fond of him and gave thanks that he wasn't some senior bureaucrat or golf-playing CEO.) Anyway, the first thing he asked me was, "Do you still use bad language?" I had no idea what he meant, given that the last time he saw me I was about two years old. Then he told me that on the tea estates in Assam where he worked, one day he accidentally burned me with his cigarette and that I glared at him and said "*chootiya*" (cunt, or imbecile)—language I'd obviously picked up in the tea pickers' labor quarters where I must have been shunted off to while my parents fought. My first piece of writing was when I was five . . . I still have those notebooks. Miss Mitten, a terrifying Australian missionary, was my teacher. She would tell me on a daily basis that she could see Satan in my eyes. In my two-sentence essay (which made it into *The God of Small Things*) I said, "I hate Miss Mitten, whenever I see her I see rags. I think her knickers are torn." She's dead now, God rest her soul. I don't know whether these stories I'm telling you are about becoming aware of the power of words, or about developing an affection for words . . . the awareness of a child's pleasure which extended beyond food and drink.

AK: How has that early view changed or become refined in specific ways in the years since?

AR: I'm not sure that what I had then was a "view" about language—I'm not sure that I have one even now. As I said, it was just the beginnings of the recognition of pleasure. To be able to express yourself, to be able to close the gap—inasmuch as it is possible—between thought and expression is just such a relief. It's like having the ability to draw or paint what you see, the way you see it. Behind the speed and confidence of a beautiful line in a line drawing there's years of—usually—discipline, obsession, practice that builds on a foundation of natural talent or inclination of course. It's like sport. A sentence can be like that. Language is like that. It takes a while to become yours, to listen to you, to obey you, and for you to obey it. I have a clear memory of language swimming toward me. Of my willing it out of the water. Of it being blurred, inaccessible, inchoate . . . and then of it emerging. Sharply outlined, custom-made.

AK: As far as writing is concerned, do you have models, especially those that have remained so for a long time?

AR: Do I have models? Maybe I wouldn't use that word because it sounds like there are people who I admire so much that I would like to become them, or to be like them . . . I don't feel that about anybody. But if you mean are there writers I love and admire—yes of course there are. So many. But that would be a whole new interview, wouldn't it? Apart from Shakespeare, James Joyce, and Nabokov, Neruda, Eduardo Galeano, John Berger, right now I'm becoming fascinated by Urdu poets who I am ashamed to say I know so little about. . . . But I'm learning. I'm reading Hafiz. There are so many wonderful writers, my ancestors who have lived in the world. I cannot begin to list them. However, it isn't only writers who inspire my idea of storytelling. Look at the Kathakali dancer, the ease with which he can shift gears within a story—from humor to epiphany, from bestiality to tenderness, from the epic to the intimate— that ability, that range, is what I really admire. To me it's that ease—it's a kind of athleticism—like watching a beautiful, easy runner—a cheetah on the move—that is proof of the fitness of the storyteller.

AK: American readers got their introduction to you when, a bit before *The God of Small Things* was published, a review by John Updike appeared in the *New Yorker* issue on India. There was a photograph there of you with other Indian writers, including Rushdie, Amitav Ghosh, Vikram Seth, Vikram Chandra, Anita Desai, Kiran Desai, and a few others.[1] In the time since then, your trajectory as a writer has defined very sharply your difference from everyone in that group. Did you even ever want to belong in it?

AR: I chuckle when I remember that day. I think everybody was being a bit spiky with everybody else. There were muted arguments, sulks, and mutterings. There was brittle politeness. Everybody was a little uncomfortable, wondering what exactly it was that we had in common, what qualified us to be herded into the same photograph? And yet it was for the *New Yorker*, and who didn't want to be in the *New Yorker*? It was the fiftieth anniversary of India's independence, and this particular issue was meant to be about the renaissance of Indian-English writing. But when we went for lunch afterward the bus that had been booked to take us was almost empty—it turned out that there weren't many of us, after all. And who were we anyway? Indian writers? But the great majority of the people in our own country neither knew nor cared very much about who we were or what we wrote. Anyway, I don't think anybody in that photograph felt they really belonged in the same "group" as the next person. Isn't that what writers are? Great individualists? I don't lose sleep over my differences or similarities with other writers. For me, what's more interesting is trying to walk the path between the act of honing language to make it as private and as individual as possible, and then looking around, seeing what's happening to millions of people and deploying that private language to speak from the heart of a crowd. Holding those two very contradictory things down is a fascinating enterprise.

I am a part of a great deal of frenetic political activity here. I've spent the last six months traveling across the country, speaking at huge meetings in smaller towns—Ranchi, Jullundur, Bhubaneshwar, Jaipur, Srinagar—at public meetings with massive audiences, three and four thousand people—students, farmers, laborers, activists. I speak mostly in Hindi, which isn't my language (even that has to be translated depending on where the meeting is being held). Though I write in English, my writing is immediately translated into Hindi, Telugu, Kannada, Tamil, Bengali, Malayalam, Odia. I don't think I'm considered an "Indo-Anglian" writer any more. I seem to be drifting away from the English-speaking world at high speed. My English must be changing. The way I think about language certainly is.

AK: We are going to entertain the fantasy that you have the time to read and write these days. What have you been reading this past year, for instance?

AR: I have for some reason been reading about Russia, postrevolution Russia. A stunning collection of short stories by Varlam Shalamov called *Kolyma Tales. The Trial of Trotsky in Mexico.* Emma Goldman's autobiography, *Living My Life. Journey into the Whirlwind* by Eugenia Ginzburg . . . troubling stuff. The Chinese writer Yu Hua. . . .

AK: And writing? You have been effective, at crucial moments, as a writer-activist who introduces a strong opinion or protest when faced with an urgent issue. Often, these pieces, which are pretty lengthy, must require a lot of research—so much information sometimes sneaked into a stunning one-liner! How do you go about doing your research?

AR: Each of these pieces I have written over the last ten years are pieces I never wanted to write. And each time I wrote one, I thought it would be my last. . . . Each time I write something I promise myself I'll never do it again, because the fallout goes on for months; it takes so much of my time. Sometimes, increasingly, like of late, it turns dangerous. I actually don't do research to write the pieces. My research isn't project-driven. It's the other way around—I write because the things I come to learn of from the reading and traveling I do and the stories I hear make me furious. I find out more, I cross-check, I read up, and by then I'm so shocked that I have to write. The essays I wrote on the December 13 Parliament attack are a good example—of course I had been following the case closely.[2] I was on the Committee for the Free and Fair Trial for S. A. R. Geelani. Eventually he was acquitted, and Mohammed Afzal was sentenced to death. I went off to Goa one monsoon, by myself with all the court papers for company. For no reason other than curiosity. I sat alone in a restaurant day after day, the only person there, while it poured and poured. I could hardly believe what I was reading. The Supreme Court judgment said that though it didn't have proof that Afzal was a member of a terrorist group, and the evidence against him was only circumstantial, it was sentencing him to death to "satisfy the collective conscience of society." Just like that—in black and white. Even still, I didn't write anything. I had promised myself "no more essays."

But a few months later the date for the hanging was fixed. The newspapers were full of glee, talking about where the rope would come from, who the hangman would be. I knew the whole thing was a farce. I realized that if I said nothing and they went ahead and hanged him, I'd never forgive myself. So I wrote "And His Life Should Become Extinct." I was one of a handful of people who protested. Afzal's still alive. It may not be because of us, it may be because his clemency petition is still pending, but I think between us we cracked the hideous consensus that had built up in the country around that case. Now at least in some quarters there is a healthy suspicion about unsubstantiated allegations in newspapers whenever they pick up people—mostly Muslims, of course—and call them "terrorists." We can take a bit of credit for that. Now of course with the sensational confession of Swami Aseemanand in which he says the RSS [Rashtriya Swayamsevak Sangh] was behind the bomb blasts in Ajmer Sharif and Malegaon, and was responsible for the bombing of the Samjhauta Express, the idea of radical Hindutva groups being involved in false-flag attacks is common knowledge.[3]

To answer your question, I don't really do research in order to write. Finding out about things, figuring out the real story—what you call research—is part of life now for some of us. Mostly just to get over the indignity of living in a pool of propaganda, of being lied to all the time, if nothing else.

AK: What would it mean for you to write fiction now?

AR: It would mean finding time, carving out a little solitude, getting off the tiger. I hope it will be possible. *The God of Small Things* was published only a few months before the nuclear tests, which ushered in a new, very frightening, and overt language of virulent nationalism. In response I wrote "The End of Imagination,"[4] which set me on a political journey which I never expected to embark on. All these years later, after writing about big dams, privatization, the wars on Iraq and Afghanistan, the Parliament attack, the occupation of Kashmir, the Maoists, and the corporatization of everything—writing that involved facing down an incredibly hostile, abusive, and dangerous middle class—the Radia tapes exposé has come like an MRI confirming a diagnosis some of us made years ago. Now it's street talk, so I feel it's all right for me to do something else now. It happens all the time. You say something and it sounds extreme and outrageous, and a few years down the line it's pretty much accepted as the norm. I feel we are headed for very bad times. This is going to become a more violent place, this country. But now that it's upon us, as a writer I'll have to find a way to live, to witness, to communicate what's going on. The Indian elite has seceded into outer space. It seems to have lost the ability to understand those who have been left behind on earth.

AK: Yes, but what do you have to do to write new fiction?

AR: I don't know. I'll have to find a language to tell the story I want to tell. By language I don't mean English, Hindi, Urdu, Malayalam, of course. I mean something else. A way of binding together worlds that have been ripped apart. Let's see.

AK: Your novel was a huge best seller, of course. But your nonfiction books have been very popular, too. In places like New York, whenever you have spoken there is always a huge turnout of adoring fans. Your books sell well here, but what I've been amazed by is how some of your pieces, including the one published in the immediate aftermath of the September 11 attacks, become a sensation on the Internet. Could you comment on this phenomenon? Also, is it true that the *New York Times* refused to publish that piece?

AR: As far as I know the *New York Times* has a policy of not publishing anything that has appeared elsewhere. And I rarely write commissioned pieces. But of course "The Algebra of Infinite Justice," the essay I wrote after 9/11, was not published in any mainstream U.S. publication—it was unthinkable at the time.[5] But that essay was published all over the world; in the United States some small radio stations read it out, all of it. And yes, it flew on the [Inter]net. There's so much to say about the Internet . . . Wikileaks. The Facebook revolution in places like Kashmir, which has completely subverted the Indian media's propaganda of noise as well as strategic silence. The Twitter uprising in Iran. I expect the Internet to become a site of conflict very soon, with attempts being made by governments and big business to own and control it, to price it out of the reach of the poor. . . . I don't see those attempts being successful, though. India's newest and biggest war, Operation Green Hunt, is being waged against tribal people, many of whom have never seen a bus or a train, let alone a computer. But even there, mobile phones and YouTube are playing a part.

AK: Talking of the *New York Times*, I read your recent report from Kashmir, just after you were threatened with arrest on the slightly archaic-sounding charge of sedition.[6]

AR: Yes, there was that. But I think it has blown over. It would have been a bad thing for me. But I think, on balance, it would have been worse for them. It's ludicrous because I was only saying what millions of Kashmiris have been saying for years. Interestingly, the whole thing about charging me for sedition was not started by the government, but by a few right-wing crazies and a few irresponsible media channels like Times Now, which is a bit like Fox News on acid. Even when the Mumbai attacks happened, if you remember it was the media that began baying for war with Pakistan. This cocktail of religious fundamentalism and a crazed, irresponsible, unaccountable media is becoming a very serious problem, in India as well as Pakistan. I don't know what the solution is. Certainly not censorship. . . .

AK: Can you give a sense of what is a regular day for you, or perhaps how irregular and different one day may be from another?

AR: My days and nights. Actually I don't have a regular day (or night!). It has been so for years, and has nothing to do with the sedition *tamasha* [spectacle]. I'm not sure how I feel about this—but that's how it is. I move around a lot. I don't always sleep in the same place. I live a very unsettled but not uncalm life. But sometimes I feel as though I lack a skin—something that separates me from the world I live in. That absence of skin is dangerous. It invites trouble into every part of your life. It makes what is public private and what is private public. It can sometimes become very traumatic, not just for me but for those who are close to me.

AK: Your stance on Kashmir and also on the struggles of the tribals has drawn the ire of the Indian middle class. Who belongs to that class, and what do you think gets their goat?

AR: The middle class goat is very sensitive about itself and very callous about other people's goats.

AK: Your critics say that you often see the world only in black and white.

AR: The thing is—you have to understand, Amitava, that the people who say such things are a certain section of society who think they are the universe. It is the jitterbugging elite, which considers itself the whole country. Just go outside and nobody will say that to you. Go to Orissa, go to the people who are under attack, and nobody will think that there is anything remotely controversial about what I write. You know—I keep saying this—the most successful secession movement in India is the secession of the middle and upper classes to outer space. They have their own universe, their own *andolan*, their own Jessica Lal, their own media, their own controversies, and they're disconnected from everything else. For them, what I write comes like an outrage. *Ki yaar yeh kyaa bol rahi hai?* [What the hell is she saying?] They don't realize that they are the ones who have painted themselves into a corner.

AK: You have written that "people believe that faced with extermination they have the right to fight back. By any means necessary."[7] The knee-jerk response to this has been, "Look, she's preaching violence."

AR: My question is, if you are an Adivasi living in a village in a dense forest in Chhattisgarh, and that village is surrounded by eight hundred Central Reserve Police Force [officers] who have started to burn down the houses and rape the women, what are people supposed to do? Are they supposed to go on a hunger strike? They can't. They are already hungry, they are already starving. Are they supposed to boycott goods? They can't because they don't have the money to buy goods. And if they go on a fast or a *dharna*, who is looking, who is watching? So, my position is just that it would be immoral of me to preach violence to anybody unless I'm prepared to pick up arms myself. But I think it is equally immoral for me to preach nonviolence when I'm not bearing the brunt of the attack.

AK: According to Macaulay, the rationale for the introduction of English in India, as we all know, was to produce a body of clerks. We have departed from that purpose, of course, but still, in our use of the language we remain remarkably conservative. I wonder sometimes whether your style itself, exuberant and excessive, isn't for these readers a transgression.

AR: I wouldn't say that it's all Macaulay's fault. There is something clerky and calculating about our privileged classes. They see themselves as the state or as advisors to the state, rarely as subjects. If you read columnists and editorials, most have a very clerky, "apply through proper channels" approach. As though they are a shadow cabinet. Even when they are critical of the state they are what a friend once described as "reckless at slow speed." So I don't think my transgressions as far as they are concerned have only to do with my style. It's about everything—style, substance, politics, speed. I think it worries them that I'm not a victim and that I don't pretend to be one. They love victims and victimology. My writing is not a plea for aid or for compassion toward the poor. We're not asking for more NGOs or charities or foundations in which the rich can massage their egos and salve their consciences with their surplus money. The critique is structural.

AK: Your polemical essays often draw criticism also for their length. (We are frankly envious of the space that the print media in India is able to grant you.) You have written: "We need context. Always."[8] Is the length at which you aspire to write and explain things a result of your search for context?

AR: I don't aspire to write at any particular length. What I write could be looked at as a very long essay or a very short book. Most of the time, what I write has everything to do with timing. It's not just what I say, but when I say it. I usually write when I know the climate is turning ugly, when no one is in a mood to listen to this version of things. I know it's going to enrage people, and yet I know that nothing is more important at that moment than to put your foot in the door.

AK: But even as we raise the issue of criticism, it is also important to say that some of these critics who accuse you of hyperbole and other sins are hardly our moral exemplars. I'm thinking of someone like Vir Sanghvi. His editorial about your Kashmir speech was dismissive and filled with high contempt. We've discovered from the recent release of the Radia tapes that people like Sanghvi were not impartial journalists: they were errand boys for corporate politicians.

AR: We didn't need the Radia tapes to discover that. And I wouldn't waste my energy railing against those who criticize or dismiss me. It's part of their brief. I don't expect them to stand up and applaud.

AK: Having read all your published writing over the past twelve years or more, I wonder: Is there anything you have written in the past that you don't agree with anymore, that you think you were wrong about, or perhaps something about which you have dramatically changed your mind?

AR: You know, ironically, I wouldn't be unhappy to be wrong about the things I've said. Imagine if I suddenly realized that big dams were wonderful. I could celebrate the hundreds of dams that are being planned in the Himalayas. I could celebrate the Indo-U.S. nuclear deal. But there are things about which my views have changed—because the times have changed. Most of this has to do with strategies of resistance. The Indian state has become hard and unforgiving. What it once did in places like Kashmir, Manipur, and Nagaland, it [now] does in mainland India. So some of the strategies we inherited from the freedom movement are a bit obsolete now.

AK: You have pointed out that the logic of the global war on terror is the same as the logic of terrorism, making victims of civilians. Are there specific works, particularly of fiction, that have arrived close to explaining the post-9/11 world we are living in?

AR: Actually I haven't really kept up with the world of fiction, sad to say. I don't even know who won the Booker Prize from one year to the next. But when you read [Pablo] Neruda's "Standard Oil Co.," you really have to believe that while things change, they remain the same.

AK: Your old friend "Baby" Bush is gone. But has Obama been any better? While we are worried about the TSA [Transportation Security Administration] at airports, in less fortunate places U.S. drone attacks are killing more civilians than militants. Shouldn't we be raising our voices against the role played by the U.S. terrorist-industrial complex instead of backing, as you suggest, the Iraqi resistance movement?

AR: I hope I didn't say we should back the Iraqi resistance movement. I'm not sure what backing a resistance movement means—saying nice things about it? I think I meant that we should become the resistance. If people outside Iraq had actually done more than just weekend demonstrations, then the pressure on the U.S. government could have been huge. Without that, the Iraqis were left on their own in a war zone in which every kind of peaceful dissent was snuffed out. Only the monstrous could survive. And then the world was called upon to condemn them. Even here in India, there are these somewhat artificial debates about "violent" and "nonviolent" resistance—basically a critique of the Maoists' armed struggle in the mineral-rich forests of central India. The fact is that if everybody leaves Adivasis to fight their own battles against displacement and destitution, it's impossible to expect them to be Gandhian. However, it is open to people outside the forest, well-off and middle-class people whom the media pays mind to, to become a part of the resistance. If they stood up, then perhaps those in the forest would not need to resort to arms. If they won't stand up, then there's not much point in their preaching morality to the victims of the war. About Bush and Obama: frankly, I'm tired of debating U.S. politics. There are new kings on the block now.

NOTES

"The Un-Victim: Amitava Kumar Interviews Arundhati Roy," *Guernica*, February 15, 2011. Reprinted with permission of the publisher.

1. John Updike, "Mother Tongues," *New Yorker*, June 23 and 30, 1997, 156–61. Photograph appears on pages 118–19.
2. Arundhati Roy, "Introduction: Breaking the News," in *13 December: A Reader* (New Delhi: Penguin, 2006), ix–xxii. See also Arundhati Roy, "And His Life Should Become Extinct," in Arundhati Roy, *Field Notes on Democracy: Listening to Grasshoppers* (2006; New York: Haymarket, 2009), 68–99.
3. See Ashish Khetan, "In the Words of a Zealot," *Tehelka*, January 15, 2011. Accessed August 1, 2014. http://archive.tehelka.com/story_main48.asp ?filename=Ne150111Coverstory.asp.
4. Arundhati Roy, "The End of Imagination," in *The Cost of Living* (New York: The Modern Library, 1999), 91–126.
5. Arundhati Roy, "The Algebra of Infinite Justice," *Guardian*, September 28, 2001.
6. Arundhati Roy, "Kashmir's Fruits of Discord," *New York Times*, November 9, 2010.
7. Arundhati Roy, *Field Notes on Democracy: Listening to Grasshoppers* (New York: Haymarket, 2009), 168.
8. Roy, *Field Notes on Democracy*, 188.

· **6** ·

Salman Rushdie and Me

The organizers of the Jaipur Literature Festival were asked to hand over to the police the videotape of a reading from a novel last month. The tape will show the writer Hari Kunzru and me reading from Salman Rushdie's *Satanic Verses*, a book banned in India since its publication in 1988.[1] We were protesting Rushdie's absence from the festival. He had been forced to withdraw after extremist Muslim groups expressed displeasure, and, more urgently, when intelligence reports revealed that hired assassins from Mumbai were on their way to kill the writer. (Those reports were later revealed to be fiction. Cops as magical realists.)

On the tape, the police will have seen that, during our reading, I told the audience that just before the start of the protests in Tahrir Square last year, the Google executive–turned-cyber-activist Wael Ghonim had entered Egypt with a message ready on his computer. It said, "I am now being arrested at Cairo airport."[2] All he needed to do was press "send."

I joked that perhaps Hari ought to do something similar. Within minutes of my saying this, the festival's producer arrived and asked me to stop reading. I didn't. When the reading was over and we came out, a bank of television cameras was trained on us. A Hindi reporter asked me, "Aren't you guilty of provoking religious violence?" And then, a little later, the police were there, informing us that we had broken the law.

I was staggered at the speed at which all of this happened. We were told that the tweets we had sent immediately before the reading, announcing our plans to read from the banned novel, had gone viral. Here was proof that we were living in the age of social media, and that, as in Egypt or Tunisia, public protest was being conveyed through Twitter.

A lot had changed in the twenty-three years since the book was banned in India. The old restrictions didn't matter. Hari and I had simply stepped into the festival's tiny office and downloaded relevant passages from the Internet. In fact, the text of the whole novel was there on the screen, readily available for anyone who wanted to read or print it. It's true that the author hadn't been allowed to come, but already we were being told that he would appear among us via a video feed.

I had felt a great sense of freedom—a liberation from fear—as I read Rushdie's words out loud in public for what I believed was the first time in the country of his birth. But then I learned that such a reading had been conducted before. On January 1, 1989, soon after the ban had been imposed, a group of Indian intellectuals had gathered in Delhi to read from *The Satanic Verses*. The risk that those readers had courted must have been greater than mine. Hari and I were reading at a festival—only a few years old—where glittering stars of the literary universe gather each year; our protest was under the public gaze of the media; and, in an India that flaunts its superpower aspirations, the festival's sponsors are the largest and richest corporations in India. Even powerful politicians are routinely present in the audience and sometimes sit among the writers on stage. What did I need to fear?

Back in 1989, when Iran's Ayatollah Khomeini issued his fatwa without ever having read Rushdie's book, the price put on Rushdie's head was $3 million. This year, following the announcement that Rushdie was going to attend the Jaipur festival, a Muslim group in Mumbai offered the rather modest sum of 100,000 rupees (roughly $2,000) for anyone who would hurl a slipper at him.

No, that is not the most depressing part of this story. The tragedy is that, in the 1980s and again now, the party in power in Delhi, the Congress Party, is trying its best to court "the minority vote." It is doing so by pandering to its most aggressive, reactionary fringe. Elections were just around the corner in five states at the time of the festival, and the country's most populous state, Uttar Pradesh, boasts of a substantial Muslim population. The Congress and its rivals are eager to take on the mantle of the protector of Muslims. As a result, neither the government nor the opposition parties have come out forcefully in support of Rushdie. In fact, on the last day of the festival, even the promised video-link appearance with the writer was canceled because protestors had come inside the festival venue and threatened violence if Rushdie's face was beamed on the giant screens.

Hari Kunzru and I, along with two other writers who also later read from *The Satanic Verses*, have had seven police complaints filed against us by members of parties of diverse hues. In the coming weeks, these cases will be taken up in court. This is serious, of course, but the entire affair isn't without very bizarre aspects. One of the complainants belongs to the right-wing Hindu party, the Bharatiya Janata Party (BJP), which has been brazenly anti-Muslim in the past. But, as a competitor for the more than 18 percent Muslim vote in the coming election, the BJP considers it a sacred duty to attack Rushdie.

The Muslims, in whose name books have been banned and writers harassed, are among the poorest people in India, which has been officially confirmed by an Indian government report released in 2006. Now that elections have begun in Uttar Pradesh for its 403-seat assembly, the Congress Party has taken up one of the report's recommendations and announced a 4.5 percent affirmative action "subquota" of seats for Muslims. Elections trump ethics. As the social scientist Ashis Nandy told me in Delhi, on the morning after I fled Jaipur, "India is not a democracy, it is a psephocracy," by which he meant that it wasn't the rule of law but electoral calculation that governed the lives of Indians.

The controversy that erupted at the Jaipur Literature Festival is neither only about the freedom of expression nor only, in any representative way, about the sentiments of all Muslims. We cannot distance it from the crazy mix of celebrity, money, and media in the frenetic landscape of a market-friendly India.

Also, although Rushdie might have been the latest casualty of censorship, he isn't the only writer to be so victimized. On the way to the airport in Delhi, I stopped at the home of the writer Arundhati Roy for a drink. Just over a year ago, she was threatened with arrest for sedition for having supported the right of Kashmiris to seek justice while living under brutal military occupation. Roy is used to having court cases filed against her. She released a statement to the press: "Pity the nation that has to silence its writers for speaking their minds. Pity the nation that needs to jail those who ask for justice, while communal killers, mass murderers, corporate scamsters, looters, rapists, and those who prey on the poorest of the poor roam free."[3] Her ear planted closer to common sense, Roy said to me that evening, "Relax, boss, have another beer."

It wasn't till I was safely on the flight back to the United States that I even contemplated putting down on paper what I had felt over the past few days. I began to write down my thoughts, but, like Gibreel Farishta in *The Satanic Verses*, I appeared only to have dreamed them. *I had to leave India to be safe. A realization filled with surpassing loss. But did I have to leave India to be brave? The truth was that I was afraid—as in countless films, when the man pleads with his killer, "I have small children." First moment of fear: Hindi TV reporter pushing camera in my face to ask, "Aren't you guilty of provoking religious violence?" Imagination makes us shape better stories, sure, but it also allows us to multiply possibilities. Imagine a different end. I read from* The Satanic Verses *because it was, in that time and place, a bold and imaginative act. If I were honest, that would be the only claim I submit to the Indian authorities in my defense.*[4]

The Jaipur Literature Festival was followed by the Kolkata Book Fair, and, during a press conference there, the Pakistani cricketer-turned-politician Imran Khan questioned Rushdie's "right to inflict pain on a society." In response, Rushdie fired off a tweet: "30 yrs ago @ImranKhanPTI was a fan at my 1982 Delhi lecture and 100% secular. Now my work 'humiliates' his 'faith.' Which is the real Imran?"[5] This exchange, widely reported in the papers in Pakistan and India, was meaningful to me for a different reason. I was in the audience that night in 1982, sitting a little behind Imran Khan, in a Delhi auditorium.

I had entered college a year earlier and had bought a copy of *Midnight's Children*. A vague ambition to become a writer must have been the reason I acquired the book. Oddly, I wasn't much of a reader. I went to all the events at which Rushdie was present, but I don't think I got much out of them; I certainly hadn't made it to the end of his novel. The first piece of his writing that I read and liked was a brief essay in a 1984 issue of *Granta* called "Outside the Whale."[6] From its very first paragraph, which pitilessly excoriated Raj nostalgia, the essay directed the reader to look at the world, and certainly at literature, in a political way. The voice was so engaged, witty, and worldly that I embraced it wholeheartedly.

Part of my enthusiasm must have had to do with the fact that I was a new immigrant in America; Rushdie's mocking of the West would have found an answering echo in my heart. But there was a bigger reason. Unlike my new classes on postcolonial theory, where a writer's meaning was glimpsed, if at all, through the thick fog of nearly impenetrable verbiage, Rushdie's words were clear, even conversational. His intelligence was evident everywhere, and yet one didn't feel that his insights were weights dragging you to the bottom of the sea.

Don't get me wrong. I did my best to sound like my teachers and wrote sentences whose texture was inevitably thicker than cement. Still, Rushdie could always be trusted to provide the perfect epigraph—by turns elegant, cutting, or comic—for the challenging edifices of prose that I was building. I would still construct my academic platforms of multiple subordinate clauses and reinforced concrete, but a line from Rushdie sat on the top, like a glorious, fluttering pennant.

I can't pin down the moment when I began to think I had outgrown Rushdie, but it is a question to which I've given much thought in recent days. It seems very plausible to me that with my deepening investment in nonfiction, and in documentary writing and journalism, I began to find Rushdie's new fiction dissatisfying. In 1999, for example, when *The Ground beneath Her Feet* was published, I read the book eagerly—as I did all of Rushdie's writing—but I thought that the representations of real events were thin and unconvincing. A politician in my hometown, famous for his corruption, was portrayed cartoonishly as someone with a bad grasp of grammar. I went to interview the man on whom the character in the novel was based because I wanted to show what I had instinctively known was the man's more complex reality.

It should have been possible for me to marvel at how Rushdie transformed news into something magical. Instead, I fretted at the ways in which he so often reduced what was startling, or intransigent, about everyday realities to, at best, a metaphor.

It went downhill from there for me. Criticism is, or ought to be, a judicious act. It is nothing if it isn't a practice of discrimination, even hypervigilant discrimination. Most often, however, it becomes an exercise in shoring up a preconceived argument. You search for evidence to build a stronger case. In effect, you are reading to prove a prejudice. At least that was true of me while reading each new, subsequent work of Rushdie's. A long, negative review I wrote of Rushdie's novel *Fury* earned me a rebuke from the writer: He told an administrator at the college where I teach, who had invited Rushdie to come speak, that he wouldn't share the stage with me.[7] My attitude only hardened after that. The incident's unpleasantness intensified when I got involved in a spat with Rushdie on my blog.

It was later, much later, that I began to feel a loss—a sense of the lost affection I had had for words that had once illuminated the condition of the world around me. Maybe it was more a question of the gratitude that a writer must have toward another writer whose words he has borrowed in the past.

This realization was brought home to me via social media. I heard Rushdie on a *New Yorker* fiction podcast—where I thought he was brilliant—and then, from the day he joined Twitter, followed his tweets.[8] A new relationship sprang up in this medium; with 140 characters, I was no longer judging the whole universe of Rushdie's output. Maybe this allowed me to put him once again on a human scale. Often I wanted to quote back to him his own lines, which is what readers often want to do. It would be like reading his words aloud. That is, after all, what I did in Jaipur.

All the inventiveness and joy of Rushdie's fiction were there in the section from *The Satanic Verses* I had read out at the festival, when Gibreel Farishta considers the advantages of transforming London into a tropical city: "Religious fervor, political ferment, renewal of interest in the intelligentsia. No more British reserve; hot-water bottles to be banished forever, replaced in the fetid nights by the making of slow and odorous love. Emergence of new social values: friends to commence dropping in on one another without making appointments, closure of old folks' homes, emphasis on the extended family. Spicier food; the use of water as well as paper in English toilets; the joy of running fully dressed through the first rains of the monsoon."[9]

It had been important to do this, to remind readers of the pleasures of the book, even as outside there were calls for book burnings and the author's head.

We were not alone; there are many who have expressed support for us. And yet, amid all the compliments that I have received about standing up for freedom of expression in India, maybe I was doing something more humble and honest. I was trying to restore a sense of balance to my own personal practice of literary criticism.

NOTES

From Amitava Kumar, "Rushdie and Me," *Chronicle of Higher Education*, February 24, 2012. Reprinted with permission of the publisher.

1. Salman Rushdie, *The Satanic Verses* (New York: Viking, 1988).
2. Wael Ghonim, *Revolution 2.1: The Power of the People Is Greater Than the People in Power* (New York: Houghton Mifflin Harcourt, 2012), 163.
3. J. J. Sutherland, "Writer Arundhati Roy May Be Arrested for Sedition after Kashmir Remarks," NPR, October 27, 2010. Accessed September 25, 2014. http://www.npr.org/blogs/thetwo-way/2010/10/27/130857674/writer-arundhati-roy-may-be-arrested-for-sedition-after-kashmir-remarks.
4. Amitava Kumar, "Twitter Feed of a Lawbreaker," *New York Times*, January 25, 2012.
5. "Who Is the Real Imran, Asks Salman Rushdie," *Express Tribune* (Pakistan), February 1, 2012. Accessed September 25, 2014. http://tribune.com.pk/story/330316/who-is-the-real-imran-khan-asks-salman-rushdie/.
6. Salman Rushdie, "Outside the Whale," *Granta* 11 (spring 1984), 123–38.
7. Amitava Kumar, "The Bend in Their Rivers," *Nation*, November 26, 2001, 32–38.
8. Salman Rushdie reads Donald Barthelme's "Concerning the Bodyguard." Accessed on September 25, 2014. http://downloads.newyorker.com/mp3/fiction/110819_fiction_rushdie.mp3.
9. Rushdie, *The Satanic Verses*, 354–55.

Bad News

In May of this year [2008], a fourteen-year-old girl named Aarushi Tal-war was found murdered in her parents' house outside Delhi. The teen's parents were both dentists. The main suspect in the killing was the ser-vant employed by the Talwars, a forty-five-year-old Nepalese migrant named Hemraj.[1] Most servants in a large Indian city like Delhi are the poor who have arrived from impoverished eastern states, mostly Bihar, Uttar Pradesh, and Orissa.

In India, even an ordinary middle-class person can employ domestic help. You provide a poor young man or woman with space to sleep, left-over food, and old clothes, and you are likely to get away with paying as little as fifty dollars a month. A hundred maximum.

Delhi is a city of seventeen million people, and six were robbed or murdered by their servants last year.[2] This is not a very high number, but a large part of the urban middle-class mythology is built around the fear of being robbed, and even killed, by domestic servants. As it turned out, in the Aarushi murder case, the police had been inept. They had simply concluded that Hemraj was guilty because he was missing. Not only were no photographs taken of the crime scene, but even the trail of blood leading to a staircase was not investigated. A day later, a retired police officer broke the lock on the door leading to the terrace above and found the servant's corpse already decomposing in the heat. The search for a new suspect was under way.

The case took a sensational turn when the police arrested Aarushi's father. There was no clear evidence to suggest that the dentist had committed the murders, but the police provided the media with lurid speculations. There were stories about the father's alleged affair with a fellow doctor. The police said that the daughter had come to know of this and confronted him. Officers also openly alleged that Aarushi was involved in a relationship with Hemraj, and the enraged doctor killed the ill-suited lovers.

None of this turned out to be based in fact. Amid criticism of police bungling and the role of tabloid journalism, the investigation was handed over to the central intelligence authorities. They released Aarushi's father, and suspicion shifted to a man in the doctor's clinic as well as a neighbor's servant. But earlier this month the investigators disclosed that they were not going to charge anyone in the crime. The dead girl's parents previously had shunned the media that had so damagingly fed the public sordid stories about them, but they now appeared on television to demand justice for their murdered child. They believed that the investigators had at last caught the killers. Why were they allowed to go free?

All through the summer, I followed the story from my home in upstate New York. Then, in mid-June, I read an article in a British newspaper about the Aarushi case, in which I found out that a popular novel had already been written this year about middle-class Indian fear of domestic servants. The novel, the article said, "tells the story of a bitter and disenchanted chauffeur in Delhi who slits his employer's throat."[3]

That is how I came to discover Aravind Adiga's debut novel, *The White Tiger*, winner of the 2008 Man Booker Prize.

Soon after I learned of the book, I met Adiga in New York City. He was born in Chennai, India, and later migrated to Australia. He then studied at Columbia University and at Oxford. After university he returned to India, where for three years he worked as a correspondent for *Time* before quitting to write fiction. Adiga told me that his novel is the fruit of his labors as a reporter in India. He traveled to various parts of the country, including places whose backwardness shocked his sensibilities. *The White Tiger* is his rebuke of the cheerful, and false, notion of a new, transformed India.

What Adiga said was exciting to me: I have long subscribed to the idea that one of the novel's primary tasks is to produce a map of the contemporary. By one definition, then, the province of the novel is what you read in your newspaper each morning or watch on your television at night. The novelist's task is to explore how the news enters people's lives and indeed becomes a part of daily life.

I also loved what I'd heard of Adiga's cheeky use of the epistolary form, that the whole book was a letter from the Indian servant to the Chinese premier, Wen Jiabao. Certainly, the narrator's voice is bold and funny. One review quoted Adiga's protagonist: "Only three nations have never let themselves be ruled by foreigners: China, Afghanistan, and Abyssinia. These are the only three nations I admire." And then, his belief that "the future of the world lies with the yellow man and the brown man" because "our erstwhile master, the white-skinned man, has wasted himself through buggery, mobile phone usage, and drug abuse."[4]

But when I started reading the book, my enthusiasm evaporated. I did not know until I began reading the novel that the protagonist, Balram Halwai, is from the state of Bihar, where I was born and grew up, and which Halwai in the entire book calls by the name Darkness. But more than the name was unsettling.

In the book's opening pages, Halwai begins to tell the Chinese premier the story of his life. We are introduced to the poverty of rural Bihar and the evil of the feudal landlords. Halwai's voice sounds like a curious mix of an American teen and a middle-aged Indian essayist. I find Adiga's villains utterly cartoonish, like the characters in a Bollywood melodrama. However, it is his presentation of ordinary people that seems not only trite but also offensive. Here is his description of the migrant Bihari workers returning to their villages after their hard labor in the cities:

A month before the rains, the men came back from Dhanbad and Delhi and Calcutta, leaner, darker, angrier, but with money in their pockets. The women were waiting for them. They hid behind the door, and as soon as the men walked in, they pounced, like wildcats on a slab of flesh. They were fighting and wailing and shrieking. My uncles would resist, and managed to keep some of their money, but my father got peeled and skinned every time. "I survived the city, but I couldn't survive the women in my home," he would say, sunk into a corner of the room. The women would feed him after they fed the buffalo.[5]

I have witnessed such men, and sometimes women, coming back to their village homes countless times. The novelist seems to know next to nothing about either the love or the despair of the people he writes about. I want to know if others, who might never have visited Bihar, read the passage above and recognize how wrong it is, how the appearance of verisimilitude belies the emotional truths of life in Bihar.

As I continued, I found on nearly every page a familiar observation or a fine phrase, and on nearly every page inevitably something that sounded false. I stopped reading on page thirty-five.

I was anxious about my response to *The White Tiger*. No, not only for the suspicion about the ressentiment lurking in my breast, but also because I was aware that I might be open to the same charge of being inauthentic. My own novel *Home Products*, published last year, has as its protagonist a journalist who is writing about the murder of a young woman.[6] The case is based on a well-known murder of a poet who had an illicit relationship with a married politician. Kidnapping and rape and, of course, murder, feature quite frequently in the novel's pages. By presenting these events through a journalist's eye, I tried hard to maintain a tone of observational integrity. At some level, realism had become my religion.

Since then, I have wondered whether my choice of the journalist as a protagonist is not itself a symptom of an anxiety about authenticity. Was it the worry of an expatriate Indian, concerned about losing touch with the society he took as his subject? To invest in an aesthetic of observation and reportage was to build banks against the rising tide of that worry. I know now that this worry informs my reading of all novels about India.

For years, in the wake of Rushdie, I imagined magical realism to be the last refuge of the nonresident Indian. If you were dealing in invented details, it hardly mattered when you mixed up names and dates. But now, more than magical realism, it is the painstaking attempt at verisimilitude that clearly betrays the anxiety about authenticity. This condition is more subtle. It has limited fiction's reach, keeping writers to what they know. Look at Jhumpa Lahiri, who has assiduously mined the experience of Bengali immigrants of a fixed class. She is one of the better ones, writing about what she knows; lesser writers have been content to churn out what we all know: arranged marriage, dowry, saris, and spices.

Quite apart from this slew of stay-at-home writers, home being in most cases somewhere outside India, are the ones who, like Adiga, have taken the bus, or at least a hired taxi, to the hinterland. They might have traveled on a boat and risked being eaten by a Royal Bengal tiger. Or they might have walked in the tight, smelly alleys in the slums and, if they were enterprising, met a hired killer or two. This brings a different frisson to the body of Indian writing in English, which, given its roots in the middle class, has often been insular and dull. And these works seem direct responses to the numbing social violence in nearly every stratum of Indian society. But reportage is only an inoculation against the charge of inauthenticity. It hides larger untruths. Authenticity does matter, but only as it serves the novel's more traditional literary demands: that the fault lines be drawn where the internal life and the larger world meet.

. . .

During the summer, a few weeks before I began reading *The White Tiger*, I read in the news that nine men and women had gone on an indefinite hunger strike to call attention to the suffering in Bhopal.[7] On the night of December 3, 1984, forty tons of toxic methyl isocyanate gas from a tank in the Union Carbide plant formed a dense poisonous cloud. In what has often been described as the world's worst industrial disaster, the gas killed thousands that night and left many more with lifelong respiratory and other ailments.

The protestors were demanding, among other things, medical care, clean water, and legal action against Dow Chemical. The chemical giant acquired Union Carbide in 2001 but has not participated in the cleanup of Bhopal, where more than twenty years after the accident children are still born with damaged brains and deformed limbs. Seven of the strikers were survivors of the disaster.

In a village in southern France, the novelist Indra Sinha fasted in solidarity, although he had to stop after seven days because he was undergoing long-term radiotherapy.[8] Last year Sinha's novel *Animal's People* was shortlisted for the Man Booker Prize.[9] *Animal's People* was dedicated to Sinha's friend Sunil Kumar, who was a Bhopal survivor. Kumar was only twelve when he became the breadwinner for his younger siblings, everyone else in the family having died as a result of the gas. He became an activist, fighting for the rights of his fellow victims. In July 2006, at age thirty-four, Kumar hanged himself from a ceiling fan. When he died, he was wearing a T-shirt that read "No More Bhopals." I had read Sinha's moving obituary of his friend, and after reading of the protests I wondered how the lives of people like Kumar, and the story of the disaster as a whole, entered fiction and found new life.

Animal's People is set in the near present in a fictional town called Khaufpur. One night, following a chemical leak in a pesticide factory, the town's inhabitants are awakened "by a wind full of poison and prophesying angels."[10] Khaufpur translates as "the place of fear." The novel portrays the struggles of the people unable to forget the desperate panic of the night that overtook their lives two decades ago. Indeed, terrible realities of that night have seeped into the present, corroding almost everything worthwhile in the lives of the Khaufpuris. On his website (http://www.indrasinha.com), the author speaks of the "double disaster" in the lives of the people residing in the "all-too-real city" of Bhopal: "first the gas leak itself which has killed around 23,000 people directly and through lingering illness" and then the second disaster, "the mass poisoning of the water supply of 30,000 more by chemicals leaking from the abandoned, never-cleaned factory."[11]

The narrative is presented as a young Khaufpuri's true-to-life account recorded on tape for a visiting foreign journalist. Animal lives in a scorpion-infested den; he introduces himself on the book's opening page with the words "I used to be human once."[12] He lost his parents on the night of the disaster, and later, when he was six, the toxins took their toll. His spine twisted "like a hairpin," he could only walk on all fours, his backside the highest part of his body.[13]

Rescued by a French nun working in Khaufpur, the orphan grew into a Dickensian street-smart kid who survived by picking pockets. But this is the backstory. The novel's main interest is in describing Animal's transformation from a scam artist into a somewhat reluctant political activist. As his creator is committed to an unsentimental, even cynical, worldly-wise hero, Animal's motivations are primarily sexual. In fact, a lot of narrative energy is expended in the repetitive detailing of Animal's erections and ejaculations. Animal is driven by his love for the beautiful Nisha, who, in turn, is in love with the man of the people Zafar, whom Animal sarcastically calls the "champion of the good and true."[14] The three of them are involved in negotiating the hopes as well as suspicions aroused by an American doctor's arrival in Khaufpur to open a free health clinic.

Is the Pennsylvania-born female doctor an agent of the pesticide company that has so far only brought misery to them? Most people around him believe so, but Animal finds himself divided. It turns out that he is a sentimentalist after all. Animal secretly hopes that the American doctor will cure him, and that when he walks on two feet, Nisha will naturally want to marry him. The plot somewhat tediously plays with these possibilities before the court case between the people and the company is reopened, breathing a new urgency into the lives of the Khaufpuris. They fear that a deal will be struck between the American corporate lawyers and the local politicos, and, indeed, matters come to a head when, hiding outside a luxury hotel, Animal spies one of the lawyers kissing the attractive doctor.

What is Sinha trying to achieve with this particular way of retelling Bhopal's story? In 1993, while working as an ad writer in London, he designed a campaign that garnered enough money to help establish a medical clinic in Bhopal that, he claims, has provided health care to more than 30,000 people. Given that Sinha has taken an activist approach to pragmatic goals in Bhopal, one could assume that the novel had specific literary goals. What is distinctive about Animal as a character in a novel? Not his sensitive heart or his buried humanity. Not, also, his back "bent as a scorpion's tail." However remarkable his physical appearance might be—he believes four parts of him are strong and appealing: his face, his powerful arms, his chest, and his enormous penis—it is Animal's language that is more immediately striking. A toxic mix of irreverence and energy, its vulgarity is a ready antidote not only to the hypocrisy of the elite, but also to the solemn pieties of those who from their space of comfort want to make a better world. Animal, early in the book, explains his point of view:

> The world of humans is meant to be viewed from eye level. Your eyes. Lift my head I'm staring into someone's crotch. Whole nother world it's, below the waist. Believe me, I know which one hasn't washed his balls, I can smell pissy gussets and shitty backsides whose faint stenches don't carry to your nose, farts smell extra bad. In my mad times I'd shout at people in the street, "Listen, however fucking miserable you are, and no one's as happy as they've a right to be, at least you stand on two feet!"[15]

One imagines that Sinha did not want simply to tell a moral tale, and that is why he found a voice that was scabrous and also playful. As an invented argot, particularly with its mix of Hindustani and gabbled English ("Kampani" for company, "jarnalis" for journalist, "internest" for the Internet, and, more interesting, "jamisponding" for spying à la 007), it appears to possess a texture that is earthy and redolent of the street. But does it? The British colloquialisms, the impromptu rhymed verse, and the French sentences that in the book form a part of the speech of the homeless Khaufpuri youth seem overwrought and—ah, that dreaded word—inauthentic. For a book that strains so hard to achieve its air of visceral realism, the narrator's language, which no street urchin in India would employ, is disturbing. It is not that this novel about Bhopal is less than literary; rather, it is too literary, trying painfully and self-consciously, through its use of a familiar romantic tale and other devices, to find distance from the well-known tragedy that is its subject. My criticism points to a historical reversal. Now that nonfiction so routinely uses fiction devices, novelists run the danger of appearing lazy and dated when they dress up real-life happenings as genre fiction. What was once newsworthy is easily made banal.

Perhaps the novel form was born to bring news, but today news is everywhere. The disaster novel of the present at its best makes news personal and intimate. It tries to contain crises of one sort or another. Containing involves a retelling. In the wake of 9/11, there came disaster novels by writers as different as Jonathan Safran Foer (*Extremely Loud and Incredibly Close*) and Don DeLillo (*Falling Man*). Each attempted to give intimate meaning and poignancy to an event that not only defied meaning but that also was too large, too public.

However, in countries such as India and Pakistan, the disaster novel is not so much a way of making real what had seemed remote; rather, for people who have experienced the bite of reality, writing offers a shot at redemption or justice. Or at least that is the alibi. Such a clear and laudable goal allows writers to contain the messy actuality: issues of complicity and the entanglement of privilege are burned away in the heat or light of righteous glory. A near-universal feature of such high-minded fiction is that despite its attention to real grievances it is often abstract and unreal. I can only call the absent element the essential quiddity of the real. With all their beauty and artifice, novels often hide the ordinary grit of reality. We find it sometimes, plain and unadorned, in the news, but it is often too generic and drained of force. It is the ir-repressible bubbling up of the everyday, not the unbending demand of a rigid aesthetic, that makes a novel satisfying, that connects it to life.

Sinha's work thus represents another crisis of authenticity. It is not enough to have local knowledge and an activist's good intentions. For a political novel to be successful, it may, in the end, have to betray its program. Art, like life, seizes us when it transcends a fixed purpose. *Animal's People*, despite its self-conscious attempts, never quite manages that liberating act.

Sinha's novel is most engaging when it, almost accidentally, opens up an absorbing conversation between art and life. Consider the daily reports I read about the hunger strike during the summer. June is a punishing month in Delhi, with high temperatures hovering around 110 degrees Fahrenheit. The police made arrests and harassed the pro-testors. I came to the closing pages of *Animal's People*: a hunger strike is launched in Khaufpur, a fast to the death, without food or water, during the nine hottest days of the year. In the middle of the strike, Zafar, one of the men who is fasting, his tongue already dry and swollen, begins to talk to Animal: "'What a place is this Khaufpur,' he says, 'where even the sky is broken and when rain comes it's just a loan against long overdue debts.'" It is a remarkable statement and much more effective than the more magical realist outpourings from Sinha's pen. Zafar goes on: "Is Khaufpur the only poisoned city? It is not. There are others and each one of has its own Zafar. There'll be a Zafar in Mexico City and others in Hanoi and Manila and Halabja and there are Zafars of Minamata and Seveso, of Sao Paulo and Toulouse and I wonder if all those weary bastards are as fucked as I am."[16] In the light of these words, the hunger strike in Delhi acquires a near-luminous glow. It also seems as if the protestors from Bhopal, and indeed the writer on his own fast in France, were living the life that had been depicted in the novel. All this is a far cry from John Updike's claim in the *New Yorker* a few years ago that the novel was "traditionally a mirror held up to the bourgeoisie, to teach its members how to shave, dress, and behave."[17] Were novels ever doing only that?

· · ·

On August 17, 1988, shortly after takeoff, a plane carrying the Pakistani military dictator General Muhammad Zia-ul-Haq crashed, killing all the passengers. Those who died along with General Zia were not only his top commanders but also the American ambassador to Pakistan and the head of the American military mission in Islamabad. The cause of the crash has never been explained.

Mohammad Hanif's elegant thriller *A Case of Exploding Mangoes* begins with that afternoon on the sun-bleached desert runway as General Zia is about to board the doomed plane. The protagonist coolly describes what will happen in the assassination's aftermath, thereby introducing us at the same time to the semifictional landscape in which his own story is being given birth:

> The generals' families will get full compensation and receive flag-draped coffins, with strict instructions not to open them. The pilots' families will be picked up and thrown into cells with blood-splattered ceilings for a few days and then let go. The U.S. ambassador's body will be taken to Arlington Cemetery and his tombstone will be adorned with a half-elegant cliché. There will be no autopsies, the leads will run dry, investigations will be blocked, and there will be cover-ups to cover cover-ups. Third World dictators are always blowing up in strange circumstances, but if the brightest star in the U.S. diplomatic service (and that's what will be said about Arnold Raphael at the

funeral service in Arlington Cemetery) goes down with eight Pakistani generals, somebody will be expected to kick ass. *Vanity Fair* will commission an investigative piece, the *New York Times* will write two editorials, and sons of the deceased will file petitions to the court and then settle for lucrative cabinet posts. It will be said that this was the biggest cover-up in aviation history since the last biggest cover-up.[18]

A fairly comprehensive failure of conventional newsgathering as the condition for the novel's emergence! Although the causes of the crash were never identified, there were plenty of suspects. On the list were the CIA; the KGB; Indian intelligence; the Israeli Mossad; several disaffected groups inside Pakistan, sections of the military among them; and the members of Zulfiqar Ali Bhutto's family seeking revenge for his hanging. To this long and impressive list of suspects, and this is only a partial list, Hanif, a graduate of the Pakistan Air Force Academy who now heads the BBC's Urdu service, adds a few more, not least a determined junior air force officer armed with love's vengeance and aided by a supporting cast—a crow, an army of tapeworms, and, of course, a case of exploding mangoes.

Hanif's protagonist is Junior Under Officer Ali Shigri, smart and capable but without any air of superiority. This is important; like Adiga's Halwai and Sinha's Animal, Shigri is a man of the people. His knowledge of the world and of history, for instance, seems to be drawn only from *Reader's Digest*. Hanif has reserved all assumptions of disdainful superiority, and therefore all signs of hypocrisy and weakness, for the rulers. Like Animal, Shigri hides his sentimentality from the world and turns resourcefulness into an art. His father used to be a colonel in the Pakistani intelligence, faithfully serving his country's (and the CIA's) mission to arm and pay the mujahideen in Afghanistan. The colonel's suicide, which his son believes was murder, is the impetus for Shigri's revenge against Zia. His carefully laid plans go awry, however, when Shigri's fellow cadet and roommate, the effeminate Obaid, tries to do away with Zia on his own.

The fast-paced story is rich with implausibility and therefore of great interest. For the reader on the subcontinent, particularly in Pakistan where the book's publisher is reportedly having difficulty finding even a printer, no officially sanctioned statement of fact is either true or benign. Nearly everyone is on the take, and therefore everyone is suspect. No one theory is capable of explaining anything, but everyone gets by as a conspiracy theorist. News, fueled by rumor, rapidly mutates like a virus.

But if the novel's plot is not believable, its exaggerated, satirical comedy rings true. It has bite. The portraits of the military leaders, all recognizable figures in Pakistani politics, are full of irreverence. In a country ruled for much of its history by men in uniform, this is heady stuff. Major Kiyani—a senior intelligence officer who is described as "a man who runs the world with a packet of Dunhill, a gold lighter, and an unregistered car"—has an extended biography that Hanif presents with all the precision and poetry of a postcolonial Graham Greene:

> One look at his skin and you can tell he has been fed on a steady diet of bootleg scotch, chicken korma, and an endless supply of his agency's safe-house whores. Look into his sunken cobalt blue eyes and you can tell he is the kind of man who picks up a phone, makes a long-distance call, and a bomb goes off in a crowded bazaar. He probably waits outside a house at midnight in his Corolla, its headlights switched off, while his men climb the wall and rearrange the lives of some hapless civilians. Or, as I know from personal experience, he appears quietly at funerals after accidental deaths and unexplained suicides and wraps things up with a neat little statement, takes care of loose ends, saves you the agony of autopsies and the foreign press speculating about decorated colonels swinging from ceiling fans.[19]

General Zia himself emerges in the novel's pages as a scared man who reads the Qur'an before his morning prayers to ascertain what the day holds for him—and to choose suitable lines that he could use in his acceptance speech for the Nobel Peace Prize he hopes to win some day. The general is also bothered by a rectal itch because of the tapeworms that are devouring his innards. In addition, his marital life is on the rocks. As the book progresses, we find the powerful man disintegrating under attacks of paranoia and piety. The parts about the general particularly test the reader's credulity, but their main weakness is that they rob the man of his menace. This happens less with other figures like Major Kiyani, and therefore, unlike the pages that paint Zia as a buffoon, those other sections of the novel pack a stronger punch.

What we have in the narrative sketches about the military men—from a lowly loadmaster who sexually molests a prisoner, to the toadying generals whose suave demeanors barely hide their instincts for torture—is a complex picture of a ruling class in transition. It reminds us of what Eqbal Ahmad wrote of the great shift that had already begun taking place in Pakistan's military by 1974. According to Ahmad, during the first twenty-five years of its existence, Pakistan was ruled by bourgeois soldiers and bureaucrats of colonial vintage, men who were largely status-quoists, greedy and paternalistic but nevertheless moderate in their beliefs and behavior. In the years that followed, new officers joined the ranks, men of petit bourgeois origin and fascist in outlook. These officers tended to be more religious and, having been trained by the Americans, resembled the Brazilian and Greek juntas. For Ahmad, the political environment in Pakistan appeared "to favor the growth of a right-wing, militarist dictatorship."[20]

That reality has obviously come to pass in the world depicted in *A Case of Exploding Mangoes*. A different way of acknowledging this development would be to say that news in the form of fiction has caught up with theory. And there is a feeling of retributive justice in the unanticipated fact that a lowly cadet has taken up the pen and merrily skewered his former bosses.

· · ·

A couple of weeks ago, I resumed my reading of Adiga's *The White Tiger*. When I left him, Balram Halwai, the book's narrator and hero, was painting a mythical image of Bihar. When I encountered him again, he was making a journey to the metropolis.

As I got deeper into the book I discovered that Halwai does not so much move to Delhi as move into a car. And because he is a chauffeur, it is vital that the important and meaningful talk between his employer and his employer's wife and other relatives takes place inside the car. Apparently the expensive apartment the employer owns in Gurgaon is only for sleeping, not for living, and this sacrifice is important for the sake of the plot. And useful also for delivering numerous bits of potted dialogue between the members of the ruling class:

"Why are we going to this place in the middle of nowhere, Ashoky?" Her voice, breaking the silence at last.

"It's my ancestral village, Pinky. Wouldn't you like to see it? I was born there—but Father sent me away as a boy. There was some trouble with the Communist guerrillas then. I thought we could—"

"Have you decided on a return date?" she asked suddenly. "I mean to New York."

"No. Not yet. We'll get one soon."[21]

The description of the journey to the ancestral village in Darkness is a clean and fine piece of writing: "We drove along a river, and then the tar road came to an end and I took them along a bumpy track, and then through a small marketplace with three more or less identical shops, selling more or less identical items of kerosene, incense, and rice. Everyone stared at us. Some children began running alongside the car. Mr. Ashok waved at them, and tried to get Pinky Madam to do the same."[22] But even at such moments, the novel reveals its great weakness. Who is looking here? The village to which the car is returning is not only the employer's village but also Halwai's—he is returning to the place where he was born and grew up and that he has only recently left. Yet does it appear to be the account of a man who is returning home? He recognizes no landmark or person, he has no emotion, he has no relationship to the land or the people.

This is at the heart of the book's bad faith. The first-person narration disguises a cynical anthropology. Because his words are addressed to an outsider, the Chinese premier, Halwai is at liberty to present anthropological mini-essays on all matters Indian. It is an "India for Dummies" that proves quite adept at finding the vilest impulse in nearly every human being it represents. I do not only mean every member of a corrupt and venal ruling class, but also the victim class itself, portrayed in the novel's pages as desperate and brazenly cannibalistic. Reviews of the book in mainstream publications, including the *Economist*, present it as a glimpse into the "real India."[23] Whose India is real; Adiga's or mine?

Almost exactly eight years ago, in the pages of *Boston Review*, the Indian writer Vikram Chandra published an inspired, polemical essay called "The Cult of Authenticity." Chandra's anger was directed against those "cultural commissars," mostly critics in India, who were suspicious of writers' use of clichéd Indian motifs.[24] These critics claimed that an easy appeal to saris and samosas, and the employment of a few well-known words like karma and dharma, were the means by which Indian writers in the West signaled their identity and coddled their readers. Chandra bristled at the suggestion that others, by dictatorial fiat, could choose his material for him. Chandra made an argument not only for artistic autonomy but also for the essential hybridity of any writing. His point is that because the culture around us is mixed up and in flux, the literature that draws on that culture will reflect its energy and impurity. It was inevitable, for example, that in his fiction he would employ words in English and other Indian languages. Just as people do on the streets of Mumbai.

Quite explicitly, Chandra also argued against the notion of any real India, an India that is accessible only to a certain kind of writer, one who lives in the hinterland; or receives poor advances; or writes only in an obscure, regional language. Against such a purist aesthetic, Chandra pushed for recognition of the actual, impure world in which we all live and write:

> There will always be a prevailing market and a prevailing ideology, and a head of department who fiercely upholds that prevailing ideology, a head of department whose cousin owns the press that publishes the books, whose cousin's best friend reviews the books for the Sunday paper, whose cousin's best friend's cousin gives out the government grants and the fellowships to Paris. All art is born at this crossroads of ambition and integrity, between the fierce callings of fame and the hungers of the belly and the desires of one's children and the necessities of art and truth. Michelangelo knew this, and [the popular nineteenth-century Urdu poet Mirza] Ghalib knew this. There is no writer in India, or in the world, no artist anywhere who is free of this eternal *chakravyuha*, this whirling circle that is life itself. To have less money does not mean you are more virtuous, to have more money does not mean you are less capable of integrity. Those who believe in the salutary effects of poverty on artists have never been truly hungry, and are suspicious of money from the safety of their own middling comforts. Finally, I suspect, whatever language we write in, we are all equally capable of cowardice

and heroism. . . . In case it makes anyone feel any better, let me state for the record my considered opinion that for sheer incestuousness, for self-serving pomposity, for easy black-and-white moralizing, for comfortably sneering armchair wisdom, for lack of generosity, for pious self-interested victim-mongering, for ponderous seriousness and a priggish distrust of pleasure, there is no group on earth that can match the little subcaste that is the Indo-Anglian literary and critical establishment. I say this with full cognizance of my own somewhat contested membership in said establishment.

Chandra's argument against the impossible-to-satisfy and hypocritical demand for purity is liberating. Yet I wonder where that leaves criticism. Does Chandra's injunction to writers—"Be fearless, speak fearlessly to your readers, wherever they are"—not also apply to critics?

His opponent in the essay is an academic critic; Chandra shrewdly graphs himself as the street-smart writer. There is a lesson in this. Such is the impurity of our enterprise, as writers or as critics, that even in the act of proclaiming our freedom from the demands of authenticity, we are never free from brandishing it.

Unlike Chandra, I don't think there is freedom at hand from the entire question of authenticity, largely because there is no escape from the yearning for the real. The painfully real; the brilliantly, euphorically real; the emphatically real. Either in our lives or in our writing. And for me, living abroad, this yearning also translates as a parsing of tales about India. In an interview on the Man Booker website after his book was included on the Man Booker long list, Adiga said: "It's a great thrill to be longlisted for the Booker. Especially alongside Amitav Ghosh and Salman Rushdie. But I live in Mumbai, where not many people know of the Man Booker Prize; I'm still standing in long queues and standing in over-packed local trains in the morning and worrying about falling ill from unsafe drinking water. Life goes on as before."[25]

I envy Adiga's way of claiming authenticity at this moment when he is himself in the news: he has access to the real India, he is standing in long lines, he is afraid of drinking dirty water. I could write a novel about this.

NOTES

From Amitava Kumar, "Bad News," *Boston Review*, November 1, 2008. Reprinted with permission of the publisher.

1. A brief but comprehensive report in the press about the case was published a few years after my review essay. See Patrick French, "Worse than a Daughter's Death," *Open*, February 5, 2011. Accessed August 2, 2014. http://www.openthemagazine.com/article/nation/worse -than-a-daughter-s-death.
2. Sam Dolnick, "Servants Often the Usual Suspects in Indian Crimes," USA *Today*, June 10, 2008.
3. "Author Aravind Adiga Reveals the Class War Simmering beneath India's Boom," *Sunday Times* (London), June 29, 2008. Accessed September 24, 2014. http://www.thesundaytimes.co.uk/sto/culture/books/article102391.ece.
4. Aravind Adiga, *The White Tiger* (New Delhi: HarperCollins, 2008), 5–6.
5. Adiga, *The White Tiger*, 26.
6. Amitava Kumar, *Home Products* (New Delhi: Picador, 2007). The novel was published in the United States as *Nobody Does the Right Thing* (Durham, NC: Duke University Press, 2010).
7. "Bhopal Gas Victims Begin Hunger Strike," *Hindu*, June 11, 2008. Accessed September 24, 2014. http://www.thehindu.com/todays-paper/tp-national /bhopal-gas-victims-begin-hunger-strike/article1275367.ece.
8. Indra Sinha, "Why I'm Going on Hunger Strike for Bhopal," *Guardian*, June 12, 2008. Accessed August 2, 2014. http://www.theguardian.com/comment isfree/2008/jun/12/india. The article also provides details of Sunil Kumar's death.
9. Indra Sinha, *Animal's People* (New York: Simon and Schuster, 2007).
10. Sinha, *Animal's People*, 37.
11. When this chapter was originally published, Indra Sinha's website provided information about Bhopal. The website no longer exists. I have let the description stand because the condition it portrays is still accurate.
12. Sinha, *Animal's People*, 1.
13. Sinha, *Animal's People*, 15.
14. Sinha, *Animal's People*, 283.
15. Sinha, *Animal's People*, 2.
16. Sinha, *Animal's People*, 296.
17. John Updike, "Mixed Messages," *New Yorker*, March 14, 2005, 138.
18. Mohammad Hanif, *A Case of Exploding Mangoes* (New York: Knopf), 2008.
19. Hanif, *A Case of Exploding Mangoes*, 73–74.
20. Eqbal Ahmad, "Signposts to a Police State," in *The Selected Writings of Eqbal Ahmad*, ed. Carollee Bengelsdorf, Margaret Cerullo, and Yogesh Chandrani (New York: Columbia University Press, 2006), 436.

21. Adiga, *The White Tiger*, 80–81.

22. Adiga, *The White Tiger*, 82.

23. "His Master's Voice," *Economist*, September 11, 2008. Accessed August 2, 2014. http://www.economist.com/node/12202501.

24. Vikram Chandra, "The Cult of Authenticity," *Boston Review*, February 1, 2000. Accessed August 2, 2014. http://www.bostonreview.net/vikram -chandra-the-cult-of-authenticity.

25. The Man Booker website does not appear to host interviews with nominees any longer.

II

WRITING

8

How to Write a Novel

I began writing my novel *Home Products* in the summer of 2003, a few weeks before my wife gave birth to our first child.[1]

But even before I began work on the book I bought a black hard-cover sketchbook. In its pages, I started writing down whatever I liked in what I happened to be reading. Among the earliest journal entries is the opening line of a review that had appeared, in the *New York Times*, of the film *The Hours*. This was also the opening line of a novel by Virginia Woolf. I cut it out and pasted it in my journal: "Mrs. Dalloway said she would buy the flowers herself."

There are no notes around that neatly cut out quote, but I can imagine why it had appealed to a first-time novelist. You read Woolf's line and are suddenly aware of the brisk entry into a fully formed world.

No fussing around with irrelevant detail and backstory. And I began to write various opening lines.

In my mind there was an image of a man sitting in a room in a prison near Patna. When he gets out, he would like to make a film. But nothing I wrote promised a swift entry into a fictional world that already existed, and I went over the same lines for at least a fortnight without any success.

Then my daughter was born. My wife had undergone a long, painful labor. I tried to imagine a birth in a prison, not a human being giving birth, but an animal. Say, a dog. The distance from actual experience, its transformation into something removed from actuality, seemed to me the proper task of the novelist. On July 16, 2003, I made the following entry in my journal: "The bitch had been sullen and sluggish through the long afternoon."

When I sat down at my computer, I saw the man looking down into the dusty yard from his cell window, watching the dog circling a clump of banana trees in distress. The animal tries to bite and lick a bone. The man stays at the window and realizes, the discovery filling him with tenderness, that what the dog is licking is a newborn puppy.

I slept very little after our child came. And my wife and I were always tired. I'd go to a café and drink coffee; while sitting there, I'd try to write. My journal shows that I made little progress. More than a month later, I had only the outline of a plot. In pencil, I have written "Main character" and then, beneath a dividing line, "Father," "Mother," and "Aunt." Under "Father," as if I were drawing a family tree, I have written "2 brothers" and "one sister." The sister is identified as "Bua," and a dotted line extending from her to the far corner of the page says "Politician in Bihar, killed at the end."

Now, looking back at this outline, I am amazed that so much was changed, but I'm equally amazed that so much wasn't. On the opposite page is a note indicating that I had read about the use of Internet cafés as sleaze parlors in Chennai, with the owners providing beds for privacy and, in some cases, filming couples for blackmail. This story made its way into the book I wrote, the cyber café transported to Patna, but if I hadn't just now looked at the journal I had kept I would've assumed that I had produced this scene entirely out of my own imagination.

When I began to get more time to write, maybe an hour or two each day, I'd start by reading a few pages of *A House for Mr. Biswas*.[2] I wanted to be reminded again and again of the comedy that informs V. S. Naipaul's writing about failure. And every time I finished work, I'd be conscious only of the ways in which I had failed. There is very little doubt in my mind that one of the hardest things a serious writer must do is write with humor. It was easy to forget this demand because I was anxious to get the words on the page. I was always afraid that the book would run aground. I'd be stranded in the sand. The journal's pages are full of notes recording scenes and snatches of imagined dialogue. Much of it was never used. But reading those pages now, I can very easily recall the panic and dread that dogged me during that time.

By the following summer, I had a draft of the novel. I know this because in a new journal, in an entry dated June 16, 2004, I find the words "Outline for Draft 2." My notes are all about altering the structure and inserting new details. There is a small printout of a quote, pasted close by. It is probably from the *Guardian*: "My favourite description was in Louis Dean's *Becoming Strangers*: 'The South African pulled his short shorts back up around his ankles and positioned his genitals gamely inside the fishing-net interior.'"

An Eastern European friend of mine, a writer, had told me that he always prints out his first draft and types out each word of his second draft. This way he avoids the temptation to cut and paste; as a result, whatever he writes the second time around has a fresh feel to it. I did the same. Twice.

My goal at this time was just to get a book-length manuscript done. I couldn't worry whether it was good or not. I did worry, of course, but I was determined to put down words on paper. Several days after the outline for the second draft in my journal, I see that I have copied down a quote from James Thurber: "Don't get it right, get it written."

I also find that in October 2004 I had written in black with a red border, "Home Products." I now had my title. Below those two words, I had written down this quote from Mark Twain: "To my mind, one relative or neighbor mixed up in a scandal is more interesting than a whole Sodom and Gomorrah of outlanders gone rotten. Give me the home product every time."

I had been writing often, a few hundred words on a good day, and I usually wrote several days a week. I sent off a copy of my third draft to my agent and to two friends who are editors. The response from them was muted: I had a made a mistake, the book wasn't ready to be shown yet. I had put down an account of events, but a novel relies more on a voice.

For the next few months, I didn't write anything new. And then I returned to write two quick drafts by the following summer. It must have been around this time that I pasted in my journal a portion of a review by James Wood: the critic had narrated a story by Chekhov about an actress, Katya, who has discovered that she has no talent. She asks an older family friend for help and advice: "Tell me, what am I to do?" The man tells her he doesn't know what to do. And then, he says at last, "Let us have lunch, Katya."

Beneath the pasted note, I had made a note about endings, and how one shouldn't insist on "closure." But isn't it probable that my eye had snagged on the heroine's confession of failure at the only thing she most wants to do?

And yet, I remember being happy every time I wrote a new draft. Each time I would think that the job had been done. But it wasn't. It would never be. It is possible I wouldn't have been able to write the book if I had known this from the beginning. My diligent editor cut out more than twenty thousand words; in the months that followed, I wrote new opening and closing chapters. I felt that things were coming together nicely.

But another year would pass, and I'd go through half a dozen more drafts, before the editor and I were happy with what we had. I had never worked harder on a book before, and still a book as a finished object remains an elusive thing for me. Full of mystery and beauty, and the result of extraordinary luck.

NOTES

From Amitava Kumar, "How to Write a Novel," *Hindu*, March 4, 2007. Reprinted with permission of the publisher.

1. Amitava Kumar, *Home Products* (New Delhi: Picador, 2007).
   This essay uses quotes that have been either copied down in a notebook (without any interest in citing the source) or cut out of a newspaper and

pasted on the page. I had not anticipated using them in an essay later. Googling did not help. In most instances, it took me to my own essay. And, alas, in the case of the very first citation, it revealed that I was wrong. The review of "The Hours" in the *New York Times* doesn't begin with the famous first line of *Mrs. Dalloway*. Did I have in front of me another newspaper, perhaps a Canadian one, because it was in Toronto that my daughter was born? I wrote the essay—and a novel—quite secure in my error. Does this prove that we should be more fastidious about footnotes—or can we claim, instead, that we have established their irrelevance?

2. V. S. Naipaul, *A House for Mr. Biswas* (New York: Knopf, 1995).

· 9 ·

Reading Like a Writer

The general elections of 2014 were around the corner in India. Each political party presented its manifesto: "Health vans will reach every part of India." "Necessary legal framework will be created to protect and promote cow and its progeny." "Every cycle-rickshaw puller will be given an auto-rickshaw or a solar-powered rickshaw free."

Here is my own manifesto for Indian writing. I hereby call for a literature that engages with "the real": not just the depiction of blood on the streets, or, for that matter, the cold air of the morgue, but also the warm, somewhat moist atmosphere of unwanted intimacy in the waiting room in which we have left behind a little bit of our past. Like the political parties, I too am trying to project myself to my home base.

The title of my novel *Home Products*, published back in 2007, was drawn from a quote by Mark Twain: "To my mind, one relative or neighbor mixed up in a scandal is more interesting than a whole Sodom and Gomorrah of outlanders gone rotten. Give me the home product every time."[1] But the title had always had another meaning for me. It was meant to signal that the story wasn't for export. It was for readers in India. In fact, when people read it I wanted them to imagine that the novel could have been written in Hindi.

Also, I didn't want to have to explain much. The book's first sentence is: "Mala Srivastava's mother lived in a two-room flat above a tiny kindergarten institution that called itself Harward Public School."[2] Not for a moment did I imagine that a reader of my novel in, say, Cambridge, Massachusetts, would immediately know anything about the unsuspecting humor behind the school's name, a name that I had seen painted on a wall near my parents' home in Patna. And yet a reader like that, a reader outside India, wasn't ever far away from my thoughts.

Soon after *Home Products* was published in India, the writer Siddharth Chowdhury, a friend from Patna, sent me a congratulatory note. He had especially liked a chapter where a boy lies awake beside a couple on their wedding night in Motihari. The groom engages in foreplay by speaking to his new wife about the high marks she matriculated with. She had scored well in both history and geography. The groom says to the bride, "People like me know that the capital of Nepal is Kathmandu or that the capital of Burma is Rangoon. But please tell me—what is the capital of Mongolia?"[3]

Ulan Bator!

Such sad seduction. If we were drinking Old Monk together, and Siddharth had made the comment about liking that section in the novel, we would laugh and improvise further lines. But I was alone in my study in upstate New York when I saw his message. I wrote back with the complaint that I was still waiting to hear from my agent in London. I wanted to know whether my book was also going to be published in the West. At that point, anxiety had swallowed any sense of irony I might have otherwise possessed. Chowdhury, who had already published his stylish first novel, *Patna Roughcut*,[4] then sent me a response that I have never been able to put out of my mind:

> I truly believe that getting published in the West is not that important. At best it is a bonus and one earns more, which is a good

thing. But as Indian writers, our primary market lies here and it is here in India that we will be finally judged, though I do realise that some critics here look towards publication in the West as final validation of a writer's worth. But tell me, is Paul Auster ever bothered about how he is perceived in India? Or whether his books sell at all in India?

I read the message from my friend and wondered whether Paul Auster had ever heard of Patna.

Although I hadn't till then read anything by Auster, I now felt a connection. A couple of summers ago, I saw a young woman on the beach reading *The Invention of Solitude*, and I bought a copy the next day. When Auster's memoir *Report from the Interior* came out last year, I again picked up a copy. Early in the book, there is mention of "the starving children in India."[5] Auster is describing a scene from his childhood. American mothers in the 1950s talked of half-naked, emaciated Indian children begging for food so that they could shame their own kids into finishing what was on their dinner plates. This pleased me, but the memory was so general that it took on the character of a myth, which is what, in the end, it was.

If I were living in a *barsati* in Delhi's Defence Colony, I would feel less anxious, I think, about being invisible to American writers. But I live only an hour and a half away from the brownstone in Park Slope, Brooklyn, where Paul Auster lives. Therefore, I want him to know where, so to speak, I'm coming from. At the very least, I want him to know where on the map Patna is located.

No, I'm misstating my intention. I would like American writers to read and engage with Indian writers in the same way that Indian readers have read and celebrated them all these years. It is intolerable to me that I love Philip Roth and I also love Shrilal Shukla, but that neither they nor their work should ever come together.

Believe me, I try to do my bit. Exercising the agility of a pole-vaulter in the Olympic Games, I use any relevant detail in a story as a kind of lever to launch me into the other landscape. For example, in Auster's memoir the mention of a polio epidemic in 1952 made me think of America more tenderly because it then began to resemble India. A young Harvard man, who lived on the street where Auster's best friend lived, lost his life to polio. Auster writes that, ever since, he has associated grief with the sight of black cars outside the dead youth's white house. When I read this story, I felt a warm glow of recognition spreading in my heart. In *Home Products* too I had written about my own distant relative who has polio. In my imagination, I saw her transposed over the figure of a young woman in a play being performed at Bombay's Prithvi Theatre—Tennessee Williams's *The Glass Menagerie*. She was Laura, the beautiful, doomed girl with a deformed leg, and—another pole-vault leap—there were worries over her marriage and her dowry.

In reading Auster or Williams this way, I was acting as a translator. Indians are adept at this. We are good at mimicking and miming, but we also perform more complex actions through which we absorb outside cultures. We make what is alien our own. We are also good at opening ourselves to the outside gaze, and we have a portable notion of Indian culture that we carry to cultural festivals across the world. One criticism of Indian writing in English is that we translate too much. Not simply that the humble samosa is described as a savory food item but that the narrative, like the menu in small Indian restaurants abroad, remains limited to the same familiar items. All too often, our writing is an act of translation on behalf of the West. Where, then, is one to look for a more challenging literature?

In an article in *Mint Lounge* last December, the Indian critic Somak Ghoshal argued that recent translations from Indian languages provided a more satisfying read than books written in English by Indian writers.[6] I thought of that argument when I was reading Auster's memoir. When Ghoshal praised Ajay Navaria's stories with Dalit protagonists, it occurred to me that here was an opportunity for Auster to participate in the heats for the pole-vaulting competition.[7] What would stories about discrimination against Dalits teach Auster? Here, ladies and gentlemen of the jury, are the relevant facts: In Auster's memoir, we learn that the man who was his barber also used to cut Thomas Edison's hair. On the barber's wall was a portrait of the famous inventor and a handwritten note: "To my friend Rocco: Genius is 1% inspiration, 99% perspiration—Thomas A. Edison." As a child, Auster believed that Edison provided his connection to greatness. When he was a little older, in his teens, Auster learned that his father, when just out of high school, had worked for Edison in his lab, except that the job at the lab had lasted only a few days—Edison, a rabid anti-Semite, had discovered that Auster's father was a Jew and fired him on the spot.

The argument I'm putting forward is a very simple one: Auster, writing a memoir that touches on the prejudice against Jews during his childhood, could learn from Indian literature. For example, he could read in English translation an Urdu story by the Bihari writer Husainul Haq, who examines the inescapable dilemmas of a Muslim man in a period— the early 1990s—that has witnessed the rise of the Hindu right.[8] Haq's protagonist is asked by his Hindu neighbor, who has returned from Ayodhya, to hide a brick from the demolished mosque. The neighbor fears arrest; he argues that the piece of rubble is also, after all, sacred to Muslims. It is a delicate story, rich in paradoxes, and deserves a wide readership. The larger point I'm making is that India isn't revealed only by tracking the dilemmas of Indians abroad. In other words, stories like "Jasmine" by Bharati Mukherjee, about a young woman of Indian origin in America, need not be Auster's only point of reference.[9] The diaspora story that Mukherjee tells is by now a familiar one. Not only that, it also sees Indian identities only in terms defined by the struggle to achieve the American dream. The backstories that such characters have are either thin or nonexistent. The subcontinent and its histories are simplified to the point of fantasy. The vernacular literatures in India are better poised to elude these tendencies and, thankfully, in recent years, we have seen a rise in translations from Indian languages. Books like Sachin Kundalkar's *Cobalt Blue*, Uday Prakash's *The Walls of Delhi*, U. R. Ananthamurthy's *Bharathipura*, and Chandrakanta's *A Street in Srinagar* have all been top contenders for the DSC Literature Prize awarded at the Jaipur Literature Festival. This is a very good sign. Pole-vaulting has grown at once simpler and also more complicated.

These days, as I read the news careening about on social media about shootings and terrorist attacks, massacres and gang rapes, I often find myself thinking that a writer's task today, more than ever before, has become one of making sense of violence. This, too, is an act of translation. Particularly because a writer often has to respond imaginatively to a report of violence from a part of the world other than the one in which he or she is living.

In late January this year I read the news of the killing in Delhi of a twenty-year-old student from Arunachal Pradesh named Nido

Taniam.[10] The tragedy of Taniam's death was brought out not by the fact that he was, seemingly for racist reasons, beaten up by shopkeepers in Lajpat Nagar, but that, as if bound to the wheel of injustice, he was detained by the police and later returned to the same place by them. And there, once again and several hours after his first ordeal, he was beaten again.

Such sad inevitability! As if each tragedy were hiding a chronicle of a death foretold. The news reports were brutal but spare; perhaps because of this quality, conveying a few unforgettable details but leaving a lot to the imagination, they brought me closer to life. But—and this is the more important point—these reports also brought me to literature. Specifically, the details of Nido's tragedy reminded me of the story "Tirich" by the Hindi writer Uday Prakash.[11] It is a story I have wished everyone to read, to be filled with the same dread I was when I first encountered it: a boy in a village tells the story of his father's death after the old man, deranged either by a lizard's bite or by the datura herbal drink he has taken as a cure, is beaten by security guards in a bank, then attacked by kids throwing stones, and then assaulted by a group armed with iron rods. The boy's story is a testimony, and therefore honest about cruelties, but his narration is sensitive, even soft. The brutality of the day's happenings is enhanced by their tender narration. The disorientation brought about by the bite or by the drug is reinforced by the fact that the old man is wandering alone, deranged, in the alien, urban streets. The story begins with the poisonous *tirich*, but the greater dread is of the inexorable violence of the city. Uday Prakash told me over a meal some years ago, while we watched India and Pakistan playing a one-day cricket match on TV, that Delhi started to change in the 1980s: "I was once at the ISBT"—Inter-State Bus Terminal—"and I suddenly imagined my father, visiting from the village, getting lost there."

I was already living in the United States when I first read "Tirich." Like much other Hindi literature I read during the mid-1990s, the discovery of Uday Prakash's story was a homecoming. I read him still because his writings bring news from the new, shining India: the explosion of money. The bewildering changes in social relations. Small, vulnerable people being ground underfoot by the moneyed bosses who come from powerful castes. In his recent fiction, Prakash boldly offers small essays embedded as editorials, as if they were op-eds written by

Arundhati Roy in Hindi. This mixed form suggests that he is not merely telling a tale but pressing on with urgent truths.

Long after putting down "Tirich," I am still haunted by the names I found there, names of towns, streets, and characters that are rarely encountered in Indian writing in English: Samatpur, Master Nandlal, Pandit Ram Autar, Sipahi Gajadhar Sharma, Deshbandhu Marg, Sardar Satnam Singh, and, best of all, Satte. The pleasure of coming across, in Hindi, names like Minerva Talkies and National Restaurant! I suspect this was a species of nostalgia, this attachment to what we might call low-rent realism, but it was a real discovery. It mirrored an earlier discovery of mine, when I was in my early twenties, and the discovery came not through Hindi but English. I was a student in Hindu College in Delhi but would skip class to go instead to the Lalit Kala Akademi Library near Mandi House. There, for the first time, I read Ved Mehta.[12] Mehta wrote about his father, a doctor in the Public Health Department in Punjab, and his own schooling in an orphanage-like school for the blind in Bombay. In an English that was plain and unfussy, Mehta made me see that the road outside my house; or my relatives in Motihari; not to mention my Punjabi math teacher in Modern School on Barakhamba Road, Delhi, could all be written about in readable prose—and were therefore real.

It would be years before I understood that Mehta, perhaps because he was blind, simplified the world in just the right way. He brought his private world into focus—and presented it to the West on equal terms. That too was translation. In the decades that followed, this act was refined by others in the diaspora, skilled translators all, writers as different as Salman Rushdie and Jhumpa Lahiri. They each performed a complicated act of cultural engineering. Every new successful practitioner showed an ability to turn what is local or of limited valence into what is broadly intelligible in its sameness as well as its startling dissimilarity. This is literature's domain, and I believe that translations from one language to another broaden literature's landscape. The best translations, whether between languages or between cultures, are similar in the sense that they are acts of confidence. As a writer you grasp so well the specificity of what you are representing that your articulation of it always carries large implications of context and history that make it intelligible in a more universal way. Weak translations, on the other hand, are unable to grant any legitimacy to their subject, which they can only prepare for surrender to a dominant tongue or culture. When they don't exoticize, they make mute.

A novel that I regard as nearly talismanic in its ability to speak in a voice that is uniquely its own is Upamanyu Chatterjee's *English, August*.[13] No one could accuse it of translating India for the West. And yet, and yet: On the one hand, it represented a successful attempt at conveying small-town Indian realities in an English that was somehow familiar and yet new; on the other hand, however, its own narration cast doubt on any easy transportation of English into small-town India. A character in *English, August* is talking to the narrator in his office at a publishing company in Delhi, and says about a manuscript on his table: "Dr Prem Krishen holds a PhD on Jane Austen from Meerut University. Have you ever been to Meerut? A vile place, but comfortably Indian. What is Jane Austen doing in Meerut?" He goes on to ask: "Why is some Jat teenager in Meerut reading Jane Austen? Why does a place like Meerut have a course in English at all?"[14] Why, indeed. And hasn't the relevance of these questions weakened today?

Chatterjee's novel was published in 1988. The questions in it still hold true, but much has also changed. A decade after the book's publication, in a landmark essay titled "Edmund Wilson in Benares," the critic and novelist Pankaj Mishra went to considerable lengths to answer the question about Jane Austen in Meerut. Mishra's essay described four months from the same year that *English, August* came out; it painted a portrait of ruin in decaying towns like Varanasi and Allahabad, their decline redeemed by the burgeoning literary consciousness in the minds of provincial youth. Mishra's thuggish friend Rajesh, who is introduced to us in the essay, had a past mired in poverty and childhood labor in a carpet factory. But on reading Flaubert's *Sentimental Education* and Wilson's essay about the book, Rajesh told Mishra: "It is the story of my world. I know these people well. Your hero, Edmund Wilson, he also knows them." For someone like Rajesh, *Sentimental Education* held a mirror to the "grimy underside of middle-class society."[15] Flaubert's fiction wasn't so much about distant France; it was a report on the corruption common in Allahabad.

"Edmund Wilson in Benares" first appeared in the *New York Review of Books* in April 1998. I bought that issue at a subway stop near Columbia University in New York City. Upon reading Mishra's essay in its pages, I forgot that this wasn't the first time an Indian writer had offered an account of the influence a Western writer exercised on him or her. Instead, I was moved by the portrait that Mishra painted because the small room in which Rajesh lived was familiar to me, as was his mother's house in the village. I had known intimately the landscape of thwarted hopes. But, more than anything else, I was ready to celebrate the gesture through which Edmund Wilson and Flaubert had been made Indian. These figures no longer appeared alien to me; equally crucial, they didn't look larger than the small people and small lives that I had once known in Bihar's small towns and villages.

A few more years passed. Watching Vishal Bhardwaj's epic film *Maqbool*, a marvelous adaptation of *Macbeth*, I once again remembered *English, August*. In the novel, our narrator was given sleeping pills "called Somnorax . . . made in Ulhasnagar, near Bombay," and there was "a supine king on each packet, with hands beneath his head and eyes wide as chasms."[16] Below the king, this quote:

> —the innocent sleep,
> Sleep that knits up the ravell'd sleave of care,
> The death of each day's life, sore labour's bath,
> Balm of hurt minds, great nature's second course,
> Chief nourisher in life's feast,—
> Shakespeare, *Macbeth*

In *English, August* the narrator read these words on the packets of Somnorax and found himself moved by this attempt to find "some use for Eng. Lit.'s most famous insomniac." But I, on watching *Maqbool*, thought, "Such glory!" Bollywood has long borrowed from Hollywood, but this wasn't like that at all. Neither was it like a writer explaining the Indian joint-family system or caste to someone in London or New York. Instead, *Maqbool* was an example of a new kind of translation: it took what was essential about the context in which the original story was told and let it speak to what is essential and specific, and therefore eloquent, about the context in which the new art was being made. In this way, *Macbeth* came to Mumbai as an underworld don.

After a book reading in Mumbai, the film director Mahesh Bhatt asked me to write a screenplay for him. Irrfan Khan, Mr. Maqbool himself, was also in the audience. As I had just written a book called *Husband of a Fanatic*—an account of my marriage to a Pakistani Muslim during the Kargil War, but also a report on violent riots in Indian cities—I was asked to write about the struggles of a Muslim youth accused of terrorism.[17] But *Maqbool* had planted a different idea in my mind, and I began work on an adaptation of Chekhov's famous story "The Lady with the Dog." In my story, the couple meet at Harki Pauri in Haridwar. The middle-aged married man who falls in love with a woman, also married, travels to Amritsar to tell her about his longing and loneliness. The film based on this story was never made, but I tied it into the narrative of *Home Products* because I wanted to pose a question to Hindi films: Don't middle-aged people fall in love? This question was asked in the interest of making art more real, and writing more meaningful, a way of working out a problem or two I would face in my own life.

There will always be many ways of doing art. I want better and more honest, and certainly more searching, accounts of whatever is happening in the world. This sometimes makes me a partisan of good nonfiction. The young woman in Delhi who was raped and assaulted with an iron rod in December 2012—where are the stories that do justice to her life and death? Close to the one-year anniversary of the attack, her father told a BBC reporter about how his daughter comes to him in his dreams and asks him if he needs money. The father offered the reporter an explanation for this. He said that this is what poverty does to you. You think about money all the time, think about whether you have enough money in your pocket to take your daughter's body home. He said this because he was thinking of the night his daughter was raped and left by the roadside. The father said that a call summoned him to the hospital, where he was told his child would live only a few hours: "My first thought was how will I take her body home?"[18]

These statements do not appeal merely as facts; they seem to embrace life's most difficult complexities and challenge the imagination.

In late August 2013, I read a news story whose horror has stayed with me. I do not ask myself how Auster will write about it, or even how I might translate it for a wide readership. Nor do I wonder so much whether the story needs to be told as fiction or nonfiction. All I ask of myself and my readers is: how to keep this story alive? This is what I wrote down of the story in my notebook:

> A young Dalit woman from Jind in Haryana left home to sit for a Teacher Training Exam. Her father, a daily-wage labourer, received a call saying that his daughter's papers were found scattered near the bus-stop. Her body, which was found the next day, had cigarette burns. Her clothes were bloodstained. The police at first refused to register a case, and then denied that the victim was raped. Her father said, "Her eyes were still wide open with fear. Nobody bothered to straighten her curled fingers. And nobody tried to close her mouth. It was as if her last scream was still inside her mouth."[19]

Before I end, let me make one point clear about what it means to read as a writer. Around the time I was starting work on *Home Products*, I read an interview with the literary agent David Godwin. When asked what turned him on in a book, his reply was: "Voice, not so much story."[20] I think it's because of their clarity that I can never put some nonfiction stories out of my mind. This is the apotheosis of voice that writers from Orwell to Naipaul dreamed about: a language so transparent that there is an illusion of an art which works without the trespass of personality. In other words, the voice propelling the story often stays out of the picture and lets the events stand out in an austere or striking light. Over the hush of a narrative voice I hear the hammer of new truths striking my heart.

My examples above might be misleading. I am not asking for screaming headlines. Or urgent voices hoarse from all the shouting at Jantar Mantar. This is a plea for the ordinary—that it be returned to the startling quotidian arrangements without being crowded into the ornate and colorful covers between which Western publishers tend to put all Indian books. I'm appealing here to an argument made by Amit Chaudhuri that to produce the estrangement effect in art one need not look at the extraordinary—rather, let's look at "the dross that surrounds us: verandahs, advertisement hoardings, waiting rooms, pincushions, paperweights."[21]

Here, then, instead of a slogan, is an image from a doctor's clinic. It comes from a story by Upendranath Ashk, newly translated from Hindi by my friend Daisy Rockwell. All along I had been looking for authenticity, and I found it in a description of a fake: but this is the value of fiction, the fake that sends a shiver up your spine. When I read it, I saw that it belonged to its own landscape, and yet it shocked me into recalling my forgotten childhood in Patna:

> A fake cockroach had been pinned to the partition behind the doctor. Under the cockroach hung a lizard with its tail crooked. The first time Mr Goyal had come to Dr Chatterji's clinic, both these creatures had looked completely real to him, and for quite some time he had waited for the lizard to leap up and seize the cockroach in its jaws. Even though he had since learnt that both were fake, he always found himself riveted by the cockroach and the lizard when he went to Dr Chatterji's clinic.[22]

NOTES

From Amitava Kumar, "The Shiver of the Real," *Caravan*, May 2014, 72–76. Reprinted with permission of the publisher.

1. Mark Twain, "Italian without a Master," in Mark Twain, *The $30,000 Bequest and Other Stories* (Rockville, MD: Wildside, 2003), 232.
2. Amitava Kumar, *Home Products* (New Delhi: Picador, 2007), 3.
3. Kumar, *Home Products*, 64.
4. Siddharth Chowdhury, *Patna Roughcut* (New Delhi: Picador, 2005).
5. Paul Auster, *Report from the Interior* (New York: Henry Holt, 2013), 18.
6. Somak Ghoshal, "Reading: The Year of Local Treasures," *Mint Lounge*, December 28, 2013. Accessed August 2, 2014. http://www.livemint.com/Leisure/DssnFdrPHWRNvaAtowFuCP/Reading—The-year-of-local-treasures.html.
7. Ajay Navaria, *Unclaimed Terrain*, trans. Laura Brueck (New Delhi: Navayana, 2013).
8. Husainul Haq, "Consecrated Brick," trans. M. Asaduddin, in *Image and Representation: Stories of Muslim Lives in India*, ed. Mushirul Hasan and M. Asaduddin (New Delhi: Oxford University Press, 2000), 146–55.
9. Bharati Mukherjee, "Jasmine," in Bharati Mukherjee, *The Middleman and Other Stories* (New York: Ballantine, 1988), 123–55.
10. "Outrage after Student 'Beaten to Death' in New Delhi," *Al Jazeera*, January 31, 2014. Accessed August 2, 2014. http://stream.aljazeera.com/story/201401311949-0023434.
11. Uday Prakash, "Tirich," in Uday Prakash, *Tirich* (New Delhi: Vaani Prakashan, 1996), 23–47.
12. Ved Mehta, *Face to Face* (New York: Little, Brown, 1957).
13. Upamanyu Chatterjee, *English, August* (London: Faber and Faber, 1988).

14. Chatterjee, *English, August*, 170.
15. Pankaj Mishra, "Edmund Wilson in Benares," *New York Review of Books*, April 9, 1998.
16. Chatterjee, *English, August*, 95–96.
17. Amitava Kumar, *Husband of a Fanatic* (New York: New Press, 2005).
18. Soutik Biswas, "How Life Has Changed for Delhi Rape Victim's Family," BBC *News India*, December 15, 2013. Accessed August 2, 2014. http://www.bbc .com/news/world-asia-india-25344403.
19. Maria Akram, "Jind: Nine Days, Three Autopsies Later, Dalit Girl's Death Remains a Mystery," *Times of India*, September 2, 2013. Accessed August 2, 2014. http://timesofindia.indiatimes.com/india/Jind-Nine-days-three-auto psies-later-dalit-girls-death-remains-a-mystery/articleshow/22217868.cms.
20. Shoma Chaudhury interview with David Godwin, "I'd Like Suketu under My Belt," *Tehelka*, February 3, 2007. Accessed August 2, 2014. http://archive .tehelka.com/story_main26.asp?filename=hub020307ID_Like.asp.
21. Amit Chaudhuri, "The East as a Career: On 'Strangeness' in Indian Writing," in Amit Chaudhuri, *Clearing a Space: Essays on Literature, India, and Modernity* (Oxford: Peter Lang, 2008), 93.
22. Upendranath Ashk, "Hats and Doctors," in *Hats and Doctors*, trans. Daisy Rockwell (New Delhi: Penguin, 2013), 26.

10

Writing My Own *Satya*

"Mumbai ka king kaun?"[1]

Remember that question in *Satya*? The words were shouted by a man with his arms raised triumphantly in the air. He was standing on a high rocky outcrop. The sea lay under those outstretched arms, and behind him, as his witness and backdrop, spread out the city of Mumbai. That man was a brash and exuberant underworld goon named Bhiku Mhatre. Mhatre spoke the street lingo of that city, a mix of Hindi and Marathi that is now as much the Bambaiyya argot as it is the lingua franca of the Tarantinoesque films made about that city. The actor who played Mhatre was Manoj Bajpai, whom I had read had been born in a village close to mine in Champaran in Bihar. He had gone to school in Bettiah, a town where I had spent parts of my childhood and where I still have family ties. While watching *Satya*, therefore, I was watching Bhiku

Mhatre as a Bhojpuri-speaking man who had taught himself to pass as a native in the Marathi-dominated metropolis.

It was a magnificent performance, of course, but for me, more than an actor's prowess what the film revealed was a talented individual's ability to rise above, and escape, his origins. And even that was not all. What was real about Bhiku Mhatre, his earthiness and his authenticity, was the subtle result of a persistence in Bajpai's performance of the enormous toil that had gone into the making of what he now was. That presence of opposites—and nothing else—made his every gesture a high-wire act.

When I first saw *Satya*, I was deep in work on a book called *Husband of a Fanatic*.[2] My wife was pregnant with our first child, and I was in a hurry to complete the project. But I immediately took a new notebook from my shelf and wrote down a set of questions I wanted to ask Bajpai. I can't say whether I wanted to get Bajpai's answers because I didn't know him—or because I believed his answers would only confirm what I felt I already knew. I remember I had drawn a star on the page: I didn't want to write a clever little book mocking Bollywood. Instead, I thought I could do a good job developing an accounting chart that told the story of what was it that Bajpai had to learn on the path to success and what he had also needed to unlearn.

A few months passed. I could see that I was coming to the end of my labors on the book I had spent the past few years researching and writing. One day, I sent a note to my friend the filmmaker Shyam Benegal, who had directed Bajpai in *Zubeida*. A message came back for me, and I called Bajpai on the phone. He said "Hello" the way we have seen actors like Amitabh Bachchan say that word on the phone: it is heavy with import, delivered in a deep bass, almost as if it was a constitutional declaration. I wasn't very clear in my mind what form the writing would take, or even if I'd have enough material for a book, but I wanted Bajpai to know that I admired him enough that I could fill 300 pages with praise.

. . .

There is something I wish to confess at this point. There have been moments when I have believed that my primary allegiance is not to India where I was born, or to the United States where I work, but to Hindi films. I am a citizen of the world created by Bollywood. It would only be honest to acknowledge this because in some fundamental way my emotions, or the language of my sentiments, have been shaped by what I have seen on screen. I also have a different debt to Hindi cinema, which is primarily aesthetic; the diction of neorealism, acquired from the films of Shyam Benegal and Govind Nihalani, has become a part of my imagination. But the original, and more long-standing, debt is to mainstream Hindi films with their melodrama, their songs, their rich and familiar set of conventions. I recognize that they are a part of whom I am.

One night, several years ago, I sat down with a bottle of single malt and a film that I had borrowed from the Indian video store. The film was Mani Ratnam's *Bombay*. I must have already been drunk by the time I saw Manisha Koirala running toward her lover beside the sea—her body and, it would appear, even her love buoyed on the rhythms of A. R. Rahman's music. I was thinking of my girlfriend, a white American, with whom I had recently broken up. That night, in a mood that must have been a mixture of maudlin sentimentality and nostalgia, and perhaps a dash of despair, I resolved that I would never marry anyone who didn't understand the words that a slightly shrill Lata Mangeshkar was singing at that very moment: "*Tu hee re, tu hee re . . . tere bina main kaise jeeoon.*"

Of course, the quick embrace of sentimentality and tearful nostalgia isn't about love or loneliness so much as it is about a certain way of talking. It is about language. That is why, unlike any other kind of cinema, in Hindi cinema you have this intense interest in the mannered delivery of lines. And the popular form that applause takes: "*Arre, kyaa dialogue maara hai!*" It is partly about inspired theater, but partly it's just the words: the two reasons come together in the habit that people have of repeating Dilip Kumar's lines from *Mughal-e-Azam*.

In my case, the hunger for language that a film like *Satya* can satisfy takes on a keener edge. I have been living away from India for two decades now. Although I visit each year, I know that the changes in the cities where I was born and grew up far outpace my understanding. Most crucially, there are new words being minted on the streets of my past. Behind my back, language is altering, shifting, becoming unrecognizable. In a film like *Satya*, more than the guns exploding on the screen, it is abuse that erupts over and over again. This is the spectacular eruption of language from the street. Fresh, energetic, highly gregarious, utterly welcome—the film's dominant idiom constitutes a full assault on ears previously attuned to hearing only syrupy declarations of platonic love.

When the film starts, a steady voice-over introduces us to the city that never sleeps and doesn't stop dreaming either. A city of inequalities and, as a result of those divisions, a city with an underworld. The camera tracks through the wreckage of cars and the tightly packed homes in the slums. The road to the city passes through the hell called the underworld. This is the universe of *supari* killings and the short, dangerous lives of the hit men called *taporis*. The film's main story begins with that staple shot of Indian cinema, the outsider from somewhere else arriving in the big city. This stranger, alone with a bag in his hand, walking outside Victoria Terminus, is named Satya. As the film unfolds in its opening minutes, his confrontation with the underworld is intercut with scenes of extortion and murder carried out by the gangs. Very soon, the two story lines collide, and then the pace hardly ever drops.

Part of the frisson of the narration is because of the reference to real-life events, including the killing of the music magnate Gulshan Kumar. Kumar belonged to the film world, and this too is a theme in *Satya*, the regular back-and-forth between the two worlds, presenting a dark intimacy between the underworld and filmmaking. This increases the viewer's experience of delight and danger.

Even the moments of release, like the one that follows Bhiku's emergence from prison, as in the famous drunken song sequence ("*Goli Maar Bheje Mein . . .* "), have their own moments of rare energy and even ominous warning. The film often follows to a charming degree the formula of a film like *Pulp Fiction*, where the men who are going to kill talk about techniques of foot massage. In *Satya*, you have an innuendo-laden talk about a particular prostitute called Shaboo mixed with a grim interview with the builder Malhotra and an expert analysis of the real-estate business in the city. But the film is also rooted in the history of Hindi cinema. There are loud echoes of numerous other movies: the orphaned protagonist, the paralyzed housebound father, the corruption in politics. There are more direct evocations too. Not only in the way in which Bhiku Mhatre asks Satya during their first, violent encounter if he imagines he is Amitabh Bachchan, but also the way in which violence, with revenge as its engine, reminds us of all the *dhishoom-dhishoom* fights we have witnessed in 1970s movies like *Deewaar*. An important sequence in the film also involves a police action at a cinema hall where the audience had been watching a recent popular hit, *Border*. In this and at many other moments in the film, the scriptwriters Saurabh Shukla and Anurag Kashyap pay homage to cinema; but their passion for the medium also shows in their clever accommodation of the conventions of Bollywood—the return to laughter through weddings, and dances, and the blossoming of implausible romance.

At the same time, the script and direction remains alert to difference or what is new. The cast is packed with characters who appear real. The mafia advocate Mule, played by Makarand Paranjape; Bhiku's Marathi-speaking wife; and Shukla's own remarkable, even endearing, portrayal of the veteran gangster Kallu Mama—these are all performances that make *Satya* special and tell the story of a film that was clearly more than a film with a stunning individual performance or even the work of a successful director. In fact, it is easy to believe that the film is the product of a collaborative and improvisatory work. One gift that art offers us is that it makes human everything it touches. And that is what is happening in *Satya*. The gangsters are made human not only with their hurts and strengths, but also with their wives and children, their loves, their friendships, their deceits, their hopes and dreams, their bad jokes.

· · ·

I flew to Atlanta and met Bajpai. I had taken a room in a hotel. Bajpai was visiting with his girlfriend, whom he married later, and I would pick him up each day in my rented car. Bajpai was a late riser and we didn't start till eleven or noon, but I had the chance to sit with him in a Starbucks for hours and talk to him till evening. We talked over three or four days. Not once did anyone recognize him except one evening, on our last day, when a flock of Indian girls rushed in, squealing, and asked for his autograph.

Had I read in an interview that he used to wet his bed when he was a boy? Or was this something that Bajpai told me during our conversation? This was a detail that struck me. It reminded me of one of my heroes, George Orwell, who once wrote an essay about this.[3] Orwell had a plain honesty about him. It is easy to forget, while reading Orwell, that this honesty is a quality that he achieves on the page. It is a performance. It is informed by a desire to acquire an audience. Bajpai was candid with me, but not about everything. I felt that he had decided to share with his audience a few things from his past. How had he decided what he would choose to share with others? I never found out. Yet it was with genuine excitement that I took notes as Bajpai spoke of his childhood, his long years of poverty, his days in theater, his failures. He spent an entire afternoon and evening speaking about his painful divorce. Bajpai had found small roles in television serials and in films like *Bandit Queen* before Ram Gopal Varma gave him his big break in *Satya*. On the day of the film's release, a friend took him to place in Mumbai where there was huge billboard with his face on it. Bajpai stood under it and drank beer from the bottle while his friend shouted at the passersby to take note of whom they were seeing. I saw in him another Satya, the newcomer in the city making it big.

Often I heard the repetition of stories that I had already read in the interviews; I would press him for details. It didn't always work. I was unsure whether Bajpai understood the difference between a journalist and a writer. But I was pleased when he granted me little snippets. One day, I remember he told me his college mates in Delhi laughed at his lack of English. As an example, he said he didn't understand it when the headline in the *Times of India* had said "University Closed Sine Die." But that wasn't English. It was Latin. I said I wasn't sure of the meaning either. I could identify with him because we both spoke Bhojpuri at home; it was also the language in which Bajpai and I often spoke with each other. Despite that sense of familiarity, I didn't ever think I was getting a new or more profound sense of a person through those interviews. I wasn't disturbed: I had just started on the project. I knew I was going back to Bihar, to Bajpai's village and mine. I was also confident I would find out more when I came to Mumbai and learned about the process through which films get made.

Over the next two or three years, I came to Mumbai for visits. I met many people who had been a part of the making of *Satya*: its director, Ram Gopal Varma, whose unyielding, arrogant affect with me spoke of a near-adolescent indifference to anything that isn't immediately gratifying or of interest; the film's writers, Saurabh Shukla and Anurag Kashyap, who generously spoke of their own growth in film; Bajpai's co-actors like Makarand Paranjape, whose new work on the stage of Prithvi Theatre was there for all to see. I also decided to interview the security guards who served at the homes of the Bollywood film stars; on another occasion, I went looking for Bihari prostitutes and talked to them about their work. I felt my story needed more: I toured the city, especially the areas where the Bihari working class lived and worked. A Hindi film journalist named Ajay Brahmatmaj told me a lot about the industry in which he worked. On one of my visits, Suketu Mehta was also visiting Mumbai, and he took me to places that he had written about in his book, which was still to be published.[4] Through Bajpai, I met Mahesh Bhatt, and we decided that I would write a script for him. I would be in my home in Pennsylvania, and the phone would ring. It would be Bhatt on the line, asking for ideas, sharing plotlines, even lines of poetry. I felt I was entering an exciting new world.

An editor friend urged me to give up the idea of writing a nonfiction book about Bajpai and *Satya*. Bajpai's story would be there, but it would be part of a rich fictional world. I began to play with the idea of two men from Bettiah living in Mumbai, one an actor in Hindi films, and another who was a film journalist. But this didn't have enough energy yet. I needed another character, and this need was filled by someone from my own family, a cousin who had been jailed, except that when I saw him in my mind he looked like Bhiku Mhatre. The man in prison possessed Bhiku's wild energy and optimism. If a film were to be made from my story, Manoj Bajpai would play the character inspired by my cousin. The story I wrote became my novel, *Home Products*.[5] The novel discusses many Hindi films like *Bandini*, or *Bhumika*, and even *Arth*; *Satya* is not mentioned even once, but in a way it is present on every page.

. . .

In an interview with a writer from London, Neeraj Dubey had said that if you really want to enjoy a Hindi film, you should go to a theatre in a small town in Bihar. "Small-town people tear their shirts open when they are feeling very excited. They do that when a hit song is on the screen. When some titillating dance is going on, you see coins being thrown at the screen. It's madness. They don't hold back any emotion, they don't care a damn what people think. If they want to cry, they cry or howl in the theatre. In cities, audiences go to the theatre with expectations. In small towns, they don't have any expectations, they come to enjoy the film and if you betray them, and you let them down and you can't hold them, then you'll see empty theatres the next day. They are extreme in their emotions; the city people aren't—I would say they don't know how to enjoy a Hindi film."

When he read those lines, Binod had felt love for Dubey. He saw him as someone who would speak honestly and in an unguarded way, even though when he thought about it more, he felt that Dubey's success as an actor was precisely in holding himself back while a part of him cried for full disclosure. It was that struggle between opposing emotions that gave his performances their particular tension.[6]

These lines are taken from *Home Products*. The words uttered by the character named Neeraj Dubey were actually spoken by Manoj Bajpai in an interview with Nasreen Munni Kabir.[7] When I read those words today, I'm reminded with sudden force why I had been so moved by Bajpai in *Satya*. A part of me was behaving in exactly the way he said the audience in Bihar would behave. Writing a novel after you have watched a film is also, after all, a demonstration of an extreme emotion.

While writing this essay, I returned to watch *Satya* once again, something I hadn't done for a long time. I was surprised how much I remembered; I was surprised how much I had forgotten. In the prison yard, Bhiku Mhatre and Satya are shown having a conversation under a tree, while in the distance some prisoners are playing a *kabbadi* match. Was this forgotten snippet the inspiration behind the scene in my novel when the two protagonists watch a wrestling match in prison? I can't know for sure. More than that, I found myself a trifle impatient and, just now and then, despite all the old, familiar appreciation, also a bit bored. Watching the film this time, I was reminded of a line from *The Great Gatsby*: "It is invariably saddening to look through new eyes at things upon which you have expended your own powers of adjustment."[8] I had at one point used *Satya* as a way of going back home; it had allowed me to tell a story about the Bihar of my boyhood. But it was now a part of my past. I had moved on, and so had the place I had written about. Going back is never easy and, after a while, it is nearly impossible. Nevertheless, I am happy that this lesson too should have come to me through a Hindi film, especially through a film like *Satya* that had once meant so much to me.

NOTES

From Amitava Kumar, "Writing My Own Satya," in *The Popcorn Essayists: What Movies Do to Writers*, ed. Jai Arjun Singh (Chennai: Tranquebar, 2011), 78–90. Reprinted with permission of the publisher.

1. "Who is the king of Mumbai?" This question is asked in the film *Satya*, directed by Ram Gopal Varma (Englewood Cliffs, NJ: Eros Entertainment [for USA and Canada], 1998), VHS.
2. Amitava Kumar, *Husband of a Fanatic* (New York: New Press, 2005).
3. George Orwell, "Such, Such Were the Joys," in George Orwell, *A Collection of Essays* (New York: Harcourt Brace, 1970), 1–47.
4. Suketu Mehta, *Maximum City: Bombay Lost and Found* (New York: Knopf, 2005).
5. Amitava Kumar, *Home Products* (New Delhi: Picador, 2007).
6. Kumar, *Home Products*, 96.
7. Quoted in Nasreen Munni Kabir, *Bollywood: The Indian Cinema Story* (London: Channel Four, 2001), 40–41.
8. F. Scott Fitzgerald, *The Great Gatsby* (New York: Scribner, 1953), 69.

11

Dead Bastards

A little boy on his way to church notices the bright reflection of the church in a lake. He tells his father that the second church is better. He wants to go there instead. The father tries to dissuade the child, but when he remains persistent, the father says, "Fine. Go in the lake, see what happens."

I'm describing a poem to you. I'm paraphrasing, reducing the poem to a narrative. Having confessed my sin, let me now go on with the story. In the poem, the boy goes into the second church and notices that everyone is wet but no one is embarrassed about it. He likes it there. Except, after a while he notices that the faces around him are turning red. People are praying for air. The boy urges them to leave, to get out and breathe.

I have read this poem many times over the past few months and am always surprised by the tight turns and details. There are hundreds of people drowning, mothers and sons, and an organ player. Bubbles are coming out of the pastor's mouth. It is sort of beautiful, the boy thinks, and then ignores his own advice and dies alongside the other drowning parishioners.

The poem was written by my student, Mikko Harvey. He has just graduated from Vassar College and was awarded last month the Academy of American Poets Prize. I was used to reading smart, surreal, often whimsical, poems written by Mikko, but he held one more surprise for me. In the thesis he turned in at the end of the year, there was a poem about Dzhokhar Tsarnaev, and it was titled "My Inability to Pronounce Your Name."

The lines that caught my attention were the following: "We had the same history teacher. / She was pretty. / Did you notice? / You must have, the way she brushed / the bangs from her eyes. / So at what point did we become / different?"

Mikko's poem, as it proceeds, turns on an examination of the small differences that lead to one destiny that is catastrophically distinct from another.

Mikko and Dzhokhar were both students at Cambridge Rindge and Latin School. Mikko doesn't remember ever having spoken to the younger Boston bomber, though he saw him in school all the time. I asked Mikko to tell me why he wrote the poem. He said: "I was trying to find out who he was after the fact of the bombing. Trying in a small way to understand the person behind the action. I couldn't just dismiss him as a monster because we have so much shared history. Teachers say he was friendly and soft-spoken; they would say the same thing about me. He smoked pot and played Fifa; I did too. We had the same history and literature teachers. We pissed in the same urinals. There is this intimacy between us, yet also a great distance." Mikko had an additional comment. He wrote to me that the week before the bombing, Dzhokhar had tweeted: "I really don't like it when I have one ear pressed against the pillow and I start to hear my heart beat, who can sleep with all that noise." Mikko said: "This is so intimate, so human, almost poetic. When I read this tweet, I know I can't dismiss him as a monster. I have to face the ways in which we are similar."

DEAD BASTARDS

I know that many will remonstrate that we all know, even from bad Hindi films, about evil men who love their mothers or who have charming failings. What is so attractive about Mikko's stance is that he locates humanity in a shared history ("We pissed in the same urinals") and yet says nothing to deny the mystery behind inhuman choices.

This attitude is a welcome departure from the certainties of experts who routinely refer to position papers that predict the regular turns on the road to radicalization. The counterterrorism authorities are like the boy who mistakes the reflection for the real church. In the world made real or recognizable only on the basis of their theories, we have been asked to take the plunge and we are drowning.

As I sit writing these words, the news on the radio is of the start today of the military trial of Private First Class Bradley Manning in Fort Meade, Maryland.[1] This trial is taking place three years after the arrest of the whistleblower, who released hundreds of thousands of classified documents to WikiLeaks. Manning has already spent months on end in solitary confinement. He has denied the most damning charge of "aiding the enemy" and helping Al-Qaida.

Will he get life in prison? If found guilty, will the judge impose the death penalty? This is the debate on the radio right now. But the real point that Manning threw up for debate through his actions is why the American administration did not regard the people of Iraq as human. As Daniel Ellsberg, the Pentagon Papers whistleblower, said at a protest for Manning during the past weekend, "He was concerned that the people of the world should be informed of the way, as he put it, the First World, or the West, he said, treats the Third World."[2]

This is how you and I first learned of the work that Bradley Manning had done. On April 5, 2010, a classified military video was released by WikiLeaks showing the slaying of two Reuters employees and others by the crew of two U.S. army Apache helicopters. The video was shot through the gun sights of one of the helicopters, and we watch the deaths through the fatal crosshairs in the center. For an ordinary viewer of the video, it is difficult to adopt this dehumanizing optic, as if all one surveyed was under a death sentence, every person merely a target.

And they are targets. As one of the voices on the video says, "Got a bunch of bodies layin' there," and a little later, another voice adds, "Oh, yeah, look at those dead bastards."[3]

This was the horror that Bradley Manning exposed. The material he released to WikiLeaks revealed, if any further proof were needed, the murderous fraud that was the U.S.-led Iraq War. We owe Bradley Manning thanks. I'd piss in the same urinal with him any time.

NOTES

From Amitava Kumar, "Dead Bastards," *Open*, June 22, 2013. Reprinted with permission of the publisher.

1. A few weeks after this essay was written, Manning released a statement that she would like to live her life as a woman. She would henceforth be called Chelsea Manning ("I Am Chelsea," *Today*, August 22, 2013. Accessed August 3, 2014. http://www.today.com/news /i-am-chelsea-read-mannings-full-statement-6C10974052).
2. Quoted in Amy Goodman, "Bradley Manning Trial: After 3 Years, Army Whistleblower Begins Court-Martial Shrouded in Secrecy," *Democracy Now*, June 3, 2013. Accessed August 3, 2014. http://www.democracynow .org/2013/6/3/bradley_manning_trial_after_3_years.
3. "Collateral Murder Video," Chelsea Manning Support Network. Accessed August 3, 2014. http://www.chelseamanning.org/learn-more/collateral -murder-video. The video is also available on YouTube.

The Writer as a Father

When our daughter was about to be born, I chose for her a short name, Ila. Ila's mother is Muslim, I am Hindu. We had got married when our two countries, India and Pakistan, were fighting a war. Ila is a Hindu name; it is also the opposite of her mother's last name, Ali.

Ila Ali. A friend of mine said it would be a name that would sway in the breeze all day. I had noticed that it formed a palindrome. Ila's name mirrored her mother's, and yet kept its difference. I liked that.

Which is all to say that even before she was born, Ila had become, like many other kids, a site of complicated, and often silly, fantasies on the part of her parents.

Ila is now six. A few days before she was born, I chanced upon an essay by Raymond Carver called "Fires." It is a memoir produced, I suppose, in response to a question about literary influences. In a characteristic move, Carver declares that more than books and writers, it was other things in his messy, real world, that had affected his work. In particular, his children. The memory of those years, when his kids were growing up, still bothered Carver. Sitting in the basement of my in-laws' house in Toronto, while waiting to become a new father, I read the following lines: "I have to say that the greatest single influence on my life, and on my writing, directly and indirectly, has been my two children. They were born before I was twenty, and from beginning to end of our habitation under the same roof—some nineteen years in all—there wasn't any area of my life where their heavy and baleful influence didn't reach."[1]

It is a searing little essay. Carver describes the desperation of his younger years, working at one, sometimes two, menial jobs and trying to put food on the table for his family. He describes his struggle to write. He wrote short stories because there was never enough time to write anything longer. His despair soon begins to feel like a dark liquid pooling on the page. You feel the writer's pain but, of course, you can also imagine the children drowning in that misery.

Around the time that I first read "Fires," I was also starting to draw the outline of a first novel. I cannot remember now whether it was Carver's essay that led to this decision in my mind, although I remember reading that piece more than once that summer, but as I played with the outline I began to think that I would write about the birth of my daughter. My wife underwent a long, painful labor. The novel began with a man in a prison near my hometown in India. I tried to imagine him witnessing a birth in a prison, not a human being giving birth, but an animal. Say, a dog. Now when I look back on it, I wonder whether some of Carver's "dirty realism" (or what Tess Gallagher has called his "benign menace") hadn't crept into my presentation of Ila's arrival as an animal birth witnessed in a prison. In any case, when the novel was published, the scene I have described above found its way into its pages. But there were many times during the writing of the book when I wished I had more time to write. Perhaps all writers complain about time, there is never enough time, and in the years following that first encounter with Carver's essay, I have often gone back to it like an alcoholic returning to drink. As far as I am concerned, despite or perhaps because of my hunger for it, that piece is like poison.

For the truth is that I also love my daughter so much that anything sweet or tender reminds me of her. I don't only mean a child on a street in strange city, wearing a dress of a style and color I associate with my daughter, who can suddenly induce heartache, but even a bird calling in an overhead branch, ku-hu, ku-hu. I remember being in a small town in India a couple of years after Ila had been born. In a dark front yard of a house where I had come to conduct a late-night interview, two young servants were busy with a black cow that was about to give birth. Lanterns swinging in their hands, the youths explained that the last time one of the cows had given birth, it had been in the middle of the night. No one was around to take care of the calf. In that crowded stall, the mother had accidentally trampled her newborn to death.

As I watched, fifteen minutes later, the calf arrived, its legs thin and crooked as in a child's drawing. I could think only of Ila as I gazed at the lovely little animal in front of me: she was also the child whose drawings had given me a way to look at it that night. The creature's arrival filled me with a sudden elation and it also made me miss my daughter terribly. It is the same when I'm in the train coming back from New York City, hoping to be home before she goes to bed. To participate in the ritual of preparing her for sleep, and then lying down next to her to read a story, offers me great joy. I will not exchange it for another hour of writing. At such moments, I have traded Raymond Carver for Wallace Stevens. When asked by Marianne Moore to turn in a piece on William Carlos Williams, Stevens said no, explaining in his letter: "There is a baby at home. All lights are out at nine. At present there are no poems, no reviews. I am sorry."[2]

Such grace. And, however impermanently, that sense of patience and grace is also mine.

I say impermanently not only because, in my case, the feeling of sweet resignation that Stevens is describing gives way, sometimes, to the rage that Carver is articulating. That does happen, but what I have in mind is this: I put Ila to sleep and lie awake in the dark for a while; the lights are, indeed, out at nine, but not for long. I come out of the room and make my way slowly upstairs to sit down and write.

· · ·

On occasion, I write about Ila. As I am doing right now. This is what writers do, they write about the world, and because their children often loom large in their world, they end up putting them into their stories too.

Carver certainly did. He wrote a poem to his daughter that invoked a similar effort by W. B. Yeats, except that instead of wanting his daughter to be plain, he wanted her to be sober: "You're a beautiful drunk, daughter. / But you're a drunk."[3] These are two lines that appear near the middle of what is certainly not among Carver's better poems. In this poem, Papa is preaching against alcoholism. As in an AA meeting, there's great value put on confessions of one's own sins, the daughter being asked why she hasn't learned from all the mistakes her parents made. No doubt because he's a writer, Carver is better at description than he is at offering advice. The poem goes on to document the daughter's degradation and her injuries at the hand of the man she loves. It's all gritty and intense. Nevertheless, I wonder what Carver's daughter herself thought of her father laying out in full public view the intimate picture of her sorry life.

I ask this as if I feel aggrieved; I'm not. I ask only as a member of the offending class. The offending class of writers. Once, when Ila was two, my wife was nursing her. Ila turned away from one breast to the other, saying, "This one not working." I remember asking myself how long it would be before I used that in my writing.

When Ingmar Bergman died, many obituaries appeared in the papers; there was one by the British critic David Thomson that discussed Bergman's isolation and his kids. "Probably no one knew the loneliness better," wrote Thomson, "than the lovers, and the children, who saw how he put their smiles, their eyes, their meals, their untidy beds on the screen."[4] The phrase that stayed with me in Thomson's obituary was a reference to Bergman's "ruthless and obsessive use" of the smiles and faces of those he loved. Any feeling of guilt that I had was displaced by a curiosity about method: in what way was Bergman ruthless or obsessive? He had been married five times; he accepted paternity of as many as nine children. Did he meticulously portray the tangle of these relationships in his films? Most important, and this was a writer's question and not a father's, did he keep notes?

Ila would come back from preschool and bring bits of her strange, alluring world to me. Everything she said I'd store like postcards from a fictional place. In my journal is a note that shows that when Ila was three she pored over a map and asked me, "Where's California? California lives in the desert, right, Dad?" I thought that was precious, but a part of me must have also believed that I could use that line in a novel. But even as I look at some of the other entries I have made in my journal, I see that there is another impulse also at work.

Consider the line that Ila offered at bedtime on April 18, 2007, when she was a few months short of four: "I know only two things. That I have to wear loose clothes when I go to sleep, and that we have to be nice to each other." These are not notes for a novel: instead, these are memos to self. "Shape up," these memos say. There are several entries in this vein in my journal. I find myself reflecting, not only on my daughter's sweetness, but also on my secret desire to be the person that my daughter thinks I am. This becomes clearer to me when I read in another entry that after a ten-hour journey, when Ila and I are picked up late at the train station by her mother and I complain about the time we have spent waiting in the cold, Ila silences the apologies by saying, "You were on time, Mom. You were on time."

My daughter thinks I am the person who will take her to Disney World. Who am I to pretend to be otherwise? This was a couple of years ago. My wife, who is an economist, refused to come with us. She said something like, "It is a corrupt consumerist trap, you cannot possibly take Ila there." I enjoyed the trip very much. I confess I had mixed motives for visiting Florida. In the pages of the New York Times, Thomas Friedman had written that post-9/11 America had become hostile to visitors and our government was exporting fear, not hope; more specifically, Friedman had complained, "If Disney World can remain an open, welcoming place, with increased but invisible security, why can't America?"[5] Friedman's remark sparked my curiosity. I suddenly felt that I could excuse my extravagance.

Once there, I noticed that bags were searched before entry, but there wasn't much more that I could observe. This becoming a research trip was unlikely. It wasn't as if while rushing from the Caribbean Beach Resort to the Magic Kingdom, I could touch Mickey Mouse's elbow and ask, "Say, where are the hidden cameras?" Not only that. Even if I had found the answer to that question, perhaps all I'd have wanted to find next was whether the cameras would reveal where the lines for the rides were shorter.

CHAPTER 12

Frankly, I couldn't have been happier than doing what I had really come to do. From morning to night, nervous about a thousand things, I took my child in a rented stroller from one overpriced event to another. There was tea with Sleeping Beauty. There were endless encounters with people in cute, but no doubt hellishly hot, stuffed-animal costumes. We met patient princesses who held their smiles while parents of the kids standing next to them figured out how to use a simple digital camera. I was anxious that in the heat my daughter looked sunburned and thirsty. But I was happy not to have to think about work. I was on holiday with my happy child.

It is not always like this. I can be in another city for work, perhaps on way to an interview, but I'll be searching with one eye for a toy shop. There was a period of time when I would take the train to New York City to attend a terrorism trial—but even while rushing to catch the subway, I'd stop at a kids' store in Grand Central station to buy a little gift for Ila. I was often late to court, and when I took a seat on a bench near the door, a witness would already be half-way into a story about illegal funds. I would hear about where the money went, but have no idea about where the money came from!

Such happenings leave me conflicted. Not about the plain fate of being a father—although one evening, when she was four, Ila looked up from a game she was playing with me and asked, "Are you tired of having a child?"—but about how I deal with my responsibilities. Last October, I was in Beijing searching for clues to two writers' lives early in the twentieth century. I went to museums and libraries, and even to cemeteries, but required more information for what I wanted to write. A lot of work needed to be done. Instead of pounding the pavements in search of people who would provide me what I needed, I found myself one morning in Beijing's Hongqiao Market looking for a Chinese costume for Ila. Her instructions had been precise. She had watched *Mulan* on TV and wanted what Mulan was wearing. Earlier, I had stopped at a store called Cinderella but it only sold bridal dresses. Hongqiao Market didn't disappoint; it was full of goods that we think of as stereotypically Chinese. The shops were packed with haggling Americans and salesgirls who, in a show of intimacy, would each grab my arm and shriek, "Very cheap, very cheap." I had a list of things I needed to buy, which included a Chinese doll and a paper kite; on the back was the outline of two little soles because, as you might be aware, Mulan also wore distinctly Chinese shoes. I had to search for these items with care, but what was also exhausting was the pressure to bargain. For thirty yuan, one could buy a pot of green tea, and, more than once, I sat down to sip tea and collect my wits. And during those breaks, I asked myself whether I shouldn't have actually been conducting interviews at the Beijing Normal University. The answer was perhaps yes, but what was undeniable was the elation I felt as I ticked off what I had purchased on the list. It was my best day in China.

In January 2004, a Seattle paper reported that a conference was going to be held in Yakima, Carver's hometown, to honor the writer's memory. The keynote speaker was Vance Carver, the writer's forty-five-year-old son. The younger Carver had declared his intention to remove the misconceptions about his father's early family life, about the bad years before the writer sobered up and did the work that earned him his name. The younger Carver had told the newspaper: "His years as a family man before 1978 are often depicted as dark years, as a baleful time that were hard on him, that somehow have no redeeming value. That's only part of the story."[6]

The detail that caught my eye in that news item was Vance Carver's mention of a famous story of his father's called "The Compartment." This was the first story of Carver's that I had read. A middle-aged man named Myers is on a train, going to visit his son whom he hasn't seen for eight years. Myers thinks his breakup with boy's mother was because of the boy's own "malign interference in their personal affairs."[7] At one point, Myers steps back into the compartment after a few minutes' absence, and finds that someone, possibly a fellow passenger pretending to be asleep, has stolen the expensive wristwatch he had bought for his son. The mood has soured, and Myers realizes he never wanted to meet the boy or make small talk with him. As it happens, more and more things go wrong, as they inevitably will in Carver's fiction, and it becomes clear that Myers isn't going to see his son anyway.

In the news story Vance Carver had pointed out that "The Compartment" was based on a trip that he had taken to Paris with his father. But that wasn't all. He also said that his father had transformed what had been a pleasant memory into a dark tale of a troubled relationship between a parent and his progeny. And yet he said that he had liked the story but simply wanted people to know his relationship with his father didn't resemble what we encounter in the story. Such pathos, such poignance! It is not only parents who have fantasies about their children. The opposite is also true.

But that is beside the point. I don't myself know what I want to believe more. That the lives of the Carver children weren't always as miserable as their father's writings had suggested, or so clear and steadfast was Carver's vision of reality that his imagination turned all he touched to something squalid. Here, I have a private fantasy of my own, which is a writer's fantasy, fatuous and self-serving, and it goes something like this: Carver was good at hiding the drunkenness and his frustration from his kids when they were growing up, but when he sat down to write he hid nothing and tried his best to cut close to the bone. Of course, a writer's greatest fantasy is that he or she will keep writing well. When Carver was doing that, a few years before he died of cancer, he claimed in an interview that he had regained his children.

At the end, Carver seemed to have found a balance in his life. I haven't found that place yet. Perhaps because I haven't felt myself at the end of my tether, or not for too long, I haven't also scripted for my life bleak little narratives of destruction. But I think of Carver often. One night we were sleeping at a friend's house. I woke up Ila at night and asked her to come to the bathroom with me so that she could pee. But she refused. I was afraid she was going to wet the bed. I tried again and again, and lost my temper when she crossed her arms and angrily turned away her face to the wall. I put off the light and said I wasn't going to lie down with her anymore; she could sleep by herself. Ila began to cry then, and when I put on the light a few moments later, she was standing on the floor. Her hands were stretched out in the dark; her eyes were still shut, and tears were streaming down her cheeks. Such shame. The squalor of love, the play of power. That is probably what made me think of Carver, although in him one would find no quick redemption through swift kisses. There is little search for forgiveness in his writing, only the clear putting down of the right words for all the wrong things in life. He came to mind the other day again when I found myself thinking that there is a word in the English language for loving one's wife too much, but none for lavishing too much affection on one's daughter.

NOTES

From Amitava Kumar, "Little Fires," in *What I Would Tell Her: 28 Devoted Dads on Bringing Up, Holding On To, and Letting Go Of Their Daughters*, ed. Andrea N. Richesin (New York: Harlequin, 2010), 174–84. Reprinted with permission of the publisher.

1. Raymond Carver, "Fires," in *Major Writers of Short Fiction*, ed. Ann Charters (Boston: Bedford, 1993), 201.
2. Wallace Stevens, *Letters of Wallace Stevens*, ed. Holly Stevens (Berkeley: University of California Press, 1996), 246.
3. Raymond Carver, *Where Water Comes Together with Other Water* (New York: Random House, 1985), 27.
4. Quoted in "No One Made Films Like Him," *Guardian*, July 30, 2007. Accessed August 3, 2014. http://www.theguardian.com/film/2007/jul/31/ingmarbergman.news.
5. Thomas Friedman, "9/11 Is Over," *New York Times*, September 30, 2007.
6. Quoted in Associated Press, "Conference on Author's Yakima Youth," *Seattle Times*, January 12, 2004. Accessed September 24, 2014. http://seattletimes.com/html/localnews/2001834734_carver12m.html.
7. Raymond Carver, "The Compartment," *Granta* 8 (summer 1983), 69.

Ten Rules of Writing

When I was promoted to the rank of professor, the library at the university where I was then employed asked me to send them the name of a book that had been useful to me in my career. I chose V. S. Naipaul's *Finding the Center*. The library then purchased a copy, which was duly displayed in one of its rooms, with a statement I had written about the book:

> This was one of the first literary autobiographies that I read. Its very first sentence established in my mind the idea of writing as an opening in time or a beginning: that sentence conveyed to me, with its movement and rhythm, a history of repeated striving, and of things coming together, at last, in the achievement of the printed word: "It is now nearly thirty years since, in a BBC room in London, on an old BBC typewriter, and on smooth, 'non-rustle' BBC script

paper, I wrote the first sentence of my first publishable book."[1] This first sentence—about a first sentence—created an echo in my head. It has lasted through the twenty years of my writing life. The ambition and the anxiety of the beginner is there at the beginning of each book. Every time I start to write, I am reminded of Naipaul's book.

But that wasn't the whole truth, neither about Naipaul, nor about beginnings. The sentence I had quoted had mattered to me, yes, and so had the book, but what had really helped was Naipaul's telling an interviewer that in an effort to write clearly he had turned himself into a beginner: "It took a lot of work to do it. In the beginning I had to forget everything I had written by the age of 22. I abandoned everything and began to write like a child at school. Almost writing 'the cat sat on the mat.' I almost began like that."[2]

And I did that too, almost. About a decade ago, soon after I had received tenure, *Tehelka* asked me to come aboard as a writer. I was visiting my parents in India at that time; it was winter, and I went to the *Tehelka* office to talk to the editors. Later, when we were done, I was taken around for a tour of the place. There was a pen-and-ink portrait of Naipaul on the wall because he was one of the trustees. And high above someone's computer was a sheet of paper that said "V. S. Naipaul's Rules for Beginners." These were rules for writing. It was explained to me that Naipaul was asked by the *Tehelka* reporters if he could give them some basic suggestions for improving their language. Naipaul had come up with some rules. He had fussed over their formulation, corrected them, and then faxed back the corrections. I was told that I could take the sheet if I wanted. A few days later I left India and the sheet traveled with me, folded in the pages of a book that I was reading. In the weeks that followed, I began writing a regular literary column for *Tehelka*, and, in those pieces, I tried to work by Naipaul's rules. The rules were a wonderful antidote to my practice of using academic jargon, and they made me conscious of my own writing habits. I was discovering language as if it were a new country. Like a traveler in a new place, I asked questions, took notes, and began to arrange things in a narrative. I followed the rules diligently for at least a year, and my book *Bombay-London-New York* was a product of the writing I did during that period.[3] Here, then, are "V. S. Naipaul's Rules for Beginners":

Do not write long sentences. A sentence should not have more than 10 or 12 words.

Each sentence should make a clear statement. It should add to the statement that went before. A good paragraph is a series of clear, linked statements.

Do not use big words. If your computer tells you that your average word is more than five letters long, there is something wrong. The use of small words compels you to think about what you are writing. Even difficult ideas can be broken down into small words.

Never use words whose meanings you are not sure of. If you break this rule you should look for other work.

The beginner should avoid using adjectives, except those of color, size, and number. Use as few adverbs as possible.

Avoid the abstract. Always go for the concrete.

Every day, for six months at least, practice writing in this way. Small words; clear, concrete sentences. It may be awkward, but it's training you in the use of language. It may even be getting rid of the bad language habits you picked up at the university. You may go beyond these rules after you have thoroughly understood and mastered them.

In their simplicity and directness, I do not think the above rules can be improved upon. A beginner should take them daily, like a dose of much-needed vitamins. Of course, rules can never be a substitute for what a writer can learn, *should* learn, simply by sitting down and writing. But I offer my own students rules all the time. On the first day of my writing class this year, I handed out xeroxed sheets of rules by Ray Bradbury, not least because he offers the valuable advice that one should write a short story each week for a whole year. Why? "It's not possible to write 52 bad short stories in a row."[4]

I have also prepared my own list of rules for my students. My list isn't in any way a presumption of expertise and is offered only as evidence of experience. I tend to teach by example. These habits have worked for me and I want my students to use them to cultivate the practice of writing.

1. **Write every day**. This is a cliché, of course, but you will write more when you tell yourself that no day must pass without writing. At the back of a notebook I use in my writing class, I write

down the date and then make a mark next to it after the day's work is done. I show the page to my students often, partly to motivate them, and partly to remind myself that I can't let my students down.

2. **Have a modest goal**. Aim to write 150 words each day. It is very difficult for me to find time on some days, and it is only this low demand that really makes it even possible to sit down and write. On better days, this goal is just a start; often, I end up writing more.

3. **Try to write at the same time each day**. I recently read a Toni Morrison interview in which she said: "I tell my students one of the most important things they need to know is when they are at their best, creatively."[5] It works best for me if I write at the same time each day—in my case, that hour or two that I get between the time I drop off my kids at school and go in to teach. I have my breakfast and walk up to my study with my coffee. In a wonderful little piece published on the *New Yorker* blog Page Turner, the writer Roxana Robinson writes how she drinks coffee quickly and sits down to write—no fooling around reading the paper, or checking the news, or making calls to friends or trying to find out if the plumber is coming: "One call and I'm done for. Entering into the daily world, where everything is complicated and requires decisions and conversation, means the end of everything. It means not getting to write."[6] I read Robinson's piece in January 2013, and alas, I have thought of it nearly every day since.

4. **Turn off the Internet**. The Web is a great resource and entirely unavoidable, but it will help you focus when you buy the Freedom app. Using a device like this not only rescues me from easy distraction, it also works as a timer. When you click on the icon, it asks you to choose the duration for which you want the computer to not have access to the Net. I choose sixty minutes, and this also helps me keep count of how long I have sat at my computer.

5. **Walk for ten minutes**. Or better yet, go running. If you do not exercise regularly, you will not write regularly. Or not for long. I haven't been good at doing this, and have paid the price with

trouble in my back. I have encouraged my students to go walking, too, and have sometimes thought that when I have to hold lengthy consultations with my writing class, I should go for walks with them on our beautiful campus.

6. **A bookshelf of your own**. Choose one book, or five, but no more than ten, to guide you, not with research necessarily, but with the critical matter of method or style. Another way to think about this is to ask yourself who are the writers, or scholars, or artists that you are in conversation with. I use this question to help arrive at my own subject matter, but it also helps with voice.

7. **Get rid of it if it sounds like grant talk**. I don't know about you, but I routinely produce dead prose when I'm applying for a grant. The language used in applications must be abhorred. Stilted language, jargon, etc. I'm sure there is a psychological or sociological paper to be written about the syntax and tone common in such things—the appeal to power, lack of freedom—but in my case it might just be because, with the arrival of an application deadline, millions of my brain cells get busy committing mass suicide.

8. **Learn to say no**. The friendly editor who asks for a review or an essay. Even the friend who is editing an anthology. Say no if it takes you away from the writing you want to do. My children are small and don't take no for an answer, but everyone who is older is pretty understanding. And if they're understanding, they'll know that for you occasional drinks or dinner together are more acceptable distractions.

9. **Finish one thing before taking up another**. Keep a notebook handy to jot down ideas for any future book, but complete the one you are working on first. This rule has been useful to me. I followed it after seeing it on top of the list of Henry Miller's "Commandments." It has been more difficult to follow another of Miller's rules: "Don't be nervous. Work calmly, joyously, recklessly on whatever is in hand."[7]

10. **The above rule needs to be repeated**. I have done shocking little work when I have tried to write two books at once. Half-finished projects seek company of their own and are bad for morale. Shut off the inner editor and complete the task at hand.

If you have read this essay so far, you are probably a writer. That is what you should write in the blank space where you are asked to identify your occupation. I say this also for another reason. Annie Dillard wrote, "How we spend our days is, of course, how we spend our lives."[8] Those words scared the living daylights out of me. I thought of the days passing, days filled with my wanting to write, but not actually writing. I had wasted years. Each day is a struggle, and the outcome is always uncertain, but I feel as if I have reversed destiny when I have sat down and written my quota for the day. Once that work is done, it seems okay to assume that I will spend my life writing.

NOTES

From Amitava Kumar, "10 Rules of Writing," *Indian Quarterly* (October–December 2013), 74–77. Reprinted with permission of the publisher.

1. V. S. Naipaul, *Finding the Center* (New York: Knopf, 1984), 3.
2. V. S. Naipaul interviewed by Ahmed Rashid, "The Last Lion," *Far Eastern Economic Review*, November 30, 1995, 49–50.
3. Amitava Kumar, *Bombay-London-New York* (New York: Routledge, 2002).
4. "Ray Bradbury Gives 12 Pieces of Writing Advice to Young Authors (2001)," Open Culture, April 4, 2012. Accessed August 3, 2014. http://www.open culture.com/2012/04/ray_bradbury_gives_12_pieces_of_writing_advice_to _young_authors_2001.html.
5. Interview with Toni Morrison in the *Paris Review*, 1993, Daily Routines Blog. Accessed August 3, 2014. http://dailyroutines.typepad.com/daily_rou tines/2008/09/toni-morrison.html.
6. Roxana Robinson, "How I Get to Write," *New Yorker* Page Turner Blog, January 4, 2013. Accessed August 3, 2014. http://www.newyorker.com/online /blogs/books/2013/01/on-writing-in-the-morning.html.
7. Henry Miller, "Work Schedule 1932–33," in Henry Miller, *Henry Miller on Writing* (New York: New Directions, 1964). Excerpted at Brain Pickings. Accessed August 2, 2014. http://www.brainpickings.org/index. php/2012/02/22/henry-miller-on-writing/.
8. Annie Dillard, *The Writing Life* (New York: HarperPerennial, 1990), 32.

III
PLACES

· **14** ·

Mofussil Junction

My son turned four the other day. Every night I read to him, and sometimes we read together a picture book about trains.[1] This is a book my
son likes very much. The pictures show trains in bright colors from
many different countries. Most of them carry passengers, of course,
but there are others that carry freight, or they clean rail tracks or plow
snow. There is only one picture from India. The picture looks dated. The
caption beneath the train reads "Timber Train." Its steam engine has a
sign on the side: "Insular Lumber Co." The palm trees in the background
suggest the picture was taken somewhere in south India, maybe Kerala.
My son, who was born and has grown up here in the United States, un-
failingly asks the same question: "Dad, have you traveled on that train?"

I was in my twenties and travelling alone to Patna from Delhi in an
unreserved compartment. There was not an inch of empty space inside.

I sat on a sack wedged between two berths. Beside me was a dying man who was being taken home by his family; a plastic bag was connected to his insides, and through the night the bag filled with waste. There was also another smell coming from the man, a strong smell of rotting flesh, and many times that night I thought that what I had in my nostrils was the smell of death. Many years later, I put that scene in my novel, *Nobody Does the Right Thing*.[2] Except that the dying man in the novel, the narrator's father, is jauntily telling stories about death. For instance, about the death of Gandhi's pet goat. When Gandhi died, kitchen fires all over the nation were put out. In Birla House, the dough that had been rolled for rotis was left untouched. That night, Gandhi's goat wandered in and ate all the dough. By morning, it was dead from a bloated stomach. Its eyes had popped out.

Once, when I was going in the opposite direction, this time from Patna to Delhi, an old man in a dhoti began to tell people that he was Jawaharlal Nehru. It was extremely hot outside. The train was crowded. We had just left Aligarh, and all around me were petty traders who had boarded the train with their goods, plastic toys, women's clothing, cheap bric-a-brac. One man on the berth above me took off his slipper and hit the old man, who, in turn, began to pour abuse on the men who were laughing and jeering at him. The traders from Aligarh had so far been playing cards. Now they had a new game. Everyone had a go at hitting the old man. He lost his dhoti. The men asked him to clean the floor of the train compartment, which he did, and all the time that he was being beaten or cursed he was always respectfully called Jawaharlal Nehru. I think I put that in the novel too. The same goes for a handcuffed prisoner whom I had seen sucking on a popsicle. He was seated between two police constables. I can't remember now whether I had seen the policemen taking money for the popsicle from the prisoner's shirt pocket or whether I made that detail up.

My novel's narrator arrives at Patna Junction and finds waiting for him there the woman he is going to marry. I had modeled this woman on someone I had known. In the novel, I have the narrator say that he hated the smell of toilets in the trains and felt that they clung to his body. He forgets the smell when he sees the woman who is waiting for him. I had once waited like that for my sister. The train was ten hours late. When my sister got down from the train, she was followed by the young woman who was to later find fictional form in my novel. I had for a long while secretly liked this woman. She didn't say much to me, and perhaps because of that I found her very alluring. No one had eyes like hers; no one possessed her shapely mouth. That night at the station, however, her lips were dark and parched. I commented on this to my sister when we were by ourselves, and she replied that the two women didn't want to risk a trip to the dirty toilet in the train. There might also have been a question of safety. They had together decided not to drink any water.

When I return home at night from New York City, my daughter will hug me and then inevitably say that I smell of the train. I make the trip from Poughkeepsie to New York City in less than two hours. My Metro North train runs along the Hudson River; the landscape is beautiful, especially in the fall when the leaves turn red, orange, and gold, but I find the trip uncomfortable. If there is any advantage to train travel, it is just that I can get time to read or grade student papers. Once or twice on the train, I have also seen Anita Desai. She lives in a nearby town. I had learned that she has been unwell, and when I saw her the last time, I asked her if I could bring her soup. She is so gentle and is such an important writer. I would love to be able to help. When I made the offer, however, she smiled and brushed it off. When I was in college and living in Delhi—I'm talking now of thirty years ago—I'd see Anita Desai walking in Lodi Garden. She looked delicate in her crisp cotton saris, her hair pulled back in a small bun. She would look on with a silent smile when her dog leaped into the water fountain in the park.

An hour from my home mofussil station in Poughkeepsie, I pass the Sing Sing prison. John Cheever taught there. I see the shining rows of barbed wire atop the prison's surrounding walls and think of Cheever's tortured art. He used to live in the town of Ossining, which is also located beside the Hudson. When the train crosses that town, I sometimes take out my iPhone and click on the Kindle app. I have Cheever's *Journals* on my Kindle and read a few paragraphs from time to time. Here is a paragraph I just found: "I take a train up the Hudson Valley on a brilliant autumn afternoon. Read, drink. Strike up a conversation with a heavy woman. Decorous. Educated as a schoolteacher, she has an accent that is prim and enlightened. She mistakes me for an Englishman and I lead her on. She is at first afraid of my intentions. Ultimately, I am afraid of hers."[3]

When I go to India these days, I seldom travel by train. Part of the reason is that plane travel has become cheaper, but part of the reason also is that trains have lost their charm for me. I'm writing this while traveling on a train: Train 2160, the Acela express to Boston. I will readily admit that I like the touch of luxury on this train. I'm also grateful that Wi-Fi is available for all passengers. The compartment in which I'm sitting is the quiet car: no loud conversation is allowed and mercifully no ringing of cell phones. It is possible to say that there is also, therefore, no romance. But I'm not complaining. I have come far from that moment in my youth when a friend told me that the long, piercing cry of a train whistle at the end of a Meena Kumari song in *Pakeezah* was the stand-in for the sound of a woman in orgasm.

Trains mean less to me now. Wouldn't this be true of so many others in India too? In *Home Products*, I inserted a mini-essay on trains: "In the work of classic film-makers like Satyajit Ray, as in the Apu trilogy, the train is a marker of the arrival of modernity. The sound of the train cutting across the frame signals the invasion of the city into the space of the village. When the train leaves, the city has claimed the innocence of the village-dweller."[4] But that space of innocence is no longer available to us, or certainly not to me. Similarly, a romance that blossoms on the train, or culminates with an escape on the train, is more than a little implausible now. Trains have aged, and so have I.

Trains take me not to the future but to the past. Several years ago, while watching the film *Trainspotting* in a theater in America, with its strung-out boys horsing around the railway tracks, my mind went back to Patna: my friends in school would get high on heroin and stand beside the tracks to feel the rush of the wind as the train blasted past them. (Yes, I put that into the novel too.[5]) When I think about this, it makes sense that writers like Ian Jack went to India to find their own past by looking at trains.[6] On a train, depending on whether you are from the city or from the village, the trip is either to your past or your future. I'm forever trying to say goodbye to nostalgia. Having said that, let me quickly acknowledge that tomorrow I will happily board trains, first Train 2155, the Acela express to Washington, D.C., disembarking at

Penn Station, and then the Metro North to Poughkeepsie, so that I can be home again.

NOTES

From Amitava Kumar, "Mofussil Junction," *Brick* 93 (summer 2014): 142–44.

1. Roger Priddy, *My Big Train Book* (New York: Macmillan, 2012).
2. Amitava Kumar, *Nobody Does the Right Thing* (Durham, NC: Duke University Press, 2010), 13–14.
3. John Cheever, *The Journals of John Cheever* (Kindle edition), 172.
4. See *Home Products* (New Delhi: Picador, 2007), 247. *Home Products*, which printed in India, was shortened and adapted to print in the United States as *Nobody Does the Right Thing*.
5. Kumar, *Nobody Does the Right Thing*, 85–86.
6. Ian Jack, *Mofussil Junction: Indian Encounters 1977–2011* (New Delhi: Viking, 2013). The title of this chapter pays homage to this fine work of reportage and travel writing.

15

A Collaborator in Kashmir

The reason I had come to Kashmir was to meet Tabassum Guru, the wife of Mohammad Afzal Guru, who is on death row for his role in the attack on the Indian Parliament.[1] However, when I reached her in Sopore, north of Srinagar, she waved me away, saying she had no desire to meet with journalists.

Mohammad Afzal Guru was the main person accused in the attack on Parliament. While two of his coaccused, S. A. R. Geelani and Afsan Guru, were acquitted, Afzal was sentenced to death by hanging in 2004. A fourth accused, Afsan Guru's husband, Shaukat Hussain, was sentenced to ten years in prison. The hanging was scheduled for October 20, 2006, but it was stayed after a mercy petition was filed with the president. In its judgment on his appeal, the Supreme Court recognized that the evidence against Afzal was only circumstantial and that legal procedures had not been followed by the police. Nevertheless, the judgment stated that the attack on the Indian Parliament had "shaken the entire nation and the collective conscience of the society will only be satisfied if capital punishment is awarded to the offender."[2] In response, a group of Kashmiri leaders passed a resolution that read, in part, "We the people of Kashmir ask why the collective conscience of the Indians is not shaken by the fact that a Kashmiri has been sentenced to death without a fair trial, without a chance to represent himself?"[3]

Afzal's family could not afford a lawyer. He was provided a court-appointed lawyer, but the lawyer never appeared. Then a second lawyer was appointed, but she didn't take instructions from her client and agreed to the admission of documents without proof. Afzal submitted four names of senior advocates to the court, but they refused to represent him too. The lawyer who was now chosen by the court stated that he did not want to appear for Afzal, and Afzal expressed a lack of confidence in the advocate. Nevertheless, under the court's insistence, this was the choice that both lawyer and client had to stay with. That is why, in the Srinagar resolution mentioned above, the Kashmiri leaders asked whether it was Afzal's fault that Indian lawyers thought it "more patriotic"[4] to allow a Kashmiri to die than to ensure that he received a fair trial.

Such questions were raised from a sense of great helplessness. Only the naïve assume that the conflict in Kashmir is between fanatical militants and valiant soldiers. The real picture is much more complicated. In this system the conventional economic nodes no longer function, and all resource lines intersect at some level with the security state. There is a sense of enormous, often inescapable, dependency on those who are clearly seen as oppressors. This has bred complex schizophrenia in the society. Arundhati Roy has written: "Kashmir is a valley awash with militants, renegades, security forces, double-crossers, informers, spooks, blackmailers, blackmailees, extortionists, spies, both Indian and Pakistani intelligence agencies, human rights activists, NGOs and unimaginable amounts of unaccounted-for money and weapons. There are not always clear lines that demarcate the boundaries between all these things and people, it's not easy to tell who is working for whom."[5]

It is this murky landscape that is so clearly illuminated by the night flare that was Tabassum Guru's statement published in *Kashmir Times* in October 2004. Titled "A Wife's Appeal for Justice," it is a unique statement, anguished and unafraid.[6] It tells the story of the way in which the police and the armed forces have turned Kashmiris into collaborators, and, although the statement is no more than fifteen hundred words long, it demonstrates more starkly than most documents about Kashmir the brutal cost of military occupation.

In 1990, like thousands of other Kashmiri youth, Afzal had joined the movement for liberation. He had been studying to be a doctor but instead went to Pakistan to receive training. He returned in three months, not having finished his training, because he was disillusioned. Upon his return he surrendered to the Border Security Force and was given a certificate stating that he was a surrendered militant. His dream of becoming a doctor was now lost; he started a small business dealing in medical supplies and surgical instruments. The following year, in 1997, he got married. Afzal was twenty-eight, and Tabassum eighteen.

After his surrender, Afzal wasn't free from harassment. He was always being asked to spy on other Kashmiris who were suspected of being militants. (This is Sartre, writing more than fifty years ago: "The purpose of torture is not only to make a person talk, but to make him betray others. The victim must turn himself by his screams and by his submission into a lower animal, in the eyes of all and in his own eyes."[7]) One night, members of a counterinsurgency unit, the Special Task Force, or STF, took Afzal away. He was tortured at an STF camp. Afzal was asked by his torturers to pay one lakh rupees, and because there was no such money available Tabassum had to sell everything she had, including the little gold she had received on her marriage.

And, as at other points in her appeal, her own particular suffering is interpreted in the light of what other Kashmiris have experienced: "You will think that Afzal must be involved in some militant activities and that is why the security forces were torturing him to extract information. But you must understand the situation in Kashmir, every man, woman and child has some information on the movement even if they are not involved. By making people into informers they turn brother against brother, wife against husband and children against parents."[8]

One of the officers mentioned in Tabassum's appeal, Dravinder Singh, has been frank about the necessity of torture in his line of work. He has stated that torture is the only deterrent to terrorism. In fact, Singh has told a journalist in a recorded interview about having questioned Afzal:

"I did interrogate and torture him at my camp. And we never recorded his arrest in the books anywhere. His description of torture at my camp is true. That was the procedure those days and we did pour petrol in his arse and gave him electric shocks. But I could not break him. He did not reveal anything to me despite our hardest possible interrogation."[9]

After his release from the camp, Afzal had needed medical treatment. Six months later, he moved to Delhi. He had decided that he would soon bring Tabassum and their little son, Ghalib, to a place he had rented. But while in Delhi, Afzal received a call from Dravinder Singh. Singh said that he needed Afzal to do a small job for him. He was to take a man named Mohammad from Kashmir to Delhi, which he did, and he accompanied the same Mohammad to a shop where he bought a used Ambassador car. The car was used in the attack on Parliament, and Mohammad was identified as one of the attackers. Afzal was waiting at a bus stop in Srinagar for a bus to Sopore when he was arrested and taken to STF headquarters and then to Delhi. Afzal identified the slain terrorist Mohammad as someone he knew. This part of his statement was accepted by the court but not the part where he said that he had acted under direction from the STF. Tabassum wrote: "In the High Court one human rights lawyer offered to represent Afzal and my husband accepted. But instead of defending Afzal the lawyer began by asking the court not to hang Afzal but to kill him by a lethal injection. My husband never expressed any desire to die. He has maintained that he has been entrapped by the STF."[10]

. . .

There had been a lot of soldiers in Srinagar, but it was different in Sopore. They stood with guns on the streets and on rooftops. We had left behind leafless apple trees and neat rows of poplar. And painted roadside signs put up by the army and paramilitary units with messages like "Kashmir to Kanyakumari India Is One." In this town, there were only small, often half-finished, houses and grimy stores. My driver, Shafi, and I entered Sopore and then asked for the hospital run by Dr. Ibrahim Guru. That was where Tabassum Guru worked.

I found her easily enough. She was at the cashier's desk in the Inpatient Block. But she told me she didn't want to talk to me. I came outside to make calls to friends in Srinagar and found out that just a week or two earlier two journalists from Delhi had done a sting. Afzal's brothers had been collecting money for his defense but using the cash to buy property instead. The journalists had brought a spy camera and asked Tabassum if she felt that she had been betrayed by the Kashmiri leadership.

I decided to wait. I had come too far. There was a line of patients who kept walking up to the entrance of the hospital. A pony cart came by and dropped off a sick woman. Shafi, having learned that I was visiting from New York, wanted to know where in America the World Wrestling Federation's matches were held. We talked for a while and then went inside the hospital again. There was a large crowd waiting in the area marked Outpatient Block. Most people were standing in the corridor, jostling against each other with a feverish energy that required good health. The few chairs were occupied, and those who were sitting had adopted postures that suggested they had been waiting for days. There was a sign on the wall that said "Utilize Your Waiting Time Effectively—Plan Things to Do—Meditate—Do Breathing Exercises—Chant a Holy Name—Read Books." I studied that sign for a while, but I was greatly agitated. I decided to go back to Tabassum and tell her that I was leaving. She nodded and half-smiled, and then said goodbye.

From the road outside the hospital, lined with walnut and willow trees, I could see the snow-covered mountains. It was bitterly cold. Shafi was full of ideas about what I could have said to Tabassum to persuade her to talk to me, but none of them seemed to excite any optimism in my heart. I thought I was getting a headache, and when I suggested lunch Shafi drove us to a cheap restaurant nearby. While we were eating the steaming plate of rice and the largely inedible meat, Shafi began to tell me that I should have persuaded Tabassum that what I wrote would have helped her husband. But I would have been genuinely reluctant to attempt that. I had seen pictures of mobs in Delhi and elsewhere burning effigies of Mohammad Afzal; activists for the right-wing Bharatiya Janata Party had exploded firecrackers on the streets outside the courthouse when Afzal was sentenced to death; the print and television media had repeatedly condemned him as a terrorist mastermind. How could I have assured Tabassum that what I wrote would be of help? There was another reason for my reluctance. When being interviewed about Afzal's brothers, Tabassum had said that she had never asked anyone for money to help in her husband's legal case. She had said, "Mera zamir nahin kehta" (My conscience doesn't allow it).[11] There was great pride and dignity in that statement. And I was reminded of that again when, in Delhi a week later, I sat watching Sanjay Kak's powerful film *Jashn-e-Azadi* (How we celebrate freedom), which documents the cost of violence in Kashmir: an indigent woman in a hamlet is asked whether she has received the promised financial compensation from the armed forces for the wrongful death of her son, and the woman, her hands beating her breast, replies, "The heavens haven't fallen on this earth as yet that we should accept money from these pigs. I'll sell his share of the land. If I don't have enough for my child, I'll do that but not take money from them. . . . We don't want to accept anything from them because they snatched him away from my bosom. He was no *mujahid*, he was not guilty."

. . .

> For against this drabness, an overwhelming impression
> of muddiness, of black and grey and brown, color stood
> out and was enticing: the colors of sweets, yellow and
> glistening green, however fly-infested.
> V. S. NAIPAUL, *AN AREA OF DARKNESS*

Soon after my return from India, I was reading Orhan Pamuk's memoir, *Istanbul*, for a class I was teaching on writing about cities. In his youth, Pamuk wanted to be a painter, and he still saw his city with the eyes of an artist. Pamuk had written of Istanbul, "To see the city in black and white, to see the haze that sits over it and breathe in the melancholy its inhabitants have embraced as their common fate, you need only to fly in from a rich western city and head straight to the crowded streets; if it's winter, every man on the Galata bridge will be wearing the same pale, drab, shadowy clothes."[12] Reading those words, I thought not of Istanbul, but of Srinagar. As it happened, I had flown in from "a rich western city." Everything in the city bore a drab look, draped in a dirty military green. Every house that was new looked either gaudy and vulgar or curiously incomplete; many structures were shuttered, or burned black, or simply falling down due to disrepair. Writing about a different city, Pamuk had felt that those who lived there now shunned color because they were grieving for a city whose past aura had been tarnished by more than 150 years of decline. I believe Pamuk was also describing plain poverty. And it was true of Srinagar too, both the grief and the wretchedness of poverty.

I thought about the film *Jashn-e-Azadi*, which had shown me another Srinagar. The film's richness lay in the space it had created, in the viewer's mind, despite the violence that was represented, for thought and for color. The filmmaker had discovered again and again in the drabness of the melancholy the gleam of memory: the memory of blood on the ground, of the beauty of the hills and red poppies, of keening voices of mothers, of the painted faces of the village performers. The memory of the numbers of the dead, of falling snow, of new graves everywhere, and always the shining faces crying for freedom. In a travelogue written more than four decades ago, V. S. Naipaul had described how out of the "cramped yards, glimpsed through filth-runnelled alleyways, came bright colors in glorious patterns on rugs and carpets and soft shawls, patterns and colors derived from Persia, in Kashmir grown automatic, even in all their rightness and variety."[13] In Kak's film, riotous color is glimpsed only when we see tourists donning traditional Kashmiri costumes for photographs, holding in their hands flowerpots filled with plastic flowers.

When I think of the melancholy of Afzal and Tabassum Guru, it isn't color that I seek, but a narrative to give sustenance to their own lives. That is what was powerful about the story that Tabassum had told, giving coherence to what had been their experience and the ways in which it resonated with the experiences of other young Kashmiri couples. As with Pamuk's *Istanbul*, I found traces of Srinagar in a story about another distant place—Palestine. The film I was watching was *Paradise Now*.[14] Directed by Hany Abu-Assad, it tells the story of two friends on the West Bank, Said and Khaled, who are recruited to carry out a terrorist attack in Tel Aviv. The two young men are disguised as settlers going for a wedding. But the would-be bombers get separated at the border, and the plan is called off, instigating some reflection and doubt on Khaled's part. But Said is determined. We learn about his motivation when, in the company of Suha, a young woman who has just returned to Palestine, he goes into a watch shop, and Suha notices that videos are also available at the shop. These are videos showing the execution of collaborators. Suha is shocked. She asks, "Do you think it's normal that those videos are for sale?" Said replies, "What is normal around here?" And then he tells Suha, quietly, that his father was a collaborator. He was executed.

In Nablus, cars keep breaking down. That is what gives Said and Khaled jobs. They have been working as mechanics. Nothing works. The houses look either bombed or unfinished. There are no cinemas because the cinema has been burned down. In all of this, Nablus resembles Srinagar. But more than any of this, Nablus is like Srinagar in the ways in which its children are scarred by the violence. I'm thinking of someone like young Ghalib, Afzal and Tabassum's son, and thousands of other Kashmiris. It is horrifying but not difficult to imagine that many of them will find words, to offer as testimony, that are similar to what Said, sitting in an empty room, speaks to the camera just before he leaves on his suicide mission:

> The crimes of occupation are endless. The worst crime of all is to exploit the people's weaknesses and turn them into collaborators. By doing that, they not only kill the resistance, they also ruin their families, ruin their dignity, and ruin an entire people. When my father was executed, I was ten years old. He was a good person. But he grew weak. For that, I hold the occupation responsible. They must understand that if they recruit collaborators they must pay the price for it. A life without dignity is worthless. Especially when it reminds you day after day of humiliation and weakness. And the world watches, cowardly and indifferent.

NOTES

From Amitava Kumar, *A Foreigner Carrying in the Crook of His Arm a Tiny Bomb* (Durham, NC: Duke University Press, 2010), 141–50.

1. *13 December: A Reader*, with an introduction by Arundhati Roy (New Delhi: Penguin, 2006).
2. Quoted in Nandita Haksar, "The Many Faces of Nationalism," in *13 December: A Reader* (New Delhi: Penguin, 2006), 24.
3. Quoted in Haksar, "The Many Faces of Nationalism," 24.

4. Quoted in Haksar, "The Many Faces of Nationalism," 24.

5. Arundhati Roy, "And His Life Should Become Extinct," in Arundhati Roy, *Field Notes on Democracy: Listening to Grasshoppers* (2006; New York: Haymarket, 2009), 97.

6. Tabassum Guru, "A Wife's Appeal for Justice," *Kashmir Times*, October 11, 2004.

7. Jean-Paul Sartre, "A Victory," preface to Henri Alleg, *The Question*, trans. John Calder (1958; Lincoln: University of Nebraska Press, 2006), xl.

8. Guru, "A Wife's Appeal for Justice."

9. Quoted in Arundhati Roy, "Breaking the News," introduction to *13 December: A Reader* (New Delhi: Penguin, 2006), xix.

10. Guru, "A Wife's Appeal for Justice."

11. Quoted in Mihir Srivastava and Harinder Baweja, "Blood Brothers, Blood Money," *Tehelka*, September 20, 2014.

12. Orhan Pamuk, *Istanbul* (New York: Alfred A. Knopf, 2005), 40–41.

13. V. S. Naipaul, *An Area of Darkness* (New York: Vintage, 1964), 131.

14. *Paradise Now*, dir. Hany Abu-Assad (Burbank, CA: Warner Independent Pictures, 2005), HD.

16

At the Jaipur Literature Festival

I lost my literary festival virginity almost a decade ago, when, at the poor Indian taxpayers' expense, I was summoned to the International Festival of Indian Literature at Neemrana in Rajasthan. It was the first Kumbh Mela of literary gatherings, the mother of all literary fests, which inaugurated the venerable tradition of tantrum throwing before the eyes of the national media, and pioneered—and this is no mean achievement—the bringing together of writers who wouldn't be caught drinking, or even pissing, together.

I may sound critical, but don't be mistaken—I was thrilled to have been invited. I had written only one academic book at the time; it had been reviewed in *Outlook* magazine, but even I couldn't understand what the review was saying. The invitation to the festival made me think I could now become one of those people who roam the circuit—and, this being in the days before Facebook, claim a famous writer as my friend.

The Bharatiya Janata Party–led government in Delhi wanted to celebrate the Nobel Prize that had been awarded to V. S. Naipaul. I was still jetlagged from my flight from New York when we were taken by bus to Vigyan Bhawan for a reception: I shook hands with Prime Minister Atal Bihari Vajpayee, who wore industrial-size hearing aids and thick socks that climbed up toward his dhoti. Perhaps the prime minister was jetlagged, too, because I saw that he had fallen asleep before I had let go of his hand.

In the bus, I was seated in front of Amitav Ghosh and Vikram Seth. Unashamedly, I eavesdropped on their conversation about the merits of Arundhati Roy's activism. Roy had just published an essay in which she had said that "writer-activist," the term used to describe her, always made her flinch.[1] She wanted to know why the novel she had written had earned her the title of a "writer" while the nonfiction only garnered the phrase "activist." The subject of discussion in the seat behind me was a recent court injunction against Roy. Seth was incensed by it. He kept saying to Ghosh, "I'm not a political person, but this . . ." Was this the beginning of a serious argument about literature and politics? If it was, it was the last such conversation I heard for the rest of the festival.

The diplomat who headed the Indian Council for Cultural Relations, our official host at Neemrana, was a nice sort but treated us like schoolchildren. A rash of Indian bureaucrats are now authors. It doesn't bode well, in my opinion. Our host wasn't a closeted writer, thank God, and was merely satisfied to regard the whole lot of us as delinquents. The writer Ruchir Joshi—maybe this was a critical postmodern antic on his part—was happy to oblige. But the most petulant schoolchild at the festival was V. S. Naipaul. He accused the American ambassador's wife of a severe lack of intelligence and requested that she leave the table where dinner was being served. On the last day, Naipaul erupted once again. When Nayantara Sahgal bemoaned the sins of colonialism, he interrupted her, shouting: "My life is short. I can't listen to banalities. Banalities irritate me."

Banalities irritate me, too, but if you are so averse to them, you ought to stay away from literary festivals. And besides, not all banalities are created equal. The first year that I went to the Jaipur Literature Festival, I was given the honor of engaging in a public conversation with my early hero, Hanif Kureishi. Hanif is a writer of clean sentences; he has a dry wit and isn't afraid to be perverse or provocative. He also speaks just the way he writes, his utterances coming out clothed in elegant perfection, their hair gelled. He was in fine form that morning but quite unprepared for what, as best as I can recall, was the very first question from the audience: "Mr Kureishi, are you circumcised?"

That was good, very good, in fact, and amused everyone. Much better than questions like, "Sir, how many books have you read?" that had been posed to me the previous day after my own panel. I'm calling such statements banalities, but I quite appreciate their directness and honesty. It's important to know where these questions are coming from. The man with the pressing inquiry about Hanif's foreskin really wanted to ask about Muslim identity; his own grandson, the questioner explained, had recently been circumcised. Why should young children undergo this trauma? Of course, we might want to ask why anyone would consider writers a source of great wisdom on such worldly matters: what exactly makes someone who does nothing but spend a lot of time alone in front of their computer uniquely qualified to answer questions about violent conflicts, or stubborn social customs, or world-historical changes?

Still, every time I've been to Jaipur, schoolchildren come up to me and ask me for my autograph—and not because they recognize me. They haven't read my books, they don't know who I am, they are uncertain even about my name. Yet I'm glad they find the abstract idea of a writer engaging. So when I sign my name, I always write in their notebooks, "Read every day. Write every day." Maybe next time, I'll keep some cheap paperbacks in my bag and hand them out for the kids to take home and read.

In fact, a little literary activism of that sort might alleviate a nagging anxiety that strikes me at every such gathering. There are so many terrific writers and so little time to hear them all, and my dominant emotion at festivals is a feeling of distracted haste; it's as if I have a plane to catch. You've just landed late on Pamuk Airlines, but then Junot Jet is about to depart in a few minutes, and you are going to really have to hurry and hop a few crowded concourses to catch Air Coetzee. I usually surrender and just slip into the café to have a tea and waste time: this aloneness is closer to the experience of reading a book.

Last year at Jaipur, however, I wasn't granted much time to waste according to my wishes, as I was part of a jury for a prize. I reread three of the books on the short list and, sitting in my hotel room, agonized about my choices. There was wine when we met. One of the judges passed on the wine, saying that her stomach was cramping. At which point one of our colleagues became concerned and, pushing his wine glass aside, asked, "Is it that time of the month?"

I needed to get out. Finally I had the chance, when my friend Akhil Sharma took me to the market in the car he had been provided by the American embassy. His wife had told him of a jewelry store that was located in a small *haveli* amid a warren of narrow, twisting streets. The *haveli* had been built by a Rajasthani nobleman who was a financial advisor in the Mughal court. I had to buy jewelry for my wife. I couldn't decide between two pieces—a pair of gold-emerald earrings and a beautiful Kundan necklace—and Akhil advised that I should buy both. Addressing me in a gentle tone, he said one should not ever have regrets in matters of love. Akhil was smiling serenely, and I did as he said, and he, clearly more secure in his love, didn't buy anything.

Just last month, I was in India, visiting my parents, but I went to Goa just to sneak in a little more than a day at the literary festival there. Now, only a few weeks later, I'm anxiously waiting for a visa to return to India. I've been invited to Jaipur. You might think I have a literary festival problem. Every time an announcement wafts into my in-box, the craving begins. But rather than checking into rehab, I've decided to make this matter a subject of artistic investment. This is now my research. For the past year or two I have been writing a novel, and the narrator, in a section I was working on yesterday, is attending a literary festival in India:

> After the panel had done its work, I went looking for a toilet. This place used to be a palace, but there isn't a decent bathroom to take a leak. I wandered into a courtyard where men sitting on their haunches around a fire were cooking food in huge vats. The literary festival, it is now confirmed, is like a Hindu wedding. Under a cement peacock, over a dark doorway, I found a welcoming pink curtain stir-

ring in the breeze. This is the room I was looking for. Except that the person standing over the urinal, his hands and eyes focused on a hidden point below, was Niall Ferguson. What was Niall Ferguson doing in India? This is what had happened while I had been gone from the country: India had changed behind my back. There were now huge literary festivals held here, and colonialism had become a respectable word again.

NOTES

From Amitava Kumar, "The Indian Litfest Bug," *Caravan*, February 2012, 20–22. Reprinted with permission of the publisher.

1. Arundhati Roy, "The Ladies Have Feelings, So . . . Shall We Leave It to the Experts?," *Outlook*, January 14, 2002. Accessed August 3, 2014. http://www .outlookindia.com/article/Shall-We-Leave-It-to-the-Experts/214223.

17

Hotel Leeward

Srinagar is dusty, the dust choking the busy streets and clinging to the dark wooden houses covered with corrugated iron. Every few feet stands a soldier with a rifle, his head under a helmet and a bulletproof vest on his chest.

Outside an army bunker is a painted sign: "Please Prove Your Identity." The eye takes in the image of the dust, the rust, and the soldier on the street. Beyond is the river, also khaki, and visible above the sky, which is clean and bright.

The partially burned-down structure of the Government Hospital for Psychiatric Diseases is set away from the street. The Mughal fort that Akbar built can be seen atop the hill nearby, the military bunker there sharply outlined against the blue. Inside the hospital, in front of the wards for the male patients, there are trees and a garden with flowers in bloom. The garden fence is made up of the hospital's discarded metal cots, set on their sides.

In the corridor, men in grimy white-and-blue uniforms squat on the floor, rocking their bodies against the wall. Dr. Sadaqat Rahman, who is the only clinical psychologist in Srinagar, is making her rounds. She has an easy, affectionate manner toward her patients, many of whom are gathered at the windows of the wards in which they are locked. They shout out appeals to the doctor in Kashmiri. They all want to go back home.

Until only a few years ago, there were between eight and ten patients visiting the hospital each day. These days, the hospital treats anywhere from 100 to 150 patients daily.

Dr. Rahman is reluctant to relate the increased problems to the violence of the valley. According to her, the malady is worldwide. Wearing a long gown and a headscarf, and speaking good English, the doctor says that by the year 2008, there will be only psychiatry, no medicine.

An ambulance, with armed men in it, is parked outside the doctor's wards. They are soldiers from the Border Security Force. When they go in to see the doctor, the soldiers carry their rifles with them. The doctor explains that the soldiers do not trust even the doctors.

Four soldiers wait in the truck. Other patients, Kashmiri men and women, move around them in the hospital yard. The soldiers sit in the ambulance, talking only among themselves. They have come to the hospital because they suffer from the effects of trauma. Many Kashmiris complain of the aggression of the armed forces; in the hospital, it is clear that violence does not spare the perpetrator either.

In a few minutes, Dr. Rahman is going to attend a board meeting to deal with the soldiers' cases. She has to decide when to advise their military superiors that the soldiers be denied access to arms and ammunition. In the security force truck, a soldier who is from a village near Allahabad—one of the first things he tells me is that he is a Brahmin, and his name is Pandey—asks if I had seen the graffiti on a wall outside saying "Indian Dogs Go Back." It is only when I say yes that he begins to talk about deep-seated suspicion and stress and depression. He feels OK when he is in his village, the man tells me, but feels disoriented outside.

The local papers that day carried reports of a security force commander being shot dead by an Indian army soldier in Kupwara. The men in the ambulance know about this piece of news, but none of them wants to comment on it. Pandey, the soldier from Allahabad, tells me that it is his first visit to the hospital, but it is true that soldiers are brought here every day.

It strikes me that, for people like Pandey, the move out from the village represented an introduction to the ideology of nationalism. Without the idea of the nation, a person like Pandey is lost. The militant from across the border, who carries the idea of the Islamic nation like a gun, is a figure that the soldier recognizes. Oddly enough, it is the armed militant who confirms for the soldier everything he believes in. But what the soldier finds more disturbing, and even incomprehensible, is the ordinary Kashmiri who, unarmed, vulnerable, and in no way committed to Pakistan, still will not grant him the gift of inviolable nationhood.

In Srinagar, a housewife, a driver, a tailor, and an old poet, sitting in front of his lovely pomegranate trees, all talk of their desire for an independent Kashmir. In Delhi, in Nagpur, or in Patna, such talk is met with rage. We repeat what we have learned at school: Kashmir is a part of our identity as a nation.

The soldier in Srinagar, however, has a more immediate relation to that reality. The anonymous, painted roadside graffito asking the Indian forces to go back signifies, for the soldier, a loss of self. In the resulting incomprehension, nationalism survives only as a neurosis. The only way out of this neurosis is for the soldier to identify each Kashmiri as a potential Pakistani. This act, full of the violence of negation, fills him with despair.

And the Kashmiri? How does he or she suffer? In a bare room, bare except for a carpet and plain green sofas arranged against the wall, the chairman of the separatist All Parties Hurriyat Conference, Abdul Ghani Bhat, tells me that he is stopped by a soldier on the street and asked to show his card. "A man from Kerala has to verify," Bhat says, "that I am a Kashmiri on the soil of Kashmir. This is humiliation. At its worst."

The sun slants into the room, lighting Bhat's head from behind. He has a thin, lined face. Before becoming a leader of the Hurriyat movement, he was a professor of Persian. His language is vivid and metaphorical. Gesturing dramatically with his hands, he proclaims: "A soldier sits on each Kashmiri's head, minus children, and occasionally women and the old. The LOC [line of control, the disputed border between India and Pakistan] exists in every room, in every office, in every street, at all levels."

A cup of Kashmiri tea is brought for me. Bhat warms to his theme. He says that the government in Kashmir exists only in bunkers. There is a pause. The Hurriyat chairman spreads his hands and then brings them together in a tight clasp. He says: "Soldiers rule. Elections are irrelevant. Development is a mirage. We are fighting a war of survival."

This could be dismissed as political rhetoric. In Delhi, L. K. Advani, the deputy prime minister, will once again say that the Hurriyat has a "soft corner" for Pakistan. But what Bhat says is echoed by common Kashmiris who do not want to be cheated of real progress by politicians exchanging election slogans. The ballot box will be a place where Kashmiris will once again be asked to stuff their dreams. There will be another occasion lost for genuine dialogue.

Parveena Ahangar is the mother of five children: one of them, Javed, has been missing since the night of August 18, 1990, when soldiers picked him up. They were probably looking for his neighbor, also called Javed, who was said to be a militant. Parveena's son Javed had a bad stammer, and when he was disturbed and could not speak he would strike his foot against the ground. Sitting on the floor in her simple room, Javed's mother says that she dreams of him each day.

Parveena wants her son back, and she does not see the point in the elections. She says, *"Mera dil jalaa hua hai. Kahan jayega hum vote daalne?"* (My heart is burned. Why would I go to vote?).

On my last morning in Srinagar, I undertake a literary pilgrimage. I look for Hotel Leeward, where V. S. Naipaul lived for four months when he first came to India in 1962. Writing three decades later about Kashmir and the hotel, Naipaul noted that "it remained a glow, a memory of a season when everything had gone well." As I catch sight of the hotel, I experience it as a discovery, the white building with blue trimmings. The *shikara* I am sailing in passes a few shops and a public phone booth on the lake, and then draws close to the hotel's concrete steps. A dragonfly whirs above the lowest step, the sun lighting its wings. But I am not allowed to step off the boat. A soldier with a Sten gun waves me away.

He tells me that the hotel is not open to outsiders. The Border Security Force uses it now as a bunker.

. . .

When the above report was published in the British paper the *New Statesman*, I sent a copy to V. S. Naipaul. I was hoping he would read it. The previous year I had written about him for the same magazine, a piece that mixed admiration for his writing with a bit of mumbling criticism of his politics. This time Naipaul surprised me with a response. One evening in my mailbox at the university, there was a fax waiting for me. "Dear Amitava," Naipaul had written in his small but legible handwriting, "It was nice hearing from you. The Leeward in 1989 had become a kind of doghouse, really; better for it to be the bunker you describe. A strategic place for a bunker, commanding three lanes of lake traffic. If you take a longer historical view (not leaving out the Hindu ruins in the valley) you wouldn't be so pained." There was shorter, second paragraph: "Everyone has to make a living, but I worry for you, being in an American university. They are uncreative, overcompetitive, full of spite and with no true way of judging talent. They can dry you up. But you will be all right. We remember you with great affection. Good luck with your writing."

I lost the faxed sheet for a while but discovered that I could recall the words written on it. This was a comment not on my memory but the arrangement and flow of Naipaul's sentences. They had a natural rhythm in which I could hear the characteristic inflections of his speech.

NOTE

From Amitava Kumar, "Here, Even Doctors Are Not Trusted," *New Statesman*, September 23, 2002, 32–33. Reprinted with permission of the publisher.

18

The Mines of Jadugoda

I grew up in Patna, but the place where I learned to ride a bicycle was Chaibasa. My seventh birthday passed unnoticed because my maternal grandmother had died the previous week, but my parents relented and bought me the promised bicycle. Yesterday, I went back to Chaibasa after more than forty years.

My father was a civil servant who had served for many years in what is now Jharkhand, a place made melodious by the humble poetry of the names of its small towns: Tupudana, Murhu, Kalamati, Chaibasa. When I was a boy, did I ever visit a town called Jadugoda? I don't now remember whether I did, but recently I went to Jadugoda, one and a half hour's drive away from Chaibasa. The visit robbed me of any shred of nostalgia.

A stocky, soft-spoken man named Ghanshyam Birulee, almost the same age as I am, began telling me a story. His father, a worker in the local uranium mines, had died of lung cancer in 1984. A few years later, in 1991, his mother passed away too. The cause of her death was also lung cancer. His mother's death confronted Birulee with a question: his mother had never worked in the mines, nor had she even gone there on a visit—how was it possible that she, too, had been affected by the uranium?

Radiation and the diseases that result from it are not common knowledge among the people of Jadugoda. It took Birulee, now an activist with the Jharkhandi Organization against Radiation, a lot of time before he hit on the truth. His father would bring back each week the uniform he wore when he worked inside the mine, and his mother would then wash it. The presence of uranium particles on the uniform meant that they emitted radiation. His mother had died from uranium poisoning. From the reading he had been doing, Birulee learned about the ugly realities of the nuclear winter in Hiroshima and Nagasaki. And he reached a conclusion: "The problem that is in Japan is also the problem that is in Jadugoda."

The Uranium Corporation of India Limited, which runs the local mines, has steadfastly denied water contamination or deaths caused by radiation exposure. But various studies conducted over the last few years have shown that contamination from the uranium mine has spread in Jadugoda, and the circumference of the tailing ponds (they hold the sludge produced by the mining process) too are polluted with uranium.

In Ichra Village, close to Jadugoda, a young woman named Budni Oraon takes care of her two younger siblings. Budni is in her mid-twenties. Her younger sister Olabati and their brother Duniya are separated by another year or two. Both Olabati and Duniya are congenitally deformed and mentally disabled.

I met the siblings in their small house in Ichra. The door opened into a room with a bed and a small television set where Hindi film songs were playing. Duniya sat on the floor, moving with the help of his hands, his thin, misshapen legs bent under him. He has large, expressive eyes, and I saw that his striped T-shirt said "Born to Party." Budni, wearing bright clothes and thin silver bracelets around her ankles, talked to me while standing at the threshold under a picture of her deceased father. A little distance away, her mother sat on a bed in the corner, her eyes taking in the scene on television. From time to time, the sound of garbled words and laughter came from an adjoining room. That was Olabati, whom I later met; she was grinning as she lay supine on a sheet on the floor.

What happened to these people? I wanted to ask Budni these questions, but she had more immediate, practical concerns. Both Duniya and Olabati receive two hundred rupees each in a disability pension each month. But the money isn't given to Budni or sent by post; the block officer has to physically see the two disabled persons. Budni has to hire an auto rickshaw and spread a sack on the floor for her brother and sister, as they cannot sit up. The expense on the trip to the block office eats into the small amount of money they receive from the government.

Budni is tall and animated and has very white teeth. She said, "If I run away one day, who will take care of them?" She pointed to Duniya and said that he couldn't even drink water by himself. She has to feed, wash, and clothe him. Duniya couldn't understand the conversation; his eyes were fixed on my face. Budni said, "If I get married and go away, their lives will be destroyed."

It seemed terrible that anyone should have to make such choices. But Budni could foresee a solution. Could the government provide a fixed ration to its disabled citizens? Budni felt that if there was such a provision, then anyone taking care of her siblings could cook for them and perhaps eat a small portion themselves.

Finally, it was time for me to put the question to Budni: why are your older siblings physically fit, and why were your younger siblings born disabled? Budni pointed to the road outside. When the road was being built, the paving materials used came from the uranium plant. After the ore had been extracted, the local company, the Uranium Corporation of India Limited, had no use for the crushed stones. It was given free to the government to build roads. Budni said that her mother, first pregnant with Duniya and then with Olabati, worked barefoot on that road as it was being built.

The fate of the people in Jadugoda has been a horrible tragedy, the result of a combination of profits and prejudice. The number of disabled youth in the area far exceeds the average in any other town, at least a hundred in a population of around fifty thousand. But what is to be done now? Ghanshyam Birulee is clear about future goals: rehabilitation for all those affected by uranium poisoning; medical treatment and compensation for the sick; ensuring safe mining; and lastly, carrying out uranium waste disposal in accordance with international laws.

If these steps are taken, we will have found a more humane and just response to this incredible atrocity. I'm already feeling nostalgic for that future.

NOTE

From Amitava Kumar, "What Links Japan and Jadugoda," *Times of India*, July 14, 2013. Reprinted with permission of the publisher.

· 19 ·

Upon Arrival in the Past

I was in graduate school, and a professor of mine said that I might want to apply for a human-rights fellowship. At first I thought of Portugal. I was enrolled in a seminar in which, just that week, I had read an article about peasant struggles in that country. The name Lisbon conjured the beauty of an unbroken beach and mild ocean air. But did I really know anything about Portugal beyond the colorful postage stamps I had collected in my childhood? It would be easier to write that I wanted to work in India.

I hadn't seen my parents for three years. They lived in Patna. The day I got news of the fellowship I called them, although it must have been the middle of the night there, to tell them I was coming home.

More than twenty years have passed since I came to the United States. I have never applied for a grant to visit any country other than

India. At first it was because I didn't have the money to go otherwise, but now it is where I go to work—to write, do research, and conduct interviews. There is hardly ever time to spend more than a couple of days with my family. And when I look at glossy ads inviting travelers to India, to the Taj Mahal in Agra or Kerala's beautiful backwaters, I realize how many places, and just how much color, I have missed during my visits.

"Welcome to India," the signs at the airport say. But I have a private sign that only I can see. It says, "You're here to work."

I land in Delhi and search for sleep, always waking up, alas, around three in the morning. Even at that hour, street dogs bark from different directions, working together like runners on a relay team. Just before the sky begins to turn light, the birds fill up the night with their calls. I usually wait another hour, reading, consuming the chocolate I have bought from the duty-free shop, and then busy myself with calls to the taxi rank close by and at least half a dozen airline services, making travel plans to far-flung towns.

Often I go to Lodi Garden, where I went for walks when I was an undergraduate at Delhi University, especially during the warm summer evenings with their sunsets that seemed to linger forever. When I was in high school, a program on Lodi Garden was shown on national television. There was only one government-owned channel at that time, and the broadcasts were in black and white. The camera panned over the graffiti on the old monuments, and a grave voice said, "History has already written on these walls, what can you and I now write on them? Please do not deface our heritage."

But the graffiti writers and the lovers will not come till much later in the day. When I take my jet-lagged self there in the early dawn, I see the walkers and joggers in hectic pursuit of health. On the lawns close to the Bara Gumbad, the Big Dome tomb, mostly middle-aged men and women perform yoga. A group of boys might be playing cricket nearby. In another corner of the garden, old men stand in a circle, their heads tilted up, laughing loudly. They are the followers of an Indian doctor who has started a worldwide movement, setting up more than seven thousand laughter clubs that claim to reduce stress.

After that first day, I will never again during that trip have time to walk in Lodi Garden. In all probability, in a matter of hours, I'll be on my way to another town to do research and interviews. The beauty I will see will only be in passing but is all the more poignant for that reason.

A bit like the tiny stretch of the sea that I glimpsed on the famous Konkan Coast, a few hours south of Mumbai. This was during my last visit to India; I was doing research for a forthcoming book on the global war on terror.[1] I had gone to a village called Walavati to interview a Muslim family who had been tortured for several days by the police for possessing missiles, except that the objects had actually turned out to be bobbins used in textile machinery. I had been in the car for six hours and was in a hurry to get back to Mumbai. Rain had washed clean the mango trees on the side of the road. We passed a crowded town. And then, suddenly, as if in a watercolor hung on a wall, the sea appeared between two houses. Later that night, or maybe only after a few days had passed, I asked myself why I hadn't stopped.

But there couldn't have been much mystery to that question. After all, it is the same during every visit. In the twelve, fifteen, or even thirty days that I have, I need to travel to scores of places and speak to as many people as I can. Even by the time the jet lag wears off, I know that any pleasure I'll experience during the trip will be unplanned, almost incidental, and fleeting.

A couple of years after I began my first teaching job, I went to India to take photographs of migrant workers. Those pictures would later appear in my book about migration, *Passport Photos*.[2] The workers I met were mostly young men who had left their villages and traveled west to Punjab to do hard, backbreaking work harvesting wheat and hauling stones out of rock quarries.

The landscape was baking in the June heat. Dust blew all day. The workers wore shorts; the only other item of clothing was a bandana wrapped around their heads. But the men's faces, especially their eyelids, would quickly get coated with gray powder. Under a shed with a corrugated iron roof that radiated heat, the workers sat or reclined on sacks of cement, seemingly indifferent to any discomfort.

Each night I would go back to my hotel in a nearby small town. After sunset, it was hotter indoors. My room was without curtains, and even when I had turned out the light, the glare from the street was so bright that I could count my money. One evening, the Sikh owner of one of the stone quarries invited me to his home for dinner. We sat on wicker chairs that had been put out on the green lawn. I took off my sandals; the grass was cool and damp under my feet. For a long time, my host plied me with whiskey. The alcohol helped, but the ice cubes that he lifted with steel tongs and put in my glass were a true blessing.

While waiting for dinner, we ate a savory dish made from fried egg and spicy minced meat. Many years have passed, but even now, when I am hungry and uncomfortable, I think of that evening with a keenness that can take me by surprise.

The tourist in India is expected to complain of the heat and the dust. I suffer terribly from the infernal conditions in which I sometimes work, but I worry that to notice it would immediately mark me as the outsider that I have now become. I am also aware that my taking comfort in small pleasures—for example, the cool air coming through a straw curtain splashed with water, is a dubious form of nostalgia. And yet I'm not always certain of the correctness of that reading. The truth is that I want to distance myself from the Indian rich, who to my eye appear more greedy and grasping than the rich in the West. This judgment governs my social behavior when I'm home. They speak English, I immerse myself in the vernacular; they stick to the cities, I go to the hinterland; they appear arrogant and uncaring, I sullenly cultivate my guilt.

If I had a moment to spare while in India, I would notice that the difference I was asserting was, for the most part, an academic one.

A year after my visit to the stone quarries, I was back in India, still struggling to finish the photography project. I was in Delhi, and, as it happened, my elder sister was also visiting that city. The night before I was to leave, I took her to a restaurant at the Hotel Taj Man Singh. We were going to celebrate her birthday.

The hotel's design and décor are inspired by Mughal architecture, although its aura owes also to its location in the heart of the most affluent district in the city. I have a memory of cool marble and delicate stone screens, antique wooden sculptures, plush carpets, and stunning oil paintings by some of the best contemporary Indian artists. In choosing that hotel, however, I had made a mistake. I had wanted to surprise my sister, and when we arrived at the Taj she complained that she was not dressed right. But I didn't want to leave this place of refuge. I could feel the sweat drying on my brow. After the noise on the street, the silence alone was a gift.

At the table, my sister would read the name of an item on the menu and then glance at its price. After a while, she said she would let me order. At one point, I think I told her that I was paying with a credit card and that the dinner didn't mean much in U.S. dollars, but of course that would only have made matters worse.

A week passed, and I was back in Florida, where I then worked, when my mother called me from India. She told me that the amount of money I had spent that evening had caused much distress to my sister. Truth be told, although I had relished the prawns that were as big as my fist, a part of me had shared her discomfort. There was something that was just unnecessary about the dinner at the Taj. In the decade since, I have eaten in other wonderful restaurants in Delhi's five-star hotels, establishments like the Imperial's Spice Route or the Oberoi's Taipan, and have always been reminded of my sister's reluctance to order food that evening.

There is innocence in that guilt, but that, too, is perhaps nostalgia. And I have to confess that I have also enjoyed those moments when a trip to India hasn't simply meant a return home—a return to the small-town, middle-class conditions I knew as a young man. The luxury comes as a relief, and it seems to come more easily as the years pass. Even if I rarely do forget that it can be a complicated thing being a tourist in that country called the past.

The first real meal I want to have when I arrive in Delhi is at Karim's. With the spanking new Delhi metro, all one needs to do is take the subway to the market area of Chandni Chowk, and then hire a rickshaw for a short ride into the alleys past the Jama Masjid. The restaurant's cooks claim a lineage that takes them back to the royal kitchens of the last Mughal emperor, the poet Bahadur Shah Zafar. This goes hand in hand with the other significant claim, only slightly exaggerated, that their cuisine, fit for the emperor, comes at a price that will also satisfy the poor.

The naans and *parathas* would suffice as complete meals, but I always order the spicy chicken and meat dishes named after various Mughal rulers: Akbari Murgh Masala, Jahangiri Korma, Shahjahani Kabab. I have nowhere else eaten mutton cooked in almond paste. Almost always, I finish the meal with Pista Kulfi, which some say tastes like you're eating flowers. The food flings me into a stupor. A python swallowing a pig must have similar aims as I do. After my long nap, I wake up refreshed.

At such times, I most want to head down to Lodi Garden. Its land-scaped lawns are dotted with stone monuments, tombs of Muslim rulers who, about five centuries ago, had intended to lay out a royal cemetery. The monuments don't interest me; I go there to look at the trees. The thin-limbed *amaltas* in flower, its light yellow blossoms heavy with dew. The scarlet and red of the *gulmohar*. Hiding among the leaves of the green neem, noisy green parakeets with red rings on their necks. And scattered near the entrance, the heavy, waxy petals of the flowers that have fallen from the giant *simul*.

The India International Centre (IIC) shares a boundary wall with Lodi Garden; I first saw the films of the European New Wave there. Visiting artists and academics stay there during visits to Delhi and offer public lectures. More than two decades ago, I attended readings there by Raja Rao, V. S. Naipaul, Anita Desai, and Salman Rushdie. The IIC members are mostly senior bureaucrats, retired officials of the armed forces, and Delhi politicians who want to regard themselves as intellectuals. They are the city's aging elite. In my late teens, I would stand outside the gates and ask the people going to the "members only" film screenings to allow me to accompany them. An old police officer with a clipped white mustache, a dignified man who never once spoke a word to me, always nodded and let me follow him inside. In the IIC's dark auditorium, I discovered the works of Bergman, Antonioni, Buñuel, Resnais, Godard, Truffaut, Forman, Zanussi.

In March last year, *Home Products*, my novel about the Hindi film world, was released at the IIC by Shyam Benegal, the director credited with having inaugurated the Indian New Wave back in the 1970s.[3] The event was held outdoors under lights hanging from trees, while the birds in the Lodi Garden kept up their insistent chorus. On that occasion, and every other time I have done a reading at the center, I was still the provincial youth from many years ago, fearful that he is trespassing, standing on a stage where he does not belong.

I am recollecting all this in tranquillity, sitting at a computer in my office in upstate New York, looking out the window at a tree whose leaves are turning orange. The other world that I work in, and that I write about, is so far away from where I live. It is not only about space, it is also about time. I know that during my visits to India, I will always experience everything as if I have to hurry and meet it in the future.

Before the present takes hold of it and consigns it to the past that is now forever lost.

I will be collecting material for a book about Hindu-Muslim conflict in the subcontinent, and I will be on a narrow highway in Kashmir, driving behind an army convoy.[4] The highway will branch away to the right, and my taxi will turn left onto a gravel road. No longer will I have to look at soldiers standing upright in their trucks, black bandanas tied on their heads, gun barrels poking out from under the green tarp flapping in the wind around them. Instead, there will be doves bathing in the dirt and beyond them almond and apple trees. In the village where I'll be going, close to the Pakistan border, I'll look for a woman called Saira. She'll be hanging her children's laundry when I'll arrive at her door. She'll guess I'm a journalist and that I'll be writing about her husband. His parents migrated from that village to Pakistan in 1953, and he, too, is a Pakistani citizen. He is Saira's cousin, and they were married in 1987. According to the police, because the man is Pakistani, he is a terrorist, and he will be taken to the border for deportation the next morning.

While I will wait, a family of ducks will emerge from the apple orchard. Behind the drying laundry, I will see sunflowers. Saira will bring me tea. Her five-year-old son will play with me, shyly. Her older son will bring his notebook to show to me. He has copied down a poem by Longfellow. By the time Saira's husband, Tariq, will return from the police station, she'll have made mutton *yakhni*, fragrant with cardamom and ginger in a spicy yogurt sauce. The rice will have saffron in it. We'll all sit down on a carpet and have our meal together. Tariq, whom I'll already be thinking of as a condemned man, will eat the food hungrily. I will say to myself that he is eating one of his last meals in his home. This terrible thought will make me appreciate the taste of what I'm eating even more.

NOTES

From Amitava Kumar, "The Anima of India," *Chronicle of Higher Education*, February 1, 2008. Reprinted with permission of the publisher.

1. Amitava Kumar, *A Foreigner Carrying in the Crook of His Arm a Tiny Bomb* (Durham, NC: Duke University Press, 2010).
2. Amitava Kumar, *Passport Photos* (Berkeley: University of California Press, 2000).
3. Amitava Kumar, *Home Products* (New Delhi: Picador, 2007).
4. Amitava Kumar, *Husband of a Fanatic* (New York: New Press, 2005).

Bookstores of New York

It would be performance art—a bit like doing brownface, except not. The idea thrilled him as soon as it was proposed by his editors. He was to go to a few bookstores in New York City and ask: "Where is your 'White literature' section?"

He began with McNally Jackson Bookstore on Prince Street.

In the display window he saw some of his friends' books; there was a reading that evening by his pal who had written about an Indian-American man who lived out in the desert with his angry wife and autistic son. Inside there was a café. At one table, two women were talking in German. He returned to the front desk, but there were several people there and he felt intimidated. Coming back to the café section, he asked for a Moroccan mint tea.

The windows had been thrown open. It was a lovely spring morning. The girl in the shop opposite had come out onto the street and was photographing her displays—three large teddy bears in short dresses. A young man sat down next to him with his cappuccino and a black, hardbound copy of Bolaño's *Antwerp*. The man went back to the front desk.

"Where is your 'White literature' section?"

The salesclerk, with his muscular body encased in a bright red T-shirt, could have been just as at home behind the counter at a bicycle store. Let's say his name was Josh. Hearing the question, Josh stopped for a second, but without betraying his amiable self. He said reasonably, "That would be the literature of white countries . . ."

Extending one finger of his right hand, and then another, he counted, "England, France. . . ." And then said, "Let's walk over there."

En route to the shelf, Josh said with a smile, "The majority of literature is white." He was pointing at rows of books in front of them. The first one he picked out was Nicholson Baker's *House of Holes*. "He's fun," he said. To Baker's right there was Don DeLillo. He got a mention as well.

Josh said, half to himself, "*Who* are the great white authors?" Immediately to his right was the seeming answer. Withdrawing a copy of *Freedom* half an inch from its place on the shelf, he gently intoned, "*Franzen*."

Josh mentioned Hemingway and immediately discounted the recommendation by explaining kindly that Hemingway wasn't contemporary. He waved an arm at a line of Cormac McCarthy paperbacks but proclaimed them too bloody. Walking over to a bank of Philip Roth books, Josh said, "He was born in New Jersey, he is Jewish. His name is Philip Roth. He is amazing."

Putting a reverent hand on *American Pastoral*, he continued, "*This* is incredible."

The grateful customer acknowledged that he had perhaps heard of Roth. He took down the book he had been shown and sat down on a chair to read from its dust jacket. Josh, his sweet-natured guide, looked down at him, still full of amiability, and said as he left, "Enjoy, buddy."

The man had actually read Roth's *American Pastoral* some years ago with great attention. There was a quote from that novel carefully copied down in his writing journal at home: "The fact remains that getting people right is not what living is all about anyway. It's getting them wrong that is living, getting them wrong and wrong and wrong and then, on careful reconsideration, getting them wrong again. That's how we know we're alive: we're wrong."[1] Some other images from the book had also stayed imprinted in the man's mind—the strength and confusion of Swede Levov; rich, detailed descriptions of glove making; more disturbing, the Swede's daughter, Merry, who became an arsonist and then a Jain—and now he returned to them in his quiet corner.

But only for a minute, because the emotion he experienced more strongly was guilt. He hadn't lied, not exactly, but he had engaged in subterfuge. Why hadn't he practiced straight journalism? Why hadn't he come into the store, produced a business card, taken out a pad and asked blunt questions like, "Who decides on these categories? Can you tell me if there is any debate between you guys?" He hadn't done that, and now he would never be allowed to appear on *This American Life!* The man saw his dreams drown in this sea of guilt. Imagining a rescue, or at least an escape, he chose Hemingway's *A Moveable Feast*, and having paid $15.75, quickly left for another bookstore.

He wanted to get this over with. Close by was Housing Works Bookstore, on Crosby Street. He waited in front of the sign that said "Information." Above him were signs marking other sections: "Health," "Diet and Fitness," "Lesbian and Gay," "Sexuality." He asked his question. Again that momentary look of blankness: the confusion of categories. The person helping him was a short, pudgy Asian man. "White literature?" he repeated, skeptically but not unkindly. Near them was a cart loaded with books. The Asian man walked over to the cart and said, "It's all mixed . . ." With his finger on Chekhov's *The Shooting Party*, the salesclerk informed him, "He's Russian." The man looked at the price on the book. Five dollars. That was tempting. He noticed that the sheet of paper stuck to the cart's side said, "'Literary Classics' (Read the books you say you've already read)." On another cart nearby were cheaper books. Paule Marshall's *Praisesong for the Widow* was available for only one dollar, but he had decided that he'd only buy books by white people that day. He put down three dollars for Henry James's *Washington Square*.

The man walked to Astor Place. He had been to a branch of Barnes & Noble there some years earlier, pushing his daughter's stroller inside and buying her chocolate milk. But he couldn't find the store now. What to do? On his list was St Mark's Bookshop, located only a few blocks away. Cool, nicely lit interior, elegant rows of books on critical theory. With some trepidation, the man approached the sales counter. The woman wearing large glasses and large hoop earrings was barely unable to conceal her contempt. "What do you mean? Literature that *white people* write?"

The man nodded.

She said, "Down at the back, turn right."

Wait, did that mean they actually had a "White literature" section?

But the woman was saying, not hiding her scorn, "It's mixed up, along with the brown and black and other literature. . . . We don't split it up."

What to buy here, if only to show that he hadn't come in looking for a white race manifesto? He chose Stephanie Vaughn's new collection of stories, *Sweet Talk* ($16.28). There was a thin book by Patti Smith on the counter. The man said to the woman with the glasses, "Is this someone famous?" The woman was very kind, her eyes turned away this time, telling him about Smith in the punk movement and her memoir, *Just Kids*.

The man had time to do one more bookstore before meeting a friend for lunch. But he needed a break. At each bookstore, after each confrontation, he wondered what the salesclerks said to each other when his back was turned. He would look at books and imagine people snickering at him. He asked himself if any of the staff at the bookstores he had visited felt like lobbing questions back at him. "Where did you come across this term, 'white literature'? Are you being ironic? Are immigrants actually capable of irony? Do those people, immigrants, really have *fun*?"

There was enough time left, but he decided to make his way to the restaurant instead. Take a well-earned rest from trying to be the Sacha Baron Cohen of literary criticism. The man's friend arrived. The friend's book on Mumbai had been a finalist for the Pulitzer in nonfiction some years ago; the man told him why he was in the city, and his friend began to laugh. They ordered food and a bottle of pinot grigio. The man was drunk in no time. When the two men came out of the restaurant, two hours had passed. There was very little time left; the man would be late picking up his second child from day care. The friend pointed to the Barnes & Noble on 17th Street. The man had forgotten about it! On the awning outside, it said "World's Biggest Bookstore." He rushed inside, alone.

An Indian woman, or maybe she was Bangladeshi, tiny, with large expressive eyes, frowned at his question. She looked at the man's earring. It occurred to him he might be slurring his words. No, it was the question itself. She called her supervisor, a tall, beefy white guy in a black T-shirt. The man's name was Richard. He was quick and full of understanding. No chance of disavowal there! He said, "Well, the running joke is that much of literature is white literature."

When they were out of earshot, walking among tall, cavernous stacks, the man said to Richard, "I felt your colleague back there was perhaps confused by my question." Richard, again full of understanding, admitted that the man's "request had not been made in that form before." Then he pointed to some thick anthologies, saying these were the best places to look. The man took out his notebook but was interrupted by another staff member who had probably been sent by Richard. This person's name was Harry. He came prepared with answers. He said that the classifications that would best aid the man were "English Literature" and "American Literature." He was holding the fat Norton anthologies. He also gestured to another set of books and said, "These are more inclusive. They are anthologies of World Literature."

Harry asked the man where he was from, and when he heard the answer, he said, "I love your country." He informed the man that he had gone to India in 2003; he had gone up to Manali and then north, to places like Leh and Ladakh. The man was feeling drowsy from the wine. Meanwhile, Harry was being helpful. He asked the man if he had any questions. The man said yes. He said, "Barnes and Noble. Were they famous White authors?"

NOTES

From Amitava Kumar, "Where Is Your 'White Literature' Section?," *Margins*, June 4, 2012. Accessed August 3, 2014. http://aaww.org/where-is-your-white-literature-section/. Reprinted with permission of the publisher.

1. Philip Roth, *American Pastoral* (New York: Houghton Mifflin, 1997), 35.

IV

PEOPLE

· **21** ·

Lunch with a Bigot

Mr. Barotia was talking to someone when he opened the door. Speaking into the phone that was held in his left hand, he gave me his right fist, which I couldn't quite decide whether to touch or to hold. Mr. Barotia said to the person on the phone, "*Haan, haan,* we will sit down and talk about it." The apartment, with the sunlight falling on the bulky white furniture, some of it covered with transparent plastic, appeared clean and bright, especially after the darkness of the corridor outside with its musty carpeting. I was happy that I had got so far. I had spoken to Mr. Barotia for the first time only during the previous week, and on the phone he had called me a *haraami*, which means bastard in Hindi, and, after clarifying that he didn't mean this abuse only for me as a person but everyone else who was like me, he had also called me a *kutta*, a dog.

Although I had no idea of Mr. Barotia's identity till recently, I had wanted to meet him for well over two years. I wanted to meet face-to-face a man who thought I was his enemy, to see if I could understand why he hated me so much, and why he hated other people who were different from him. My name had appeared on a hit list put on a website in the year 2000.[1] The website belongs to a group called Hindu Unity—none of whose members, including Mr. Barotia, were named on the site—and it presented links to a variety of right-wing Hindu groups. My name was on a list of individuals who were regarded as enemies of a Hindu India. There was special anger for people like me, those who were Hindus but, in the minds of the organizers of this list, were damned as traitors to Hindutva, the ideology of a resurgent, anti-left, culturally ultranationalistic Hindu cause.

The summer after the website was established, the *New York Times* carried a report on the alliance that Hindu Unity had formed with Rabbi Meir Kahane's group. This is how the report began: "A Web site run by militant Hindus in Queens and Long Island was recently shut down by its service provider because of complaints that it advocated hatred and violence toward Muslims. But a few days later, the site was back on the Internet. The unlikely rescuers were some radical Jews in Brooklyn who are under investigation for possible ties to anti-Arab terrorist organizations in Israel."[2] The Zionist organization as well as the Hindutva group had come together in New York City against what they considered their common enemy, Islam. The news story had mentioned that Hindu Unity was a secretive group. It had been difficult for the reporter to meet the men who ran the website. I had written several e-mails to the address provided at the website—the address where one was supposed to write and report the names of the enemies of the Hindus—but no one had written back in response to my request for an interview. Then, while I was having lunch at an Indian restaurant with a leader of the Overseas Friends of the BJP, Mr. Barotia's name came up. The Bharatiya Janata Party is the right-wing Hindu party in power in Delhi; the Overseas Friends is an umbrella organization of Hindu groups outside India, zealously presenting to anyone who cares to listen the details of what they regard as the menace of the minorities in India—the non-Hindus, in particular the Muslims and the Christians. I quickly said to the man that I'd like to meet Mr. Barotia, and he took out his cell phone and gave me a number. And just as casually, the BJP man also mentioned that it was Mr. Barotia who had established the website for Hindu Unity.

Half an hour later, I was on the phone with Mr. Barotia. When I gave him my name, he recognized it. His voice lost its warmth and, from the way he was speaking, I formed an idea of him as being old and angry, a man with a lean face who was in his seventies. Mr. Barotia told me that he had read my article describing a visit to Pakistan, and he asked me, in order to confirm what he knew about me, whether I had married a Muslim. "You have caused me a lot of pain," he said. I didn't really know what to say, and, holding the phone and looking at the rain falling outside my window, I said, "I would very much like to meet you." It was only then that Mr. Barotia informed me of his low opinion of me. He also said that people like me were not secular, we were actually confused. We would learn our lesson, he said, when the Muslim population increased in India, and the Muslims came after us and chopped our legs off.

I was afraid that Mr. Barotia was going to hang up on me. I was held by the anger and perhaps more by the conviction in his voice. And I guess I could say that I felt his pain when he said that he didn't understand what had happened to the Hindu children, how it had come to be that they were surrounded by so much darkness. I said to him that I was not a child anymore, and then I thought for a moment that I sounded like one when I said this to him. Mr. Barotia said that he would talk to me, of course, and that I should come and eat in his home. I was pleased and I said yes, even when Mr. Barotia said that he was sure that after he had talked to me and given me "all the facts," I would change my mind about Muslims. This belief was important to Mr. Barotia. He was the secretary of an outfit that he called the Indian-American Intellectuals Forum; he was also the organizing secretary of the Hindu Swayamsevak Sangh, the overseas wing of the Rashtriya Swayamsevak Sangh (RSS), the militant organization whose member had murdered Mahatma Gandhi. The Internet had come as a gift to Mr. Barotia's propaganda. It made him a better long-distance nationalist. He said to me: "If the Hindus will be saved, it will be because of the Internet. I send out an e-mail and am able to talk at once to five thousand Hindus." Now, on the phone, he was telling me that he was prepared to talk to me about "all the facts." And so it was that less than a week later, I went to New York City and took the 7 Train to Elmhurst to meet Mr. Barotia.

. . .

In the summer of 1999, when India and Pakistan were engaged in a conflict near Kargil, in Kashmir, I had gotten married. The extraordinary thing was that in the days surrounding the event, I often told myself that my marriage was unusually symbolic: I was doing my bit in helping bring peace to more than a billion people living in the subcontinent. I am Indian; the woman I married is Pakistani. While I am Hindu, my wife, Mona, is Muslim.

It was in June that the wedding took place, and it was hot when I drove up to Toronto, where Mona's parents had recently moved from Karachi. It was in that same sticky heat that I drove back alone after the wedding, past Niagara Falls, where I had heard that honeymooners often go, and I felt good when I looked in the car mirror and saw myself as one who had married the enemy. The thought gave me a small thrill. I began to compose in my mind a brief piece for a newspaper about how my marriage had opened a new track for people-to-people diplomacy.

Every day in Toronto the news bulletins brought to us the war in Kashmir. But we had other preoccupations. Along with Mona's brothers and father, I would wake up at five in the morning to watch India and Pakistan battling it out on the cricket fields in England, where the World Cup tournament was being played. A day before our wedding, India had beaten Pakistan in the match in Manchester. During that game, one lone spectator had held a sign, "Cricket for Peace." Sitting in front of the television and watching the match, I wondered whether I too could walk around with a placard hung from my neck, saying "Marriage for Peace." The governments of India and Pakistan allowed eleven men from both sides to meet each other on the cricket field. But I began to think that it would be good to see a brisk traffic of common people across the border, accompanied by festive wedding processions and music bands.

I had not been entirely sure in my mind about the marriage. The plans had been made in a bit of a hurry and there seemed to be no easy way of getting rid of my doubts and questions. There was also the issue of religion. When I had called my parents in India from Toronto to tell them that I was going to get married, my mother had asked with a slight touch of panic in her voice, *"Woh log uss tarah ke musalman to nahin hain na?"* "They are not that kind of Muslims, are they?" A suitable gloss on that would be, "Are they fanatics?"

I had been impatient with the question. I wanted someone to assure me that Mona and I would be happy, and that, because of our love, we wouldn't tear each other apart when living under the same roof. This anxiety shared nothing with the anxiety about our God. And yet, the truth was that the difference in our religion, not to mention the fact that we belonged to enemy countries, kept coming up in various ways during the time that I spent in Toronto. I was also nervous that by going ahead with the wedding, despite my skepticism, I was showing myself to be indifferent and shallow. It is possible, therefore, that I had started thinking about my marriage together with peace in the subcontinent as a way of giving greater weight and even a touch of idealism to my decision.

Now when I reread the newspaper article that I wrote in the days after the wedding, I can catch a sense of my weak striving for resolve: "I like the way in which my neighborhood deli has changed the old slogan, 'Make Love Not War.' A large cloth banner, hung along the back of the store, colorfully proclaims, 'Make Soup Not War.' We need everything we can get to stop war. It need not necessarily be love. Soup will do too. And marriage."[3] This way of thinking about my marriage and peace was absurd, of course, but it also put a burden on us that was exaggerated and certainly unwanted. After Mona and I had been married, we quarreled and had fights, terrible fights that broke out incessantly in the first year of our marriage, and I would say to myself that if two people who claimed to love each other could fight like this, how was it possible for two entire nations to remain friends? In other words, whenever we exchanged hostile words—after an argument about some new item of furniture, or a broken piece of crockery, or the choice of food that one of us had brought from a nearby restaurant—a part of me also saw the mortar shells being lobbed in Kargil. Less surprisingly, others did the same. After the publication of my article about my wedding, Indian reporters looking for copy would write to me and ask questions about our married life. Did we not fight on the subject of Kashmir? Was beef eaten in our house? What about pork? If we had children, what would their religion be?

But not Mr. Barotia. He was not curious about my marriage; he simply disliked the idea of love between Hindus and Muslims. When he read my articles about my marriage and my visit to Pakistan, he denounced me as an enemy of India. Here, it is Mr. Barotia—my enemy—that I want to describe. I use that term for this man, *my enemy*, because that is how he thinks of his relationship to me. We hardly know each other. But the issue is not personal, it is political. I went to meet him in his apartment in Elmhurst, Queens, because I wanted a dialogue with him. It is also true, however, that I wanted to see his face. I found the idea of a faceless enemy unbearable. This wasn't a psychological problem so much as a writer's problem. I wanted detail and voice. Mr. Barotia had said to me on the phone that the rioters in Gujarat, who burned, raped, and slaughtered more than a thousand Muslims earlier that year, in 2002, had taught the Indian minorities a lesson they would never forget; and I wanted to meet Mr. Barotia so that I could ask him about the process through which he had come to think of the Muslim as the enemy.[4] I did ask the question, but the response revealed little to me, or at least little that was new. Nevertheless, our meeting was a discovery because it made me think not simply of our differences but also our similarities. What is it that divides the writer from the rioter? The answer is not very clear or simple. There could be more in common between the two than either of them might imagine—for example, that vast hinterland of public memory and shared prejudice that made us cultural citizens. Was it an excess of sympathy on my part—or, on the contrary, too little of it—that made it difficult, if not also impossible, for me to draw a plainly legible line between a man in a mob and myself?

. . .

There was a woman in the house—she was Mr. Barotia's niece—and she called out to him when she saw me enter the living room. He was being asked to put on a shirt. I saw that Mr. Barotia, who was short, didn't have the lean face I had imagined; his face was round and with gray eyebrows; he put on a pair of gold-rimmed spectacles after I told him that I doubted his statement that we had met before. Mr. Barotia touched his glasses and frowned. He said, "But your face looks familiar." I suddenly thought of the Hindu Unity website. They—Mr. Barotia—had put up my photograph there. This was the picture that had been picked up from some of my newspaper pieces. Perhaps that was the reason why Mr. Barotia thought that he had seen me before. He had seen my face right next to the hit-list threat that he had put against my name and address. But, for some reason, I couldn't bring myself to say this to him. Instead, I drank the tea that I was offered. And then Mr. Barotia began to tell me about what he called "the poison of Islam."

The litany of complaints was familiar and quickly wearying. Mr. Barotia began with the names of all the male Indian film stars who were Muslim and married to Hindu women: "Sharmila Tagore is now Ayesha Begum, and that pimp Shah Rukh Khan is married to a Hindu girl. Her name is Gauri." These women had been forced to convert, he said, and now they were having sex with Muslims. When Mr. Barotia told me this, he moved his right forearm back and forth against his paunch in a pumping action. He was using a Hindi word for what he was describing, a word common on the streets in India, and he said it so loudly, and so repeatedly, that I was startled and immediately thought of his niece in the kitchen. I was a stranger and she had not come in front of me; it was Mr. Barotia who had had to get up and go to her to bring the tray with tea and cookies. Her manner had suggested that there was a great deal of traditional reserve in the household. What did she think of Mr. Barotia carrying on so obscenely about circumcised cocks and fucking?

The BJP leader in the Indian restaurant, when he had given me the phone number, had told me that Mr. Barotia's family had been massacred during the riots in 1947. I found out now that this wasn't true. Mr. Barotia said that his family had left Sindh and crossed the border quite safely more than a year after the partition. This revelation left me without a convenient explanation for his bigotry. When I asked Mr. Barotia to tell me about how he had come to acquire his rather well-defined worldview, he spluttered with rage: "I was liberal like you, I was stupid, ignorant. In Islam, there is no space for your secularism. There is no humanity in it. They extol the virtue of violence, they want to kill infidels. . . . Islam is not a religion, it is a political ideology to capture land and rape the women."

I had begun taking notes. Mr. Barotia would now and then point at my notebook and say, "Write!" And then he would say things like: "Hindus were being killed in Pakistan and Gandhi was giving speeches. *Saala tum ghoomta hai haraami.* . . . When Gandhi was killed, that day I felt re-laxed." A little later, a friend of Mr. Barotia's joined us, a fat, bearded man with a red *tilak* on his forehead. This man pedantically recited Sanskrit *shlokas*—verses from the *Vedas*—when he made his polemical points, and I sometimes turned back to Mr. Barotia's plainer speech, and his abuses, with a sense of relief.

Soon, it became clear that Mr. Barotia was going to buy me lunch. We walked to an Indian diner about a ten minutes' walk away in Jackson Heights. Mr. Barotia behaved like a friendly host and, urging me to try the different dishes, put bits of warm naan on my plate. He also ate with gusto, refilling his plate several times, and as I looked at him, his shirt-front flecked with the food he had dropped there, I saw him as a contented, slightly tired old man who was perhaps getting ready to take an afternoon nap. Earlier, Mr. Barotia had told me that because the Hindus had killed so many Muslims earlier that year in Gujarat, a change had come about. "We have created fear," he boasted. *"Yeh garmi jo hai, main India mein phaila doonga.* This heat that is there, I will spread it in India. And those who write against us, their fingers will be cut." But, for now, he was quietly stuffing *pakoras* into his mouth: a retired immigrant worker eating in a cheap immigrant restaurant.

Mr. Barotia had told me earlier that day that it was in 1972 that he had arrived in America. For twenty-five years he had worked as a legal secretary in New York City—the BJP man in the restaurant the previous week had told me that Mr. Barotia had been "a typist," and I had seen from the gesture of his hand that he was being dismissive. Mr. Barotia was also aware of this dismissal in a general way, and he had tried weakly to suggest to me that he had achieved more than he actually had: he said that he had gotten along well with his colleagues at work and they treated him as "a partner in the firm," and one of them had even called him after the attacks of 9/11 to say: "Jagdish, we thought you were obsessed with Muslims. But you were right."

After our lunch, one other matter of business remained. Mr. Barotia was going to give me newspaper cuttings and booklets. We walked back to the apartment through the crowded streets of Jackson Heights, and the exercise brought Mr. Barotia back to life. His home is in a locality where Indians and Pakistanis immigrants live together, and, indeed, Elmhurst is said to be the most diverse zip-code area in the whole of

United States. I asked Mr. Barotia about his experience of living in this part of the city, and he looked at the Muslims milling around us, the men with beards and caps, women with headscarves, and he spat out abuse. They harass our women, he said, and there is a lot of tension here. Then, suddenly, he began to talk of my wife, whom he has never met. We were passing in front of the Indian grocery and jewelry stores packed together, and Mr. Barotia turned to me and said: "It is okay. You fuck her. And you tell everyone that she is Muslim, and that you keep fucking her! And through her, you keep fucking Islam!"

"What did you do when he said that?" This is what Mona, my wife, asked me when she heard the story. I had called from a public phone near Mr. Barotia's apartment. Above me was a large sign with black letters painted on a white board: "LEARN ENGLISH APRENDA INGLES." There was a pause before I replied to Mona's question. I said that I had done nothing. Wordlessly, I had kept walking beside Mr. Barotia. It would have been more accurate to say that I had made a mental note of what he had said. I had told myself that I needed to write down his words in my notebook as soon as I was back on the train. And that is what I did. Sitting in the train, with three men on the seat opposite me, each one of them wearing identical yellow jerseys and holding aluminum crutches against their knees, I took down notes about what Mr. Barotia had said during our walk back from the lunch. The strange thing is, although perhaps it is not strange at all, that later Mr. Barotia's words crossed my mind, just when my wife and I had finished having breakfast in our kitchen and there, next to the sink with the empty bowl of cereals, I had begun to kiss her.

· · ·

Language was important for Mr. Barotia, and in that, he and I were both alike. Just before we said goodbye, he had declared that for the first time the leadership of the World Hindu Council (Vishwa Hindu Parishad, VHP) had adopted his language in India. The previous week, he said, someone from the VHP had called Sonia Gandhi, the Italian-born leader of the Indian opposition, a bitch. The surgeon-turned-fundamentalist, Praveen Togadia, the international general secretary of the VHP, had said in Gujarat, "After Narendra Modi did such a good job here of controlling the riots, some dogs in Gujarat barked, then they barked in other parts of the country and now an Italian dog has begun to bark." A news weekly in India, reporting on what it called "the new, extra-constitutional world of India's loony right," wrote of the effect that the extremist demagogues had on the central government: "When they sneeze in Mumbai, Nagpur or New York, New Delhi catches a cold."[5]

During lunch, Mr. Barotia told me that I was ungrateful if I forgot how Hindu warriors had saved our motherland. He must have gotten to me, because when he asked me why I believed in coexistence with Muslims, I said a phrase in Hindi that essentially meant "we are Nehru's bastards." It was an admission of guilt, of illegitimacy, as if Nehru, the socialist first prime minister of India, had done something wrong in being a liberal, and those of us who believed in his vision of an inclusive India were his ill-begotten offspring. Nehru is often accused by his detractors of having been a profligate person, and my remark had granted him a certain promiscuity. But the more serious charge hidden in my comment was that the former prime minister had produced a polity that was the result of a miscegenation with the West.

I was being disingenuous—and so was Mr. Barotia. Our lives and our histories, with or without Nehru, were tied up with links with the wider world. I am an Indian writer who writes in English. Mr. Barotia's parent party, the RSS, had been inspired by the Nazis and revered a German man, Hitler. Today, Mr. Barotia is a fan of the Internet. We both live and work in the United States. We are both struggling, each in our way, to be like Nehru, whose eclecticism was exceptional. But Nehru was also exemplary because, unlike many of his Hindu compatriots, he had an unwavering belief that Hindu-Muslim conflict had nothing to do with tradition but was a modern phenomenon, which could be corrected by means of enlightened policy.

In the train, flipping over some of the papers that Mr. Barotia had given me, I began to read what the Hindutva brigade had to say about Nehru. An article provided "circumstantial evidence" that Nehru was a Muslim. One item of proof offered was the following: "He had 'Muslim' morals while 'chasing and pursuing' a married woman (Edwina Mountbatten) and professing love to her. If he were a Hindu he would have respected married women and looked at the unmarried girls as 'devis' (goddesses)." Another piece—this one about Gandhi, who had preached love between the different religions—began by asserting that there are two kinds of bastards. There are those who are "born of illicit sex," and then there are those who are "despicable in word and conduct." "The remarkable thing about Mohandas Karamchand Gandhi," the writer continued, "is that he was a bastard on both counts."

Mr. Barotia had given me a set of typewritten sheets collected under the title "Wake Up! America! Wake Up!" These pages, each one carrying exhortations printed in emphatic bold letters and followed by a series of mercilessly underlined sentences, were his response to the tragedy of 9/11: "The macabre massacre of around 15,000 people (mostly Disbelievers) in less than 120 minutes. The inciter, the instigator QURAN is the CRIMINAL CULPRIT, which incites millions of Muslims around the World to the ghastly, ghostly crimes of this enormous destructive nature on the Disbelievers; and UNASHAMEDLY at the same time, tells [us] these are all HOLY! So, Oh Disbeliever World! UNDERSTAND THIS COLD, CHILLING TRUTH." As I read these words, it was as if I could hear Mr. Barotia's hectoring voice. His interest in alliteration had not been evident to me before, but it didn't distract me from his real interest in producing a phony history and linking it to language. "As the history of Mohammed goes, he was a serial rapist, a serial murderer, a chronic criminal, a treacherous terrorist who was banished by his family and the society of his times," Mr. Barotia wrote. He followed this a little later with a bogus disquisition on the etymology of the name for Muslims. The Prophet, in order to avenge the lack of respect shown him, founded "gangs of powerful youth (Muscle Men), offering them girls of their choice, food and wine." And "the illiterate Mohammed mispronounced the word 'Muscle Man' as 'Musalman.' Over a period of time, this mispronunciation became an accepted pronunciation!" The ten-page text ended with a question not about 9/11 but about an earlier unresolved crime that is still an obsession for many conspiracy theorists in America and to which Mr. Barotia was only giving a new twist: "Who was behind the planning, plotting and planting the Death of the Dearest JFK?" The answer: "It was ISLAM, ISLAM and ISLAM, the ever valiant villain."

There are various things that could be said about Mr. Barotia, and one would be that he is a fringe element that gives a dangerous edge to an increasingly powerful and mainstream ideology in the subcontinent. His party is the party that rules in New Delhi, although it is in retreat in parts of India.[6] Mr. Barotia is also a member of the group that claims success in raising funds in the West—including investments made by expatriate Indians, allegedly to the tune of four billion dollars—to support the Indian government after economic sanctions had been imposed on India following the nuclear tests in 1998.

But what is of interest to me, as a writer, are the words that Mr. Barotia uses. Their violence and ferocity—their absoluteness compromised and made vulnerable in different ways, not least by the repeated eruption of a sexual anxiety—carry the threat most visible in the rhetoric of the rioter in India today. This is the threat of a worldview that has no place in it for the middle-class gentility of Nehruvian liberalism.[7] Indeed, its incivility is a response to the failures of the idealism represented by the likes of Nehru and Gandhi. Mr. Barotia's voice is the voice of the lumpen that knows it is lumpen no longer. It almost has the legitimacy of being in power, and its aggressiveness is born through its own sense that it is in a pitched battle against those who have held power for too long. I am not sure whether I would ever, or for long, envy Mr. Barotia's passion, but what gives me greater pause is the feeling that I would be more sympathetic to his perception that the English-speaking elite had not granted the likes of him a proper place under the Indian flag. Once that thought enters my head, I am uneasily conscious of the ways in which I had found myself mocking Mr. Barotia's bigotry by noticing how badly he had constructed his sentences. Like Mr. Barotia, I was born in the provinces and grew up in small towns. For me, the move to the city meant that I learned English and embraced secular, universal rationality; Mr. Barotia remained truer to his roots and retained his religion as well as a narrower form of nationalism that went with it. His revenge on the city was that he also became a fanatic. I do not envy him his changes, but I can't think of those changes without a small degree of tenderness.

There is also another reason why Mr. Barotia's words hold my attention. His stories about heroism and betrayal share something with the fantasy world of my own childhood, whose half-understood atmosphere of rumor and prejudice was a part not of a private universe but of a largely public one. What Mr. Barotia and I share in some deep way is the language of memory—that well from which we have drawn, like water, our collective stories. After my meeting with Mr. Barotia, I thought of a particular incident from my childhood. I wondered whether he, too, had similar memories, linking him and me, all of us, to all the bigots of the world.

My memory concerned a dead lizard. I must have been five or six at that time. The lizards, the *girgit*, were everywhere. In the small garden outside our home in Patna, they would creep out of the hedge and sun themselves on the metal gate. Many years later, in a mall near Washington, D.C., I saw similar lizards being sold as pets. I was reminded of my fear of the *girgit* in my childhood. These lizards were yellow or brown, their thin bodies scaly, and many of them had bloated red sacs under their chin. Although I was scared of the lizards, I also wanted to kill them. I often daydreamed about killing a lizard by throwing a stone at it when it was not looking. I would try to imagine what its pale exposed belly would look like when it fell through the air.

A boy who was a year ahead of me in school killed a lizard. He brought the dead lizard to me in the polythene bag of the sort in which we were sold popcorn by the Christian nuns during recess. And it was he who told me that the lizards were Muslim. He pointed out the sacs under their chin and said that they used to be beards. During the riots that accompanied the partition of India in 1947, the Muslims were running scared of the Hindus. If the Hindus found the Muslims, they would murder them. If the Hindus did not kill the Muslims first, the Muslims would instead butcher the Hindus with their swords. Or they would take the Hindus to the new country, Pakistan, where the Hindus would be converted and become trapped forever.

Once the Hindus saw a bearded Muslim running away. They caught him and were about to chop off his head. The man was a coward. In order to save his life, he pointed with his beard toward the well where the other Muslims were hiding. Because of this act of treachery, that man was turned into a lizard with a sac under his chin. That is why when we Hindus looked at these lizards they bobbed their heads as if they were pointing toward a well.

NOTES

From Amitava Kumar, "Prologue: Lunch with a Bigot," in Amitava Kumar, *Husband of a Fanatic* (New York: New Press, 2005), 1–14. Reprinted with permission of the publisher.

1. The Hindu Unity website used to display the "hit list" (later renamed "black list") with a noose and an animated image of dripping blood. The list has now been removed from the site. More information about the organization can be found on Wikipedia (http://en.wikipedia.org/wiki/Hindu_Unity).

2. Dean E. Murphy, "Two Unlikely Allies Come Together in Fight against Muslims," *New York Times*, June 2, 2001.

3. Amitava Kumar, "Marriage for Peace," *The Hindu*, June 22, 1999.

4. For a report on the riots, see Kumar, *Husband of a Fanatic*, 15–47.

5. Saba Naqvi and Ranjit Bhushan, "Fangs and Fury," *Outlook*, November 4, 2002. Accessed August 4, 2014. http://www.outlookindia.com/article /Fangs-And-Fury/217756.

6. When this essay was written, the right-wing BJP had just come to power. Later, it lost its hold on power and gave way to the Congress Party, which emerged victorious in the general elections of 2004 and 2009. In the elections of 2014, the BJP returned to power with a massive majority. For a report on the fund-raising done by overseas Indians with links to the BJP, see "The Foreign Exchange of Hate," Sabrang Communications, 2002. Accessed August 4, 2014. http://www.indianet.nl/reportsacw/index.html.

7. An excellent introduction to Nehru's secular ideals is provided by Sunil Khilnani, *The Idea of India* (New York: Farrar, Straus and Giroux, 1997).

22

The Boxer on the Flight

The Indian boxer was returning from the London Olympics. He was standing in the aisle of the plane I was on, coming from London to Delhi, and he was going to sit next to me. He had an attractive face, vaguely slanting eyes, and a moustache over pouty lips. The person who was with him was wearing an India blazer with an Olympic logo—I thought he was a wrestler whose picture I had seen in the newspapers. I was wrong, he was only the coach. The boxer had a slightly swollen eye, not dark enough to qualify as a black eye. When he sat down next to me, the boxer asked the flight attendant if he could be moved to business class. On the way to London, he told her, the captain had "adjusted" them. I thought it good to inform the attendant that the man had rep-resented India in the Olympics. She asked, in a good-natured way, "Oh yeah! How was London for you?" He shrugged and then said, "Thank you for seating me next to a pretty girl."

He didn't mean me, of course. It was a young German woman on the other side, who had a seat next to the window.

I will call the boxer Shyam Kumar. Shyam asked me where I lived, and when I said the United States, his first question was: "Are electronics very cheap in the United States?" He then asked about sex. "Is sex free over there?" I said, "No, it is almost like it is in India, in the sense that there are customs and conventions." He said, "But there are no blocks, parents and others saying things?"

I didn't quite know how to answer that. He now turned to the German girl. He asked about her nationality. "How old you are?" "Twenty," she said. "Boyfriend?" The young woman laughed at his questions and leaned forward in her seat to meet my eye. I think she was amused by his queries. She began to explain to him that she was going to meet her fiancé, an Indian man, who owned a security agency in Gurgaon.

"I also going to Gurgaon," Shyam said, and then tried to indicate through gestures that he was headed elsewhere, Gurgaon was only a place he was going to pass through. He had little fear or hesitation, and, despite my initial irritation at his questions, I began to find him endearing. Shyam asked the girl if the man she was going to meet was her "first boyfriend." The woman had trouble understanding the question; she said yes. He asked her more about the boyfriend, what caste he was, and then he loudly declared that they were both from the same caste, the boyfriend and he. Maybe I misheard him, but I think he asked her which of the two men was better looking.

Earlier, Shyam had asked me what I did for a living. I said I was a writer and a professor of English. He said, "You've expressed the thought that was in my mind! My English is well. Other boxers don't speak English. But I want to improve."

Shyam said he was going to travel to the United States soon to increase his weight. Could he take classes there?

Despite his infelicities with the language, he was doing okay with the German. After dinner, I had taken down my laptop in an effort to work. This inspired Shyam. He took down his laptop too. The machine came on after a while, and Shyam began showing the girl pictures of himself in the ring, and then a few news clips of his fights. I leaned over and asked him to show again one of the pictures that I had glimpsed. It was a nice shot, his right arm outstretched, the muscles of his lean body standing out in terrific tension. He then showed the German girl photos of a woman from Bhiwani who was his fiancée. Once he asked, "What do you think of her body?"

I had the aisle seat. The woman sat next to the window and Shyam in the middle. I went back to the work I was doing and fell asleep.

When I woke again, the two of them were still talking. I was grateful for a selfish reason. Shyam was slim, but he had broad shoulders and his elbows would press against me unself-consciously. It was quite uncomfortable for me, although I didn't mention this to him. But when talking to the woman he sat turned away from me, his elbows out of the way.

We might have been two hours away from Delhi, this was in the morning, when the German girl got up and went to the bathroom with a small bag clutched in her hand. While she was gone, Shyam said to me, "*Bhaiyaji*, she is very frank. She has told me everything. She has even said to me that her mother has told her she should try other people, not just think of the Indian man."

I offered the observation that he had charmed her. He said, "*Apni toh hunar hai.*" (I am talented that way.) He told me that all he needed to do now was cry in front of her, and she would be his.

The girl came back from the bathroom. She was wearing an Indian outfit. I suppose she had made the change for the sake of her fiancé's mother. She looked attractive and I heard Shyam complimenting her. He had more questions and comments, but I didn't hear them except his asking her whether she would miss him. I don't know what she said.

He took her picture on his phone: he had pressed himself against her seat and they were facing the camera. I think the girl didn't like how she looked in Shyam's photo; she took out her wallet and gave him a passport-size picture of herself. It was evenly lit and showed her smiling. Shyam held the photo in his hand for a while and then returned it to her. "I cannot take it," he said. She was surprised, and they had a conversation that I did not hear. The two were silent after that.

We were close to Delhi. After breakfast, Shyam asked the attendant if he could buy a toy car from duty free. He said he wanted to give it to the girl as a memento. But duty free was now closed. The reading light above me was on, and Shyam asked me if I would shut it

THE BOXER ON THE FLIGHT

off. I did. I continued to read in the dim light of the cabin, and I heard Shyam asking the girl something and then they fell silent. I didn't hear them talk for the rest of the trip, which must have lasted for another fifteen or twenty minutes. When the plane was taxiing to a stop, Shyam made a few calls. He wanted someone to be present at customs. Then, as I was getting up, he said, "*Bhaiyaji*, is there any offense for kissing in the plane?" He used the words *pappi dena* (for kissing). I paused. I said there was no rule against kissing, no, but, and here I looked at the girl next to the window and said, you cannot do anything that someone doesn't want you to do.

Shyam looked serious, even sad. He said, "I will do it, for certain." Then it was my turn to get up and join the line of passengers exiting the aircraft. Shyam remained seated and beyond him, unable to get out, the German girl. I didn't see them again.

Which is all a roundabout way of saying that I'm very proud of Mary Kom and happy that women are boxers.[1]

NOTES

From Amitava Kumar, "The Boxer on the Flight," *Hindu*, August 11, 2012. Reprinted with permission of the publisher.

1. Mary Kom is an Indian boxer. She won the bronze medal at the 2012 London Olympics.

23

Amartya's Birth

The baby was only ten minutes old. That is what the infant's father said to me, but it was more likely that half an hour had passed since the time he was born and then rushed to the clinic because he wasn't crying.

The clinic is new. It is located on the ground floor of the house where I grew up in Patna. My elder sister is a doctor and owns the clinic with her husband. When I first saw the baby, around nine in the morning, he already had a thin tube in his tiny nostril. This tube brought oxygen to his lungs. The child was wrapped in a soft white dhoti but my sister, or her assistant, had covered it with puffy sheets of white cotton.

The baby was making an unearthly, prolonged, painful sound. With each breath he took, the baby was grunting, the sound too loud for a body so small. I don't know how else to say it: the cry was that of a dying animal, and the look on the faces of the people in the room showed that it had a shattering effect on them.

I stepped out of the room and saw that my sister, the doctor, was standing beside the stairs; she had put both her hands on the staircase and was leaning over it with her eyes shut.

I had come back to Patna to see my parents. They are old. I'm aware of their mortality, of course, and perhaps as a result of it, I wonder also about the days that are left to me. The question becomes poignant when it is posed in Patna. I remember how some years ago, while I was writing a book about post-9/11 legal trials in the United States, I had met Hemant Lakhani, a man convicted of selling an Igla missile to an undercover agent pretending to be from a terrorist organization.[1] Lakhani was an old man and the long sentence he received means that he will die in prison. On the day of his sentencing in a New Jersey courtroom, Lakhani pleaded with the judge, begging for leniency because, he said, everyone wants to die in their homeland.

Home is where you go to die.

The greater truth, of course, is that my hometown Patna is where the people are dying. The day I began writing this piece, children were brought to Patna, dying or already dead, from having eaten their pesticide-laced mid-day lunch in a village near Chhapra.[2]

A week earlier, meeting some medical sales representatives in my sister's clinic in Patna, I had asked what medicines and diseases they were most in the market for. Antibiotics, they said, and added that people also suffered from tuberculosis and diarrhea. One of them, Ajay Pathak, told me that even if you go to Patna Medical College and Hospital only to meet a doctor, you still run a good chance of contracting TB. He was talking about himself. A month earlier, he had also started suffering from hepatitis E.

There were four of them, the medical salesmen, and each agreed that the worst thing about their job was seeing patients suffer because there was such an overwhelming lack of medical facilities. You have to pay a bribe to find a bed in a hospital. There are other perversions in the business. My friend Ravish Kumar, an anchor for NDTV, told me that when his father fell sick in Patna, Ravish went to a pharmacy to buy medicines. The man behind the counter looked at the prescription and was able to rightly guess the caste of the doctor. The doctor had pre-scribed medicines that had been manufactured by companies owned by businessmen from the same caste. This is routine practice in Bihar. As Ravish put it, even medicines have a caste.

While I was talking to the salesmen, one of them mentioned that the lack of facilities meant that people had to travel long distances to get help. In the room adjoining where we were sitting, there was a couple who had come from Jharkhand. They had brought their small child, a four-year-old boy, who had not been able to urinate in three days. It turned out that the problem was even more complicated than not get-ting help where they lived. My sister told me that the parents of the child had first taken him to a local doctor who told them he was going to have to clean the boy's genital area. That doctor inserted a catheter in the little boy's penis and this ill-advised action had hurt the boy. It was the reason he wasn't peeing. He was given medicine while I talked to the salesmen, and before the child left with his parents he had been able to release at last what my sister called "a trickle."

But that had been the previous week. No past success could offer sol-ace, or suggest a cure for the grunting baby. His pulse, oxygen satura-tion, as well as respiration, was being translated into a flow of brightly colored numbers on a monitor. A special lamp was keeping him warm, the temperature close to what he was accustomed to inside his mother's womb. An IV feed, attached to his tiny arm and secured by means of a cardboard splint, brought fluids into his bloodstream. A clamp glowing red was attached to his ear. Three or four sensors were stuck to his skin, thin tubes radiating from his pink form. Every second or so, one of the machines, perhaps the one recording his pulse, beeped. The infant's cry was louder, or more noticeable. It went on for an hour, and then more. The baby had come at nine, and at noon he was still at it. I wondered whether he would die from sheer exhaustion. When I put the question to my sister, her reply seemed to suggest we needed to wait and see. Meanwhile, she called a local business and bought a ventilator.

It was explained to me that when a baby cries after coming out of its mother's womb, the crying helps get rid of the water in its lungs. This had not happened with this particular child. This baby, who didn't have a name yet, was grunting because it was finding it a struggle to breathe. Hence, the tube of oxygen. Hence, too, my sister's attempt to drain fluids from near the baby's throat by using a vacuum machine. And assorted medications through injections.

It was difficult to watch, or hear, the baby. His maternal grandmother, who is the mother of three daughters, stood distraught, one hand squeezing the other as if she were putting on a tight bangle. The baby's father, a man with a broad, serious face, was sitting on a bench outside. I sat down next to him and found out that he was the manager at a local bank. He told me he was the father of two daughters. He revealed that in his upper-caste society, people were inclined to "indicate" (he used the English word) if you didn't have any male progeny. There had been cause for concern because of the baby's gender. The mother had complained that the fetus wasn't kicking that day, and her gynecologist had taken quick action, delivering the child about ten days prematurely. Would there have been less precipitous haste if there hadn't been the pressure of having the family's first male child? My sister said that the baby's mother had two other sisters, one of whom was mentally disabled; the baby's father was the only child of his parents.

By evening, the baby had settled down and was sleeping peacefully. There was still concern, but he had stepped out of danger. We were all enormously relieved; in fact, I felt giddy. I was in my hometown, and I felt enough at ease to declare happily to the baby's father—the mother was still in the hospital where she had undergone a cesarean procedure that morning—that now my sister had earned the right to name the child. My sister laughed off the idea, but I eagerly proffered the name Amartya.[3]

Over the next three days, I visited the baby's room often. I met his mother when she arrived, in tears, to see her baby for the first time. Your hometown is always where your roots lie, but I think it can also be about the spreading branches and, in a new season, fresh blossoms.

It would have been neat to end the tale here. But there is a story standing beside it. There was another baby at my sister's clinic. This baby, who was three months old and already had a name, Sneha Kumari, had come from a village in East Champaran. Her sternum was foreshortened and weak, and she was having trouble breathing. She was also suffering from pneumonia, and that was my sister's main concern. Sneha's father and grandfather are manual laborers. She had been brought to my sister's clinic by her grandparents and her mother; they were staying in what had formerly been our family's garage and had been converted into a space for those who couldn't afford the rooms inside. Sneha's grandfather told me that he had spent fifty thousand rupees on the baby's treatment so far, going from one doctor to another near their village. This money had come from loans he had taken from rich peasants in the village: the interest on the loan was three rupees each month on every hundred he had borrowed. He told me he belonged to the caste that traditionally prepared oil. His daily earnings were anywhere between fifty and hundred rupees.

For Sneha's family, my sister and even I were objects of suspicion and resentment. I saw it in their looks. Unlike the family of the other baby, who were grateful that my sister had saved their child's life, Sneha's mother never stopped frowning when she spoke to me. She addressed angry questions at my sister. She knew that the system was tilted against her. In fact, it promised her annihilation. Why should I have expected the young mother to feel at home in Patna? I doubt she had any education. She was tall and slim, with a pretty face, and all she had was her anger. It shone on her face. I didn't blame her for hating Patna, or, for that matter, for hating me.

NOTES

From Amitava Kumar, "Pangs of a Patna Visit," *Open*, August 17, 2003. Reprinted with permission of the publisher.

1. Amitava Kumar, *A Foreigner Carrying in the Crook of His Arm a Tiny Bomb* (Durham, NC: Duke University Press, 2010), 33–57.
2. Jason Burke, "Indian School-Lunch Poisoning: Doctors Race to Save Children," *Guardian*, July 17, 2013.
3. The name Amartya would loosely translate as "not touched by death" or "undying." It is also the name, of course, of a Nobel-winning economist of Indian origin.

· **24** ·

The Taxi Drivers of New York

Each employed immigrant has his or her place of work. It is only the taxi driver, forever moving on wheels, who occupies no fixed space. He represents the immigrant condition. And yet there is no one more adept than he is at mapping our streets and cities. He is not an alien. The cabbie has made familiar, though not without faltering, nor without arduous, repeated labor, all that was strange and forbidding. Perhaps among us he is most American.

This is the hour of the immigrant worker—after the milkman and just before the dustman. I read that in a book somewhere and imagined a pink dawn at the end of an empty city street, as in a picture postcard and already belonging to the past.

But the present looks different. It accommodates throngs of patient maids, hidden restaurant workers, and, at all hours of the day and night, in their pale blue uniforms, armies of quiet hospital staff.

It is always the taxi driver who, in the bright yellow cab, is the most visible of them all. He is also the most vulnerable. The New York Taxi Workers Alliance (NYTWA) cites studies that taxi drivers are thirty times more likely to be killed on the job than the average worker.[1]

On August 24 in New York City, around 6:00 P.M., a driver named Ahmed H. Sharif picked up a fare at East 24th Street and Second Avenue. The passenger was twenty-one-year-old Michael Enright, who asked the cabbie a question that has now been heard around the world: "Are you a Muslim?" When the driver said yes, the passenger first greeted him in Arabic and then said, "Consider this a checkpoint." Enright pulled out a knife and, in the words of an assistant district attorney, slashed the cabbie's "neck open halfway across his throat." Sharif managed to lock his attacker in the car, but he soon escaped. Enright was later arrested; both he and his victim were taken to the same hospital.

Later, Sharif released a statement via the NYTWA: "I feel very sad. I have been here more than 25 years. I have been driving a taxi more than 15 years. All my four kids were born here. I never feel this hopeless and insecure before," said Mr. Sharif. "Right now, the public sentiment is very serious (because of the Ground Zero Mosque debate). All drivers should be more careful."[2]

We might wish to make allowance for the role of the NYTWA in injecting the correct dose of political context, as in the critical parenthetical insertion in the remark quoted above; nevertheless, an event like this, especially in New York City, cannot be insulated from the vicious rhetoric that has swirled around us in recent weeks. The blogosphere is already alight with accusations that Sarah Palin and Newt Gingrich have blood on their hands.

Tempting as it may be to repeat this analysis, I don't wish to discount another factor: the sense of power, and even the false intimacy with the Other, that Enright would have experienced in Afghanistan. His behavior inside the cab also goes to show how embedded he is in the narrative of the U.S. military adventure. Are only Palin and Gingrich to be blamed for it?

Several years ago, I spent a summer in New York City with taxi drivers. These were men from the Indian subcontinent, trying to find a footing in this country. This is what I remember most about their life. Each day, they would pick up their vehicle after paying for the daily lease. It would cost a little over $100 at that time. The cabbie was also responsible for the cost of gas. In an eight-, ten-, or—most likely—twelve-hour shift, there was first a mountain to cross. This was the payment that the driver had already made for the lease on the cab and gas. It was possible, on a bad day, that the cabbie would actually lose money. Hours passed, the men drove in desperation, stopping after several hours, if at all, for a quick meal at a Punjabi *dhaba* on the East Side. You drove hard, searched the streets for a passenger, tried to get a larger tip when you were asked to help make a meeting on time, and this didn't prevent you from getting a $200 ticket.

I'd be riding shotgun and on occasion try to engage a passenger in conversation. The people I saw in the backseat were polite sometimes; hard-headed pragmatists most of the time; and, every now and then, unbelievably mean and contemptuous assholes. What amazed me most was the way in which the taxi drivers retained their equanimity: I wondered what motivated their behavior, whether it was professionalism of a sort, or powerlessness, or a mixture of greed and need.

A decade later, I was sitting in my home, drinking coffee in the morning, when I saw a letter in the newspaper. It described a trip made by the letter writer from La Guardia Airport to her home in the Bronx. As I read it, my heart was touched with a certain sweetness. I was recalling my time with my cabbie friends in New York City, but I was also touched by the letter writer's sensitivity to not only the work the cabbie was doing but also his precious, fragmented life:

> As we moved slowly through the traffic, I heard a woman's voice in the front seat of the cab. The driver told me that he had recently returned from Pakistan, where he had gotten married, and this was his bride calling from Pakistan on his cellphone. He said he was doing the paperwork so that she could come here in about six months.
>
> I could hear her voice and his as they began to sing a duet. He would sing a line from the cab creeping along in the traffic not far from Yankee Stadium, and she would sing a line in response from Pakistan. I could not understand the language of their song, but he told me she was thinking of him so much that she could not sleep.[3]

NOTES

From Amitava Kumar, "The Venerable, Vulnerable Taxi Drivers of New York," *Vanity Fair.com*, August 26, 2010. Reprinted with permission of the publisher.

1. The New York Taxi Workers Alliance reports this figure on their website, nytwa.org.
2. Eric Lach, "NY Cab Driver Allegedly Stabbed For Being Muslim: 'I Feel Very Sad'," TPM, August 25, 2010. Accessed August 5, 2014. http://talkingpoints memo.com/muckraker/ny-cab-driver-allegedly-stabbed-for-being-muslim -i-feel-very-sad. For more details of the stabbing, see N. R. Kleinfield, "Rider Asks If Cabby Is Muslim, Then Stabs Him," *New York Times*, August 25, 2010.
3. Shirley de Leon, "Dear Diary," *New York Times*, July 16, 2007.

· **25** ·

On Being Brown in America

The recent bombings in Boston threw up many questions. One of the most pressing, in my somewhat narrow view, is the meaning of being brown in America.

On April 17, two days after the bombs went off during the Boston Marathon, killing three people and injuring almost 200 others, CNN's John King went on the air to say that the suspect was a "dark-skinned male."[1] In the CNN video, which shows that the time of the broadcast was 1.15 P.M. on Wednesday, we see King pointing to a photograph from the front page of the *New York Times*. A positive identification had been made based on a surveillance video from a Lord and Taylor store just outside the frame of the picture in the *Times*, King said. A little later that afternoon, King would assure viewers that a subsequent arrest had been made.

No one had been arrested that day, of course, and, alas, there was no dark-skinned male. What is remarkable is that even while first reporting his piece of exclusive news, CNN's King felt it necessary to qualify what he was saying. The qualifications he offered were not about the haste with which he was sharing a piece of misinformation, or the bewildering lack of specificity in his description, or even the absence of adequate verification. Instead, his remarks appeared to suggest to his viewers that he couldn't be more open with them because of politically correct sentiments that complicated open disclosures of "game changers" that the police had uncovered.

"I was told they have a breakthrough in the identification of the suspect, and I'm told—and I want to be very careful about this because people get very sensitive when you say these things—I was told by one of these sources who's a law enforcement official that this was a dark-skinned male. . . . The official used some other words. I'm not going to repeat them until we get more information because of the sensitivities. There are some people who will take offense even in saying that."[2]

Some people! Who are they?

Frankly, I'm not among them. I was listening to King and wishing we were back in the days when we could say what we were really thinking. I mean the good old days even before television. Consider, for instance, W. Somerset Maugham's famous short story from the 1920s about an Englishman, a detective named Ashenden, charged with the responsibility of catching a dark-skinned male named Chandra. Chandra was an Indian nationalist plotting against the colonial rule, a man "at the heart of plots to embarrass the British in India." He had also been involved in two or three bombings that had killed "a few innocent bystanders" and, more seriously, shaken "the nerves of the public and so damaged its morale." Here is the detective's response when shown Chandra's picture: "To Ashenden, unused to Oriental faces, it looked like any of a hundred Indians that he had seen. It might have been the photograph of one or other of the rajahs who come periodically to England and are portrayed in the illustrated papers. It showed a fat-faced, swarthy man, with full lips and a fleshy nose; his hair was black, thick, and straight, and his very large eyes even in the photograph were liquid and cow-like. He looked ill-at-ease in European clothes."[3]

Vivid language. And such ease of description. This is an advantage of being white—one of the advantages, at least, although I know I'm merely speculating about a large group—you can judge others and yet never suspect that you are merely telling your version of the truth. Even I, with my swarthy skin and timid soul, am taken in by the pose. And I nearly fall over with gratitude when, a paragraph later, looking at another photograph of Chandra, Ashenden concedes that "in his turban and long, pale tunic he was not without dignity."[4]

I'm inclined to feel a bit sorry for John King, ruffled by the sensitivities of others. But the fact is that he needn't have worried about at least a portion of his audience. Even after his mistake had been corrected and the Tsarnaev brothers identified as the suspects, the Internet presented stark examples of bigotry and ignorance: "I Can't [sic] believe that pair in the Boston bombing was NOT Towel heads!!! They are Czechoslovakian!"[5]

So it would appear that some Americans cannot tell the difference between nations. An even larger number, certainly thousands of users on the Internet site Reddit, were unwilling to distinguish between individuals. The amateur detectives on Reddit saw fit to declare from the photographs circulating on the Web that they had identified the suspect as a Moroccan American youth, Salah Eddin Barhoum, a spectator at the marathon. Others found it equally easy to spread the entirely baseless rumor that the FBI was saying Suspect No. 2 was Sunil Tripathi, a Brown University student missing since the middle of March.

This behavior isn't entirely the product of the Internet. In fact, it is not even new. It has its roots in history and, arguably, in law. Let us go back to the days even before Maugham had his detective Ashenden looking at the photograph of a dark-skinned male. I'm referring here to the 1917 Immigration Act in the United States—also known as the Asiatic Barred Zone Act—which regarded as undesirable aliens all those individuals who had their origin in Asia, a region spanning the so-called Middle East to the Pacific Islands, thereby lumping them in with "homosexuals," "idiots," "feeble-minded persons," "criminals," "insane persons," "alcoholics," "professional beggars," and others.[6]

You've heard the words of the old blues song: "They say if you's white, should be all right, / If you's brown, stick around, / But if you's black, mmm mmm, brother, get back, get back, get back." That old racial imaginary is changing. Brown is staining the edges of the racial divide. Richard Rodriguez has written, "Brown bleeds through the straight line, unstaunchable—the line separating black from white, for example."[7] If we are going to be optimistic, we can even say that brown is the color of the future.

A new book by a Boston-based academic and filmmaker, Vivek Bald, describes the formation of what he calls Bengali Harlem in the early decades of the last century. Starting with the migration of Bengali peddlers to the United States in the 1880s, and a later group of seamen, mostly Muslims, in the 1930s and 1940s, those who came to this country didn't establish separate ethnic enclaves like later immigrants. Instead, they formed "networks that were embedded in working-class Creole, African-American, and Puerto Rican neighborhoods and entwined with the lives of their residents."[8] This radical mixing and assimilation, Bald argues, is an unnoticed aspect of the history of U.S. immigration.

The invisible assimilation of working-class immigrants in that early phase has given way to an entirely different order of mixing in contemporary America. The attacks of 9/11 might have drawn a line in the sand, but the reality of sand is that it keeps shifting.

Pico Iyer, who is surely the Dalai Lama of diversity, has written that "perhaps the greatest danger of our global community is that the person in Los Angeles thinks he knows Cambodia because he's seen *The Killing Fields* on-screen, and the newcomer from Cambodia thinks he knows Los Angeles because he's seen *City of Angels* on video."[9]

I'm guilty of making a vast generalization about America from having watched a stoner classic: Harold and Kumar have not only come to America, they are on their way to White Castle. Indeed, if we follow the career of one of its stars, Kal Penn, he has reached even the White House as an official in the area of public liaison.

Let me go further. As an Indian, I'm raising my kids in the firm belief that sooner or later, everyone in this country is going to look like Kal Penn.

NOTES

From Amitava Kumar, "On Being Brown in America," IndiaInk Blog, *New York Times*, April 25, 2013. Reprinted with permission of the publisher.

1. CNN's John King can be heard engaging in baseless conjecture in video hosted by Huffington Post and others ("John King: Boston Bombing Suspect

A 'Dark-Skinned Male,'" accessed September 24, 2014, http://www.huffing
tonpost.com/2013/04/17/john-king-boston-bombing-dark-skinned-male
-ifill_n_3102195.html).

2. "John King: Boston Bombing Suspect a 'Dark-Skinned Male,'" Huffington
Post.

3. W. Somerset Maugham, "Giulia Lazzari," in W. Somerset Maugham, *Collected
Short Stories* (1921; New York: Penguin, 1977), 3:88–89.

4. Maugham, "Giulia Lazzari," 88.

5. The Tumblr account Public Shaming collected screen captures of this and
similar Twitter posts following the identification of the Boston Marathon
bombing suspects on a post titled "The Definitive 'People Who Thought
Chechnya was the Czech Republic' Collection," at http://publicshaming
.tumblr.com/post/48547675807/the-definitive-people-who-thought
-chechnya-was-the. Accessed September 24, 2014.

6. Vivek Bald, *Bengali Harlem and the Lost Histories of South Asian America*
(Cambridge, MA: Harvard University Press, 2013), 2.

7. Richard Rodriguez, *Brown: The Last Discovery of America* (New York: Viking,
2002), xi.

8. Bald, *Bengali Harlem and the Lost Histories of South Asian America*, 9.

9. Pico Iyer, *The Global Soul: Jet Lag, Shopping Malls, and the Search for Home*
(New York: Knopf, 2000), 65.

· **26** ·

Missing Person

My mother's nails were painted red before I lit her funeral pyre on the banks of the Ganga. Ma was wearing bright new bangles on her arm. Her body was draped in a pink Banarasi organza sari and a burgundy shawl. A shiny gold leaf pattern covered the shawl, and it had an embroidered border with mirrors and tiny silver bells.

Minutes before we left our home, my father was brought into the room where Ma's adorned body lay on a stretcher on the floor. He was asked to put orange *sindoor* in the parting of Ma's hair. My father was sobbing by now, but he was asked to repeat the gesture thrice. Then all the women in the family, many of them wailing, took turns rubbing the auspicious powder in Ma's hair.

When we were in the car, driving to the river for the cremation, my elder sister told me that my mother was lucky. At her death, Ma had been dressed up in new clothes. Papa had put *sindoor* on her head, signifying that they were getting married again. Ma was going out as a bride.

Had my father died first, none of this would have happened. If Ma were still living, *sindoor* would have been wiped away from her head. She would be expected to wear white. The women from the family who were now wailing would still be wailing but, if Ma was the widow, these women would have had the task of breaking all the bangles on her wrist before Papa's corpse was taken out of the house.

As I listened to my sister, I understood that even in the midst of profound grief it was necessary to find comfort. One needed solace. And it was possible to hold despair at bay by imagining broken bangles and the destiny that my mother had escaped. I would have found unbearable the sight of my mother's bare arms.

That morning, while my sisters were washing my mother's body and preparing it for the funeral, my father and I went to a hair salon to get our heads shaved. Papa asked the barber the name of his village; it turned out that the barber's village and ours were in the same district. My father knew a politician from the barber's village. The radio was playing Hindi songs. *Zulfein teri itni ghani, dekh ke inko, yeh sochta hoon . . . Maula mere Maula mere. . . .* The barber was a small dark man with a limp. He was extremely polite to my father, listening quietly while he discoursed about inflation and the changes in the economy. At one point, my father said that when he started life in Patna, he could buy a chicken for ten rupees and that now it would be difficult to get an egg for that amount.

I listened to what my father was saying with a mild annoyance. But he too was finding comfort. There can be so much pathos in accounting. Lives and histories reduced to neat numbers. Everything had changed, but the past was still connected to the present, however altered or unrecognizable the world had suddenly become. Papa's stories were attempts to bridge where he had once been and where he now was.

I had tried to make all this easy for myself. As my parents grew older, I began to prepare for their death. This will sound cruel or callous, and perhaps it is. A few years ago, I wrote a novel in which the protagonist, Binod, describes his father's death and then his cremation. In my story, when the father coughs, he is unable to dislodge the phlegm. It appears that he wants to say something, but he becomes breathless instead. Binod runs down the hospital's corridor searching for a nurse. Soon the father dies, and Binod tells himself that he should have spoken to his father: "In English films, people said 'I love you.' But his father had always been formal." Later, the body is to be taken to the electric crematorium. Binod looks at his mother as she sits gazing emptily at each person as they hurry back and forth: "Her hair was spread open, she had wiped away the red *sindoor* from the parting in her hair, and her arms looked bare without her bangles."[1]

In other words, I had tried to imagine my mother grieving after my father's death. But this wasn't my real fear. I knew that my mother would go first. She was the one who was sick more often, her voice wheezing from asthma. For a while she had dyed her head with henna, but she had had an allergic reaction and for years her hair had been white. This was in marked contrast to my father's hair, which has very little gray in it. He retired from his job as a bureaucrat but has never stopped working. He now does volunteer work, helping direct a project to build public toilets. So it was my mother that I worried about. I saved the birthday cards she sent my children. I'd feel guilty when I erased any of the messages she left on our phone. When I wrote my last book, a biography of my hometown, I was unabashed about expressing my fear in its final pages: "To return to Patna is to find the challenging thought of death, like the tip of a knife, pressing against my rib."[2]

Did my mother read what I had written? She usually read everything I wrote, but I was embarrassed to ask her about those last few pages. There was a party in Patna when my book was released; my mother was in the audience, and she stood in the line with others to get her copy autographed. I cannot know whether she read what is on the last page:

> There is no way to avoid it: when I step on Patna's soil, I only want to see how much older my parents look. Rheumatoid arthritis has seized my mother's limbs and she finds it impossible even to comb her hair. My father's memory is as sharp as it has always been, certainly better than mine, but the contours of his body have begun to sag. He goes for a walk each morning, but I noticed last time that he was limping. I arrive in Patna and a few days later I leave. Each time I leave, I wonder about the circumstances under which I will need to return.[3]

You think you are prepared for the news of a loved one's death. You have read somewhere that there is no way of readying yourself for such news—and because you take this as a warning, you think you are prepared also for the surprise. When it finally comes the news sweeps aside, with gigantic force, all the matchstick barriers you had put in place. All you can see spreading as far as the distant horizon is the sudden and undeniable reality that your mother is now gone forever. The world you have known since birth is now less than what it always was for you. You don't necessarily put this into words. Instead, a part of you separates from your self, and, like a bird sitting on a distant branch, watches you weeping on a bench below. You don't know how long the new reality is going to stay this way.

Ma was taken sick on New Year's Eve and had to be put on a ventilator. I spoke to her a couple of days later, and she was better. For some reason, I choked up during our conversation and began to cry. It was perhaps because of the way in which Ma kept saying, in English, as if driving home an important, final message, "I love you. I love you all." I told her that I was going to come to Patna in two months' time. I asked her to take care. But then a few days later there were complications. A reaction to the medicines given for asthma led to my mother experiencing bleeding from her vagina. Then her body stopped producing any urine, and for the first time in her life she had to be put on a dialysis machine. I was worried by this news that came late at night and began to search online for a plane ticket to India.

. . .

Ten years ago, almost to the day, I was on a highway outside Washington, D.C., and I thought that my mother had died. She was visiting us from India because my first child had been born. That morning I was driving with Ma to my sister's home. I was to take a plane later that day to Atlanta where I was going to interview the actor Manoj Bajpai.

Only a few miles from my sister's house, as I was driving, I looked at Ma on the seat beside me. Her eyes were open, but her gaze was unfocused. She certainly didn't appear to hear me. Her body had gone rigid.

Ma, I said softly, and then Ma again, louder and louder. We must have been driving at seventy-five miles per hour and I began to change lanes, moving to the slower lanes and then exiting and finally coming to a stop on a suburban street.

Did I sprinkle water on her? I cannot say. But my mother seemed to awaken from a sleep. She remembered nothing. And soon she was fine. Before I said goodbye to her at my sister's house, Ma asked me if she should prepare some *suji-ka-halwa* for Manoj Bajpai.

This is how one can think of many women in our society: they are survivors. They have endured so much, carried such burdens, weathered so many storms. And we, who are their children, are the beneficiaries because at the end, we are asked if we want some mango, or milk, or *suji-ka-halwa*.

. . .

When I was a child, hanging in our family's drawing room was a black-and-white studio photograph. It showed my young mother with her BA degree in Hindi literature from Patna Women's College. She was graduating at the top of her class. On a small table next to her, the photographer had placed Ma's gold medal. My mother was the daughter of a policeman; two of her brothers were in the prison bureaucracy. She didn't grow up in a literary milieu, but she wanted to be a writer and a Hindi scholar. I believe she never overcame the bitterness of having her dreams thwarted by marriage and motherhood.

As a result, rightly or wrongly, I felt that by writing books I was living her dream.

In conversations on the phone, I would mention my battle with various deadlines. Ma encouraged me. I would tell her of literary festivals I was attending in cities all over the world. She used to express pride. But I always wondered whether Ma heard in my voice the guilt I felt about not coming to Patna more often than I did.

During my last conversation with her, soon after New Year's, I told Ma that I would visit her in mid-February because I had received an invitation to the Patna Literature Festival. Within minutes after our conversation, my sister sent me a photo of Ma smiling on her bed. My sister is a doctor. I felt reassured by her presence at Ma's bedside.

Now, on the night that Ma was put on the dialysis machine, my sister seemed to hesitate. By midnight I had bought a ticket on a plane that was going to leave the next morning. When I woke up, there was no news from my sister, but there was a message from a distant relative on Facebook, expressing condolence. I realized that I had missed a very important deadline.

In my novel, Binod takes his father's ashes to Benares and pays the boatman sixty-five rupees to row him out to the middle of the river. When I went to Benares with my sisters and hired a boat, I ended up paying a hundred. We had marigold petals and rose petals that we first scattered on the water. The boat kept moving, and the petals made a colorful pathway behind us. A priest had approached Binod and pointed out that there was a whole ritual that accompanied the act of immersing the ashes in the Ganga. But Binod wanted none of that: "Here he was aware only of a profound solitude. He was now alone with his father, and he didn't want to let him go."[4] We had avoided the priests, but I was a bit uncertain about what to do next. Or maybe, like Binod, I didn't want to let go. In any case, the boatman stopped rowing and looked at us. He wore a Golden State Warriors T-shirt. He simply said that there was a current there and waited. "Binod untied the red cloth that covered the mouth of the clay pot, and regretted that he had not brought any flowers, particularly marigolds, which he would have liked to have strewn on the water. He had seen the flowers floating on the river after a funeral in so many Hindi films." At least we had the flowers! Perhaps unnecessarily, maybe feeling under pressure to say something, I told my sisters that we should shut our eyes and think of our mother. I didn't dare look at my sisters. I think they were crying. They held my arm as I tipped the earthen jar into the water. Did I say this loudly, or only in my head? "I love you, Ma, I love you."

Half an hour earlier, in the parking lot, I had untied the large pot with my mother's ashes. I divided my mother's remains—black and gray charcoal mixed with flat bones, thin and white, and, a surprise that caused particular anguish to my younger sister, the surgical screws that had been put in Ma's knees and had remained untouched by the fire—into three small pots. We were going to put one pot here in the waters in Benares and a second one at Prayaag that evening, at the place where the Ganga and Yamuna met; then I was going to take the third one by myself to Haridwar, because my elder sister said that it was a place where our mother would have liked to live.

During the trip to Benares and Prayaag, my sisters had been with me; when I went to Haridwar, by car from Delhi, I was alone. Now and then during the trip, I told myself with some disquiet that my mother was making her last journey in the trunk of the car. It was a long drive. After a procession of busy small towns, we reached a long stretch of the narrow highway surrounded by sugarcane fields covered in mist. Lines of tall poplars gave the landscape a touch of symmetry. The general elections were several months away, but campaign posters were everywhere. Local leaders but also Narendra Modi waved to the passing cars from giant billboards on the side of the road. "Har Har Modi, Ghar Ghar Modi." Repeated appearances of roadside vegetarian *dhabas* with names like Shuddh Vaishno Bhojnalaya. Painted signs planted in fields and by the roadside for Dilli Ka Mashoor Chawla Band.

It was late night when I reached Haridwar and found an old hotel that was built on the riverbank. In the morning, I opened my window: mist spread into the distance, but a short drop below was the Ganga. In the water's pale green flow, I could see flowers and short lengths of white or red cloth unraveling like snakes. These were offerings made by pilgrims upstream. Putting the pot with Ma's remains in a polythene bag, I walked toward Har Ki Pauri where the evening *aarti* used to fascinate my mother: among the ringing of bells, and chanting of prayers, the flotillas of oil-lamps lighting up the dark waters. But it was early morning now, the ghats sparsely populated with pilgrims, some of whom were braving the cold and taking a quick dip in the water. Half-naked men and women stepped out of the Ganga, shivering, and changed their clothes on the red stone steps. Sadhus in dirty saffron sat huddled around fires, smoking chillums. Lines of lepers were being fed puris and *halwa* by generous pilgrims. (Four puris, *halwa*, and *sabzi*, for each person, for twenty rupees. If only two puris, then ten rupees.) An aunt had told me that I should remember to feed priests. I didn't have to look for long; they came looking for me, with a feral intensity in all their negotiations. It was too early to have a meal, the priest said to me, and I could give him cash instead. Cash for a meal, for clothes, cash for the poor, cash also for the salvation of my mother's soul. He asked me to reconsider the amount—*Yeh aapke Mataji ka samay hai* (This time is for your respected mother)—and, observing that I stayed silent throughout, he expressed concern—*Aap khush hain*? (Are you happy?)

Ever since I first got news of Ma's death, I had been like the actor who, having performed scenes on stage in which he is confronted by his mother's death, now must react to the same event in his real life. This was because of what I had written in my novel; the other reason was that despite the fact that I was now fifty, I had never before attended a funeral. I made notes and took pictures with my phone because it seemed the whole world was telling me something about my mother. I wasn't so much the anthropologist collecting information on the customs and lives of others; instead, I was the native in the familiar stereotypical anthropological tale, taking signs as wonders. For instance, the trucks on the highway, bearing the legend "OK TATA" but also the words "Ma Ka Aashirwaad" spoke to me. (The ubiquitous sign "Ma Ka Aashirwaad" or "Mother's Blessings" didn't appear overly sentimental to me on the highway. Instead, it spoke to me of love's persistence.) And in Haridwar, so did the fliers stuck to the walls all along the length of the ghats and on tree trunks and telephone poles. These were fliers for missing persons. *Papa jaldi ghar aajao. Ghar mein sab pareshan hain* (Papa come home quickly. Everyone worried at home). *Koi bhi jaankari milne pe sampark karein. Mahila ne laal rang ka suit aur shawl pehen rakha hai* (If you have any information, please get in touch. Woman is wearing red suit and shawl). These were fliers about people from other cities: did their families think that their loved one had left them and sought salvation in Haridwar? Is that what my mother had wanted to do? I stopped to take pictures of these fliers because I knew that from now on Ma was my missing person. *Ghar laut aao, Ma.* (Come home, Ma.)

I was self-conscious about the notes I was taking—and later I felt both disturbed and consoled when I came across the following line from Kafka's diaries: "Have never understood how it is possible for almost everyone who writes to objectify his sufferings in the very midst of undergoing them."[5] But in those first days, it was my writer friends who gave me words to understand what was happening to me. One of them, Ravish, a friend from my hometown and an anchor for a Hindi TV channel, told me that after his father passed away he no longer savored his accomplishments: "Our successes from now on will only be of use to our children; all our struggles had only been for the sake of our parents." Sangu, who had been in a writer's colony in Massachusetts with me, sent me a line from Catherine Chung's book, *Forgotten Country*: "After this, every death will call you back to this one, every great sorrow will lead you back to this."[6] Then there was Cheryl, an old friend who had written an entire book about her mother's death from cancer and her own descent into grief and self-destructive behavior. She wrote: "You're alone now in a way you've never been. But if you let it your grief will bring you closer to a more entire and also essential version of her than you've ever known." I would read these messages out loud to my sisters, and in the middle of doing this one of us would break down and we would end up crying together.

In other words, even as a writer, you are capable of objectifying your sufferings only half of the time. The rest of the time you feel like someone trapped in a house in a flood. There is no dry space. Water has filled every hidden corner. Still, there were practical matters to deal with. My father, who had been married to my mother for fifty-four years, busied himself with tasks like finding keys for the locks in Ma's closets. He wanted the money in her purse used or given away, her clothes distributed among relatives, her jewelry divided among my sisters and others. I didn't have much to do. As the days passed, I discovered that it was my resentment of the rituals that offered me a small refuge or escape from the waves of sadness. Which is not to deny that I was happy to be home. Many times during my ten-day stay in Patna I told myself that I would have felt bereft if I hadn't had a chance to mourn my mother's death with my father and my sisters. I had needed to feel the fresh, and undeniable, sense of loss: in the first few minutes that I was back in the room where I had last seen her, only a few months earlier, what stopped me was the sight of her walking stick, her clothes on the hangers, the two pairs of white shoes with Velcro straps. The shock of what is gone, and yet still lingers. So that, stepping into the bathroom to wash my hands, I realized that the bar of Pears soap in the dish was the one that my mother had put there just before she died.

I was washing my hands because I had touched my mother's cold cheeks and then tried to get her earrings out. Her body was in a casket filled with ice. One of my aunts said that we should remove the jewelry because, otherwise, the *doms* at the funeral would snatch it out. (*Doms* were men from the supposedly untouchable caste; they were the custodians of the funeral ceremony.) The nose stud came out easily enough, but the earrings were a problem. My younger sister struggled with one of them, and I with the other. I didn't succeed, and someone else had to complete the task. At one point, I found myself saying it was better to use surgical scissors right now than to watch her ear ripped by the *doms* at the ghat. I caressed my mother's cheeks, which felt slightly moist—as if even in death she had kept up her habit of applying lotion. A thin line of red fluid, like betel juice, glistened between her lips. In a few hours she would be taken to the burning ghat. My sisters and I slept on mattresses we had spread on the floor beside the casket. When I woke up after perhaps four hours of sleep, I saw that my younger sister was awake, sitting quietly with her back to the wall, looking vacant and sad. Outside, after an hour, it was light enough to see the fog, and the fog was still there on the water when we arrived at the river to cremate my mother.

At the ghat there was a press of strangers, many of them beggars and curious children. I had to ask people to move back. I stayed with my sisters, while other relatives moved my mother's body. She lay on straw and firewood; we were asked to pile the sticks over the rest of the body, so the sticks formed a tent from both sides. The face was left bare. The priest told me to put five pieces of sandalwood near my mother's mouth. Some of the *sindoor* that had been put in my mother's hair had scattered and lodged in her eyebrows and on the eyelids. The young man who was going to help with the fire had a wound on his face. There was an *x*-shaped bandage under his right eye. His eyes were bloodshot. His head was wrapped in a brown and blue muffler. He wore jeans and a thin black jacket. He had an air of insouciance about him that would have bothered my mother, but I liked him. His presence made things real. I was asked to sprinkle *gangajal* again—the endless purification with the Ganga's polluted water—and was then given the pile of straw that the *dom* had lit. I was to walk around the pyre three times. Then follows the ritual that is called *mukhaagni*. Now I understood suddenly why the priest had given me the five pieces of sandalwood, the size of small Snickers bars. In that moment—while I was performing *mukhaagni* inadequately, inefficiently, even badly, in my grief and bewilderment—the thought passed through my mind: is this why my mother had wanted me to be present at her death? The meaning of *mukhaagni* is present in its name for anyone who knows Hindi or Sanskrit, but what it means in practice is that the male who is closest to the deceased, often the son, sometimes the father, and in some cases, I imagine, the husband, puts fire into the mouth of the person on the pyre.

NOTES

A different version of this essay was published as "Pyre," *Granta* 130 (2015), 70–81.

1. Amitava Kumar, *Nobody Does the Right Thing* (Durham, NC: Duke University Press, 2010). For an account of the funeral and the immersion of the ashes at Benares, 139–52.
2. Amitava Kumar, *A Matter of Rats* (Durham, NC: Duke University Press, 2014), 107.
3. Kumar, *A Matter of Rats*, 107.
4. Kumar, *A Matter of Rats*, 107.
5. Franz Kafka, *The Diaries of Franz Kafka, 1914–1923*, trans. Martin Greenberg with the assistance of Hannah Arendt (New York: Schocken, 1949), 183. The entry is from September 19, 1917.
6. Catherine Chung, *Forgotten Country* (New York: Riverhead, 2012), 283.

CNN, 196–97
Cobalt Blue, 88. *See also* Kundalkar, Sachin
Cohen, Sasha Baron, 165
colonialism, 70, 142, 145; colonial India, 22,
    47, 197; colonial power, 16; colonization
    and language, 14–15, 24; division between
    colonizer and colonized, 17; postcolonial-
    ism, 55, 68
Committee for Free and Fair Trial
    for S. A. R. Geelani, 43
Communism, 29; Maoists, 39, 44, 49; guer-
    rillas, 71
Congress Party, 53
Cornershop (band), 24
corporatization, 44, 48, 52. *See also*
    privatization
corruption, 55, 71, 91, 100
cricket, 30, 54, 89, 156, 172; World Cup
    tournament, 172
criticism, 48, 59; critical theory, 165; Indo-
    Anglican critical establishment, 73; liter-
    ary criticism, 23, 56–57, 65, 71–73, 165
"The Cult of Authenticity," 71

dams, 44, 48
De, Shobha, 22–23
Dean, Louis, 81
death penalty. *See* capital punishment
Deewaar, 101
Delhi, 14, 38–39, 52–54, 58, 61, 66, 70,
    91, 102, 127, 129, 135–37, 142, 147, 149,
    156, 158–60, 183, 185; Bara Gumbad,
    156; bathroom, 30; Connaught Place, 7;
    Defence Colony, 86; Delhi University, 156;
    Hindu College, xi, xiii, 90; Hotel Taj Man
    Singh, 158–59; Inter-State Bus Terminal,
    89; Jama Masjid, 159; Jantar Mantar,
    94; killing of Sikhs, xii; killing of student
    from Arunachal Pradesh, 88–89; Lodi
    Garden, 129, 156, 160; Modern School, 90;
    New Delhi, 178–79; restaurants, 158–59;
    Vigyan Bhavan, 142. *See also* India Inter-
    national Center (IIC)
DeLillo, Don, 66, 163
democracy, 53
Desai, Anita, 41, 129, 160
Desai, Kiran, 41
Dewas, 15–17
Dhanbad, 61

dharma, 72
diaspora, 88, 90
Dillard, Annie, xii–xiii, 124
disability, 153
Disney; Disney World, 114–15; *Mulan*,
    115–16
displacement: books and libraries as mark-
    ers of, 7–8
Dow Chemical, 62–63. *See also* Union Carbide
drones, 49
drugs, 27, 60, 107, 130

East Is East (film), 26
Economist, 71
Edison, Thomas, 87–88
"Edmund Wilson in Benares," 91–92. *See*
    also Mishra, Pankaj
education: and choice, 26; college, 55–56, 60,
    129; graduate school, 29, 155
Egypt, 16, 51
el Edl, Mohommed, 16
El Salvador, 18
Ellsberg, Daniel, 108
England, 16, 19, 22; representation in books,
    20–21; Machester, 172
Enright, Michael, 193
Entreprise Culture, 19
English, August, 23–24, 91–92. *See also* Chat-
    terjee, Upamanyu
erotic aesthetic, 23
"Erotic Politicians and Mullahs," 20. *See also*
    Kureishi, Hanif
ethics, 53

Facebook, 34, 45, 142
Falling Man, 66. *See also* DeLillo, Don
fascism, 70
fatwa, 26–27, 52
feudalism, 21, 60
Fifa (video game), 107
film: European New Wave, 160; Hindi,
    99–101, 103–5, 108, 152, 160; Indian New
    Wave, 160. *See also* Bollywood; *Home
    Products*s
Finding the Center, 119. *See also*
    Naipaul, V. S.
"Fires," 110–11. *See also* Carver, Raymond
Flaubert, Gustave, 91–92
Florida, 114, 159

Foer, Jonathan Safran, 65
Ford Foundation, 6
form: epistolary form, 60; the novel, 67. *See also* style
Forman, Milos, 160
Forster, E. M., 15–19, 21–22
Fox News, 37, 46
France, 63, 67, 91, 163; Paris, 31, 72, 116
Franzen, Jonathan, 163
Freedom, 163
freedom of expression, 38, 53, 57
French, Antonia, 22. *See also* Kureishi, Hanif
Friedman, Thomas, 114
fundamentalism, 46, 177; and fanaticism, 26; Islamic, 27, 51, 52, 173, 175; radical-ization, 108; and sex, 26. *See also* sex; violence: religious
Fury, 56. *See also* Rushdie, Salman

Gallagher, Tess, 111
Galeano, Eduardo, 41
Gandhi, Indira, xii
Gandhi, Mohandas Karamchand, 35, 171, 175, 178–79, 180; Birla House, 128
Gandhi, Sonia, 177
Gandhi (film), 20
Geelani, S. A. R., 43, 132
genocide, 33. *See also* Gujarat: Gujarat riots
Ghalib, Mirza, 72
Ghodra: train burning, 35
Ghonim, Wael, 51–52
Ghosh, Amitav, 41, 73, 142
Ghoshal, Somak, 87
Gita. *See* Bhagavad-Gita
The Glass Menagerie, 87. *See also* Williams, Tennessee
globalization, 5, 27
The God of Small Things, 40–41, 44. *See also* Roy, Arundhati
Godard, Jean-Luc, 160
Google, 32, 51
Gopal, Surendra, 11–12
graffiti, 147, 156
Granta, 20, 55
The Great Gatsby, 104
Greene, Graham, 69
Green Revolution, 6
The Ground Beneath Her Feet, 55. *See also* Rushdie, Salman

Guardian, 81
Gujarat, 33–35, 174, 176–78; Gujarat riots, xiv, 32–35; Gujarat Urdu Sahitya Akademi, 33–34. *See also* violence: Gujarat
Guru, Mohammad Afzal, 43, 132–36, 138–39
Guru, Tabassum, 132–39; "A Wife's Appeal for Justice," 133–34

Hafiz, 11, 41
Hanif, Mohammad, 67–69
Haq, Husainul, 88
Haridwar, 93
Harold and Kumar Go to White Castle, 199
Haroun-ul-Rashid, 11
Harvey, Mikko, 107–8
Hemingway, Ernest, 163–64
Hindi: books and literature, xiii, 10, 85, 89; language, 34, 42, 45, 90, 94, 97, 169, 175–76, 178; lecturer, xi, xiv; newspapers/magazines, 9, 29; and nostalgia, 15; reporters, 52, 54; writing in Hindi, 10. *See also* film: Hindi; language: code switching
Hindu Holiday, 21–22. *See also* Ackerley, J. R.
Hindu, 110, 170–72, 174–75, 178; ancient traditions, 5; cremation, 6; dress (dhoti), 128, 142, 187; rise of Hindu right, 88; ruins in Kashmir valley, 150; *Vedas*, 176; weddings, 144. *See also* Muslims: Hindu-Muslim conflict; Vishwa Hindu Parishad, VHP
Hindutva, 170, 178; radical groups, 44
Hindu Unity, 170–71, 174
Hitler, Adolf, 178
Home Products, 61, 84, 87, 93–94, 103–4, 160; process of writing, 79–82
homosexuality, 16–21, 164, 198; and pornog-raphy, 20; and representation, 20. *See also* pornography; sexuality
The Hours (film), 79
A House for Mr. Biswas, xiii, 81
Humayun, 12
Husband of a Fanatic, 93, 98

immigration/immigrants, 19–21, 165, 176–77, 192. *See also* America: coming to; London: Bangladeshi immigrants
imperialism, 21. *See also* colonialism
India: civil service, 23; elites in, 7, 38, 44, 46–47, 65, 180; independence, 42; India

Reddit, 198

relief camps: Khan Gumbat, 32; Shah-e-Alam, 33

Report from the Interior, 86–88

Resnais, Alain, 160

Reuters, 108

Rhodes scholarship, 30

Right to Information Act (India), 34

rituals, 5, 23

Roberts, Gene, xii

Robinson, Roxana, 122

Rockwell, Daisy, 94

Rodriguez, Richard, 199

Roth, Philip, 20, 25, 86, 163

Roy, Arundhati, 37–39, 54, 90, 133, 142; interview, 39–50

Roy, Nilanjana, 34

RSS (Rashtriya Swayamsevak Sangh), 44

Rushdie, Salman, 15, 20, 26–27, 41, 51–57, 62, 73, 90, 160

Sahgal, Nayantara, 142

Sammie and Rosie Get Laid (film), 20

Sartre, Jean-Paul, 134

Satanic Verses, 51–54, 56. *See also* Rushdie, Salman

Satya (film), 97–105

Scott, Paul, 15

secularism, 54

sedition, 38, 45–46, 54

self-help, xiii–xiv, 136

Sentimental Education, 91. *See also* Flaubert, Gustave

Seth, Vikram, 41, 142

sex, 15–17, 85, 175, 184; and freedom, 26; and fundamentalism, 26; and illegitimate children, 179; as nexus, 26; pleasure, 130; promiscuity, 60; and sexual desire, 25, 27

sexuality, 164; and anxiety, 180; and liberation, 25; and motivation, 64; and the ordinary, 23–24; representation and idealization, 19. *See also* homosexuality

Shakespeare, William, 41, 92

Sharma, Akhil, 144

Shatir, Aqeel, 33–35

Shiva, Vandana, 6

Shukla, Saurabh, 101, 103

Shukla, Shrilal, 86

Singh, Dravinder, 134–35

Sinha, Indra, 34, 63–66, 68

small town, 17, 91–92, 103–4, 111, 151, 157, 159, 180; hinterland, 62, 72, 158, 174

Smith, Patti, 165

socialism, 19, 178

social media, 52, 56, 88. *See also* Facebook; Twitter; YouTube

Sodomy Laws, 16

Special Task Force (STF), 134–35

STD/PCO shop, 33

A Street in Srinagar, 88

style (of writing), 31, 47–48, 55, 65; first-person narration, 71; motifs, 72; and natural rhythm, 150. *See also* writing: advice

suicide, 68–69; as form of protest, 63

Supreme Court (Indian), 43, 132

Sweet Talk, 165

Syal, Meera, 20

Tahrir Square, 51

Talwar, Aarushi, 58–59

Taniam, Nido, 88–89

taxis, 192–94; New York Taxi Workers Alliance (NYTWA), 193

teaching, xii, 56, 119, 121, 129, 137, 157, 184

technology, 129–30, 171, 184. *See also* Internet; social media

Tehelka, 120

television, 15, 19, 38, 52, 54, 59, 60, 89, 115, 152, 156, 172, 197; India Now, 38; NDTV, 188; and represenation of Indians, 15

terrorism, 88, 93, 161, 170, 179, 188; bombing of the Samjhauta Express, 44; Boston Marathon bombing, 107–8, 196, 198; counterterrorism authorities, 108; and film, 138; global war on terror, 49, 157; and Gujarat riots, 33, 35; Mumbai attacks, 46; Parliament Attack (December 13), 43–44, 132–36; post-9/11, 49, 65, 114, 176, 188; September 11 attacks, 45, 179, 199; and torture, 134–35, 157; trial, 115; U.S. terrorist-industrial complex, 49

Thatcherism, 19

Third World, 67, 108

This American Life, 164

writing for India, 86. *See also* activism; censorship

writing: advice and rules, xi–xiv, 121–23; and artistic autonomy, 72; authenticity, 62, 65, 71–73, 95; about cities, 137–38; Desi writing, 23; documentary, 55; earliest lessons in, 4; endings, 82; and failure, 81; finding time to write, 44, 111–12; first writings, 40; freedom to write, 26; honesty and transparency in, 22, 93–94, 102; and humor, 81, 85; Indian-English, 42, 62, 87, 90; learning to write, xii, 8, 40; length and context of, 48; making writing more meaningful, 93; manifesto for Indian writing, 84; opening lines, 80; and the ordinary, 94; positionality and

dislocation, 61; positionality and the crowd, 38, 42, 174; process, 79–82; about race, 22; real events in fiction, 55–56, 62, 63–64, 65–66, 67–70, 88, 93–94, 128–30; research, 43–44; about sex, 22–23, 25; storytelling, 41; timing, 48 understanding, 17, 41, 86–88, 119; value of fiction, 95; voice, 60, 65, 91, 94. *See also* censorship; form; language; style

YouTube, 45

Zanussi, Krzysztof, 160
Zia-ul-Haq, General Muhammad, 67
Zionism, 170
Zubeida (film), 98